Fresh Eggs and Dog Beds 4
Laughter and Tears in Rural Ireland

Nick Albert

Book four in the Fresh Eggs and Dog Beds series

This one is for Katherine Brandon and everyone else who yearns to be back in Ireland.

Feicfidh mé go luath thú
(See you soon)

Contents

1 – Veg of the Day 7

2 – An Extended Stay....................................19

3 – Unwelcome Visitors....................................33

4 – Welcome Visitors....................................45

5 – A Slow Boat to Nowhere 57

6 – G-strings and Lycra....................................67

7 – Drunk and Disorderly....................................79

8 – Paths and Palpitations 91

9 – Jogging in Pyjamas 101

10 – The Good the Bad and the Angry 111

11 – Fur Coats and Soft Rushes 119

12 – Rules and Rulers 129

13 – And then they were Four...........................139

14 – The Final Straw................................151

15 – A Familiar Spirit 161

16 – The Cat in the Hat 171

17 – Skunk and Disorderly................................181

18 – Chainsaws in the Mist................................191

19 – A Row of Ducks................................201

20 – A Matter of Routine 213

21 – Lost and Confused 223

22 – Good Days and Bad Days 233

23 – The Final Leg 243

24 – All Good Things…................................255

25 – Back to Normal 263

26 – Fit to Drop 273

27 – Good Friends and Lost Socks 281

28 – A Taste of Honey 289

About the author 298

Contact the author 298

Ant Press Books 299

1 – Veg of the Day

"Happy birthday," I said, symbolically clinking my wife's cappuccino cup with my glass of soda water and lime. "Was your meal okay?"

"Yes, thank you." Lesley dipped her head demurely. "It was lovely, but I've eaten too much."

"Ack!" I waved dismissively. "If you can't fill up on your birthday, when can you?"

"I didn't expect cabbage, mashed potatoes, roast potatoes and chips to come with my roast beef."

"I think that's what they call Veg of the Day," I laughed. "It's good healthy Irish food and it sticks to your ribs too!"

"All the same, I'm full to bursting." My wife was using the menu card to fan her face. "And I'm roasting hot too."

"I'm not sure how, what with the cross-breeze here."

As if to consolidate my point, at that moment the doors behind me flew open and a party of four entered the pub. As had already been the case a dozen times since we had taken our seats, they paused in the open doorway whilst scanning for a vacant table. In those few seconds, the cold February wind blew through so violently a chill ran down my spine and Lesley's hair swirled around her head as if she were flying in an open-topped helicopter. In keeping with what was fast becoming a local tradition, as soon as the door had slammed shut, the four new entrants removed their wet coats and gave them a good shake.

"I see it's still raining," I tutted ironically, trying to wipe some of the water from the back of my neck. I nodded towards my wife. "You look like you've had your head out of a car window."

Lesley gave me The Look and the cold chill returned.

"It's very 1980s," I added quickly, hoping for some comedic latitude.

Poet's Corner was one of our favourite eateries and the perfect place for a birthday treat. The pub/restaurant is attached to the Old Ground Hotel, situated at the top of O'Connell Street in the Clare county town of Ennis. It's a very attractive pub, certainly not in the 'spit-and-sawdust' category. Brimming with polished dark wood highlighted with gleaming brass fittings, complemented by several leaded glass windows, Poet's Corner wouldn't have been out of place on a film set for the Titanic. The 'Poet's' tag comes from the many pictures of famous Irish poets and authors adorning the walls, whereas the 'Corner' moniker probably stems from the pub being squeezed into one corner of the hotel, rather like a bent elbow. The food is always excellent and keenly priced, but on the downside, its location and layout can leave one feeling rather like you're trying to eat in a draughty corridor.

Lesley pointed at the wall and grinned. "They still haven't got your picture up there."

"I don't think golf books count, regardless of how well they're selling," I tutted. "Perhaps when I've finished writing this memoir…"

"When?" Lesley exclaimed with an unintentional snort.

"Ouch!" I winced.

Of course, my dear wife had a valid point. For several months I'd been writing the story of how Lesley and I came to be in Ireland. Long before I had typed the first words, I'd made careful plans and written my beloved lists, outlining the story I'd wanted to tell. For me, order and process are like milk and honey. Yet once the writing began, my brain became an excitable butterfly. Constantly flitting between ideas, it soon led me astray and the timeline of the story unravelled like a ball of knitting wool in the paws of an excitable kitten. Unnamed and unfinished, my manuscript was slowly degenerating into a serpentine ramble of unconnected thoughts and half-recalled scenes from our life in County Clare.

Even though I'd had hundreds of golf instructional articles I could recycle from when I'd been writing for the local paper, my golf book had still taken a year to produce. In all that time, through the edits and rewrites, I'd remained confident and focused. But writing this memoir was proving to be a different matter. As the storyline drifted aimlessly into cul-de-sacs and dark corners, and the page count rose without reaching a conclusion, my confidence was ebbing away. I needed a boost, some hint of encouragement.

"This writing lark is harder than you might imagine," I said defensively. "It's a different skillset."

Lesley slowly sipped her cappuccino. Her cool blue eyes held my gaze without flickering. With her face hidden behind the cup, I was unable to read her expression.

"I'm sure you'll work it out," she whispered, her voice devoid of any clues as to her true feelings.

"Perhaps I should jack it in," I suggested, cautiously fishing for some reassurance.

Replacing her cup, she sighed and sat back. "Stick with it." She added a short nod of affirmation. "It's not as if you've much else to do just now."

And she was right.

It was eight years since we'd moved to Ireland on the kind of whim which couldn't reasonably be excused as 'An idea conceived in drink'. In that time, using nothing more than an aged DIY manual and dogged determination, we had gutted Glenmadrie, our draughty tumble-down farmhouse, and rebuilt it into a warm and attractive family home. Once I'd finished churning our land with diggers and dump trucks, Lesley had created an attractive garden, with a productive vegetable plot and orchard. As if that wasn't enough, my wife had developed a thriving cottage industry baking for a local market and making toys for the Christmas craft fairs. With all that going on, she somehow found the time to run a dance club. At the same time, I'd built a successful golf teaching business and then watched it flitter away to almost nothing on the shirttails of the worst recession in Irish history. Aside from walking the dogs, the occasional visit to the golf course and the odd bit of house maintenance, writing was now my life – so I might as well buckle down and make a go of it.

With our meal finished, I paid our bill, visited the loo and returned to the table.

"Did you leave a tip?" Lesley demanded.

"Of course," I replied. "You won't believe it, but that lad who served us used to be in my junior golf academy. His name is Cormac. I hardly recognised him."

Lesley looked across to the six-foot-tall, bearded hulk, who was currently serving drinks to a group of tourists at the bar.

"Are you sure?" she frowned. "He looks about 30."

"It's definitely Cormac. We were just chatting," I explained.

"He's about 20 now, so he would have been around 12 years old when I was coaching him. He's become a fine golfer and a jolly nice chap too. Apparently, he's married with a baby on the way."

"Good grief! Doesn't time fly? It feels like five minutes since we arrived in Ireland and yet…" Lesley sighed. "When we came here Joanne was still a teenager, just starting out on her own. Now she's married."

My wife closed her eyes and shook her head. A small smile played across her lips.

"I guess it's because we've been so busy," she continued. "What with the renovations and everything, we haven't had a moment to ourselves. It's little wonder time has flown by unnoticed."

"Perhaps we're living in Tír na nÓg," I suggested.

"What?" Lesley laughed.

"Tír na nÓg," I repeated, smiling. "There's an Irish legend of a beautiful green land hidden in the west where time has stopped. Apparently, it is forever green and when you enter you stop ageing. Perhaps it's where we live now."

"Glenmadrie is certainly forever green, but neither of us has stopped ageing!"

In surrender, I smiled and raised my palms. "One out of two isn't bad."

"I think it's stopped raining." Lesley pointed to the door. "Shall we head out?"

"I know you usually spurn the concept of birthday gifts," I said as I helped my wife don her coat. "But we could still walk around the shops for a bit. You might see something you want."

Lesley took my wrist and squinted at my watch. I guessed what she was thinking.

"The dogs will be fine for a while longer. I gave them all an extra biscuit before we left."

"Well…" My wife chewed her lip. "Okay. There is something I'd like, but it's not for me."

"Go on." I nodded encouragement.

"I'll tell you in a minute," she said. "Let's get out of here first."

Turning right out of the pub, we strolled casually downhill towards the town centre. The narrow one-way street was lined with dozens of small differently-coloured shopfronts, like the spines of books haphazardly stacked on opposing shelves, each demanding our attention. Although the pavements were busy, there was no hint of hustle or rude impatience. A steady stream of traffic drove slowly up the hill. Now and then a car would pause to permit someone to cross the road. There were nods, smiles and friendly waves. Shoppers and the usual lunchtime foot traffic were politely navigating around the strolling tourists and stationary groups of people who, in the best Irish tradition, had stopped to chat. The street was litter free and the shopfronts showed no sign of vandalism or graffiti.

The severe downturn in the Irish economy, particularly in the west, was a fact. Yet, despite the high unemployment, home repossessions and crippling emergency taxes, Ennis gave the impression of being a thriving town. But just below that veneer, the problems were obvious. I pointed to yet another shop emblazoned with bright orange 'Closing Down Sale' banners.

"If it wasn't for all the empty shops, you'd hardly know we were still in the depths of a recession."

"Apparently things are getting better in Dublin," Lesley replied, trying to add a hint of optimism.

"About time too," I sighed. "I fear it'll be a good while before we see an upturn here though. According to the local paper, unemployment is still rising in the rural areas."

"Then it's a good thing you haven't got a proper job!" Lesley joked.

I changed the subject to something lighter. "What did you want me to buy for you?"

"Ah." Lesley held up a finger. "It's not for me, it's for the children. They need a shelter."

"Children?" I frowned. "Do you mean chickens?"

"That's what I said," she replied.

"But you said–"

"I said chickens," my wife insisted.

I left it at that.

"We've only got three chickens left," I tutted, proving again my tendency to point out the blatantly obvious.

Despite my best efforts to fortify the chicken run, over the autumn and winter we'd lost all of our ducks and 26 chickens to fox attacks. The most recent casualty was the mighty Bruce, our magnificent Orpington rooster.

"We wouldn't have the three we've got, if you hadn't spotted the hole where the fox was getting in."

"I wish I'd found it earlier," I mumbled. "But with it being hidden behind that tree trunk…"

My wife reached over and gave my hand a squeeze. "I guess that's why they're called sly foxes."

"The chickens have already got a coop. What sort of shelter did you have in mind?"

"I was thinking of a little gazebo," Lesley explained. Her blue eyes twinkled mischievously and a playful smile danced across her lips. "Somewhere where they could shelter from the rain, or the sun. It would keep their food dry too."

"Really? A gazebo for chickens?" I laughed.

"Perhaps you could make something," my wife suggested.

We walked on for a time, comfortable in silence while I thought.

"What about a little tent," I suggested, clicking my fingers. "The sort of thing they make for kids to play in."

"That would work." Lesley nodded.

I pointed forward. "Memory serves, there's a camping shop down there."

Memory didn't, but we found the shop anyway. It was the kind of place which sold all sorts of outdoors stuff like water bottles, cooking stoves, waterproof clothing, torches, compasses, survival kits and hunting knives. It was a pretty impressive range for a store not much larger than a two-car garage. We were just four paces inside the shop when a young assistant emerged from behind a display case and greeted us with a genuine smile.

"How can I help," he enquired. His gently lilting Clare accent fitted perfectly with his well-groomed ginger hair, dark eyes and strong chin. I guessed he was around two years younger than my oldest pair of socks.

"We'd like a tent," Lesley said.

"What size?" he asked.

"Three chickens," I answered, careful to keep a straight face.

His eyes flicked to the rear of the shop. "I think I've got just the thing…"

Ten minutes later we were heading towards the carpark.

"Not bad for 16 euros," I said, patting the small pup-tent I had tucked under my arm. "Happy birthday!"

Lesley grinned. "Did you notice he didn't bat an eyelid when you told him what the tent was for?"

I couldn't help but laugh. "I guess we weren't the first to ask for a three-chicken tent."

My wife shook her head. "Only in Ireland!"

***

Back home, our dogs greeted us as if we'd been away for months rather than hours. As we'd negotiated our driveway, I could hear our black collie Kia beginning to woof. By the time I'd reached the front door, her excited barking had been joined by two others and overlaid with a comically high-pitched howl, as if a diminutive ambulance was turning tight circles in our porch. As soon as I opened the door, three dogs burst forth. Racing across our muddy driveway, they bounded up to Lesley and took turns marking her jeans with their wet and dirty paws.

"Get down!" she ordered, half-heartedly. It didn't matter, the dogs were ignoring her orders anyway.

Kia was first out of the door, but second to greet her mummy. That first-place prize was reserved for top-dog Lady. She's a slim Foxhound, as fit as a butcher's dog, but with all the arrogance of a teenage supermodel. Lady has dark intelligent eyes and soft white fur on her snout, chest and legs. Her shoulders, head and floppy ears are light brown, but her back and sides wear a saddle of dark chocolate. Lady trotted over to Lesley, jammed her face in between my wife's knees and waited until she'd received a head pat and ear rub. When the deed was done to her satisfaction, Lady gave a dismissive snort and trotted away to find something more interesting to do. With the coast clear, Kia stopped circling and stepped forwards for her fuss. Her silky soft fur is jet black, except for a flash of white on her snout and down her chest, as if she'd been carelessly lapping an ice-cream. Like Lady, Kia came to us as a puppy, via the Ennis dog pound. We rescued them together on a Friday afternoon, just moments before they were due to be euthanised. These two beautiful dogs are now as inseparable as sisters.

Not to be outdone, Amber howled like an ambulance once again, then jumped up, painting muddy paw prints on Lesley's legs – but only as high as her knees. Bouncy and endlessly energetic, Amber is a Wirehaired Terrier Pomeranian cross. At under a foot at the head, she's by far the smallest of our dogs; easily able to walk underneath the other pooches without being detected. She has long beige fur, a curly tail and large upright ears framing a pointy snout and black button eyes. Like most terriers, Amber is fearless, energetic and endlessly playful – traits which make the little dog an absolute delight, or extremely irritating, depending on how tired or busy we are.

With our most urgent canine fussing duties completed, we went through the porch to greet our fourth dog. Jack, as neurotic as ever, was still in the conservatory, hopping from foot to foot, smiling widely and woofing at his own ears, but unable to cross the porch for fear of inadvertently stepping on the cracks. He's a Rough Collie and the youngest dog in the house. Jack had arrived unannounced at our doorstep about 15 months ago. As an 'outdoors dog' at his previous home, he was free to roam as he pleased – which one freezing cold winter night, turned out to be a long trek up the hill to Glenmadrie where he took pride of place in front of our fire. After many attempts to return him to his rightful owners, they and we agreed he should remain for as long as he wished. Since then he has become a permanent fixture and a ambivalent member of our family. Jack has those classic Rough Collie features made famous in many Lassie films. His coat is long and silky soft and largely dark beige, except for a lion's mane of white fur. Jack is a large dog, with a long thin face, dark eyes and tall pointed ears – although one flops over in an attractively rakish fashion. He is an extraordinarily nervous dog, terrified by thunder, hail, loud noises, running water and tiled floors.

"I'll take Jack out the other door," Lesley sighed. "You can put the kettle on."

"What a silly dog," I whispered, watching him obediently follow Lesley outside.

We had recently discovered Jack has very poor eyesight and almost non-existent depth perception. This unexplained disability is probably the cause of his odd behaviour. His OCD extends to an annoying habit of refusing to pass through certain doors, or only going through when following certain people – usually me. As a consequence, whereas Lady, Kia and Amber will happily come in the front door, to get Jack indoors I lead him for some 50 yards around our house to reach the French doors at the rear. Furthermore, he won't pass through the kitchen at doggy meal times, at least not without being carried, so I have to guide him out through the French doors and then back indoors through the conservatory. All this kerfuffle so he can reach his personal feeding station, the only spot in the house where his food tastes just right. As this procedure seems to me like a lot of unnecessary messing about, on wet days I have toyed with the idea of hand-feeding Jack where he lies by gently spooning food into his sleeping mouth while he is breathing in the right direction. However, my dear wife says if I'm pandering to Jack, I'd have to do it for her too, so I scrapped that plan.

Not to be outdone, no sooner had we settled down with our drinks than Lady decided she wanted to go outside again.

"She's already done her business," Lesley complained as she opened the French doors.

"I guess she just wants to check out her territory," I replied.

True to form, ten minutes later, having woofed at the world from all four corners of our few acres, Lady demonstrated her new trick. There is a low window at the front of our house, directly opposite where I sit. It is the perfect height for an average size Foxhound with delusions of grandeur. True to form, five minutes after the distant barking stopped, Lady's head appeared at the window. She looked me directly in the eye and politely tapped on the glass with a muddy paw. As I frowned back, she turned her head away and stared at the sky with an air of innocence as if to say, "It wasn't me."

"Why can't she ever come back in the door she just went out through?" I growled.

"That would be too simple," my wife sniggered. "Anyway, she wouldn't feel so important,"

Lady tapped the window once again before exiting stage right, with all the aplomb of a Shakespearian actress. A moment later, I could hear her trademark double-bark at the front door.

"I suppose I should go and let her in," I groaned.

"You'd better hurry," Lesley warned.

On this occasion, I was too slow by around four seconds. Dissatisfied with the tardy service from her servants, Lady waited until she heard me approaching the door then turned tail and trotted away. By the time I'd returned to our sitting room, this regal pooch was already laid in front of the fire. As soon as I'd opened the door, she had stomped off down the side of the guest wing, nipped behind the shed, trotted along the farm track, hopped nimbly over the wall, walked across the courtyard and come back in through the French doors. The vexatious pooch's eyes were closed, but her beautiful face wore an expression of satisfaction.

"That'll teach him!" she huffed, or so I imagined.

As I raised cup to lip once again, the phone rang. It was our daughter, Joanne, calling from her home in England.

"How's married life treating you?" I asked.

"Well, I haven't shot Mark yet, if that's what you're wondering," she joked.

"You haven't been married a year," I exclaimed. "Keep your powder dry."

"Powder? What?"

"Gunpowder. For your gun," I laughed. "Oh, never mind…"

"Is Mummy there?"

"Yes, she's sitting right next to me. I'll put her on speaker, so we can both hear."

"How's the weather in Essex?" Lesley bellowed.

I covered my ears and mimed, "There's no need to shout." Lesley responded with a glare and a loving backhanded swipe.

"It's been grim," our daughter said. "Cold and raining."

"Just like here then," Lesley replied at a slightly lower level of decibels.

"Happyyy birthdayyyy too youuu!" Joanne sang.

"Thank you for the lovely birthday text," Lesley joked. "It was what I've always wanted."

"Pfft! I know you don't like getting cards and wasteful presents," my daughter replied defensively. "Anyway, I've been so busy at work I almost forgot."

"It's okay," Lesley replied with good humour. "Thank you for phoning."

"I miss you," Joanne sighed.

"I'll see you soon," Lesley said. "I'm over in May."

"You should come over here," I suggested.

"We will, in August. That's the other reason I'm calling," Joanne replied. "I have some good news. Becky's getting married."

"Oh, how lovely!" we both said.

Rebecca was one of Joanne's closest childhood friends and our honorary second daughter. Until recently, they had shared a house together in Chelmsford. Despite our fears Becky's fearsome reputation as a hardcore party animal would become an intolerable irritation, particularly as Joanne had started a new job in London, their friendship had survived intact. In truth, after a short but distinguished stint of military service, the young and wild Becky we knew from years earlier had matured into a fine respectable woman.

"They're holding the wedding in Ireland," Joanne explained.

"Whereabouts?" I asked.

"Killarney," she said. "Mark and I are coming over for the wedding. Mummy and you are invited too."

"That's great," I said, my mind racing ahead into full planning mode. "I'll see if we can get the house-sitter we used before. It'll be lovely to visit Killarney again. Perhaps we can stay for a few days."

"I thought the same," Joanne laughed. "We'd love to come over early and stay with you for a day or so. Then we can all go to Killarney together. Do you think Mummy can take a break from baking for a few days – perhaps miss one weekend at the market?"

I looked at my wife for approval, she nodded enthusiastically.

"That's no problem," Lesley said. "I could do with a break."

"Wonderful. Mark and I will look forward to it."

"I'll get planning," I added.

"Good for you, Dad," Joanne replied, her voice twinkling with mischief. "Perhaps you can make another of your lists."

2 – An Extended Stay

"Welcome home," Lesley said, leaning forward to give me a kiss. "How was your flight?"

"Very smooth. No delays." I waved dismissively.

"Did you have a nice time?" she asked, once we were on the open road.

"It was grand." I gave a contented sigh. "But I'm pleased to be home."

Lesley gave me a long look, suspiciously searching my face for clues. "Did you have a good time?"

"It was fine. Pl…please…" I pointed ahead and tried to speak without squeaking. "Please look where you're driving."

"No need. I know the way," she snapped, hauling the car away from the approaching ditch. "So, what's the matter then?"

"Nothing really." I looked out of the window and watched the bushes flashing by. "My mum was delighted to see me. She loved the chocolates we sent and enjoyed looking at all the pictures of the renovations. It's hard for her to get a sense of scale from photos on a tablet, but I think she has a better idea of what we've been doing for the last few years. Both of my sisters were there and Joanne met us in Norwich, so we all went out for a family meal."

"Where did you go?"

"That new Italian place," I replied. "It's run by Jimmy someone. That young chef."

"Jamie," Lesley corrected. "What was it like?"

I frowned and chewed my lip. "It was rather like eating lunch in a derelict warehouse. All peeling paint and exposed steel beams. I guess it's fashionable, but for me it was too bright and noisy – especially for a family meal where the guest of honour is elderly and hard of hearing. On the other hand, the food was excellent."

Lesley wrinkled her nose. "You stink of garlic,"

"Go figure," I laughed. "Mind you, I had an entire row to myself on the plane."

"I'm surprised the pilot didn't open the window!"

"I think the sudden decompression and urgent use of oxygen masks would have been rather welcome."

For a while, we drove in silence. I looked out of the window and smiled, pleased to see the small green fields and dry-stone walls of County Clare once more. As we started the long uphill climb towards Glenmadrie, Lesley spoke again.

"Did you see my mum?"

I nodded slowly and blew a long sigh. "Joanne and I spent most of today there."

Muriel, my mother-in-law, was a widow of 15 years. She lived alone in Braintree, around 20 miles from Joanne. Now in her 70s, Muriel had recently been diagnosed with dementia. Even though she was still managing, despite the home help we had arranged and the Meals-on-Wheels food service, Muriel was becoming ever more reliant on the assistance of her neighbour and frequent visits from our daughter. Dementia has no cure. It is a horrid, progressive and terminal condition, slowly stealing the mind – the very essence of a person – whilst leaving the body largely intact, but unable to function. It was inevitable that Muriel's situation would eventually become unsustainable and she would need around-the-clock care. Knowing Muriel would never consent to living in a care home, Lesley and I had recently discussed moving her mother to live with us in Ireland. We believed it was the only viable option, but Muriel was resistant, stoically soldiering on.

"We changed her home insurance to a cheaper provider," I explained. "Then I fixed her TV, reprogrammed the set-top box, changed two light bulbs and repaired that window she was complaining about."

"What about her car?" Lesley asked. "Did you get it sorted?"

"Yep. It was drivable, but not worth fixing. I took it to that scrap yard the other side of Witham, then cancelled her insurance. Your mum was sad to see her beloved car go, but she accepts it's for the best. The upside of this whole sorry mess is that she won't be driving anymore."

"No news from the police?"

"Same story as before." I shrugged. "They know who drove into Mum's car, but they can't prove it. Apparently, he's well known for racing up that cul-de-sac. Plenty of people heard the crash, but nobody is willing to stick their neck out and point a finger."

"I wouldn't blame them," Lesley sighed. "He's a nasty piece of work."

I nodded stoically. "Anyway, the police said there was a trail of bits leading back to his house, but his car has mysteriously vanished. Case closed."

"So, is that why you're upset?" my wife asked.

"No. That was an injustice." I shook my head. "Irritating, but nothing more. It sickens me to think someone would wreck an old lady's car, but not own up to it. Especially as he lives in the same street. Anyway, I'm not upset, just unsettled. I guess three days of racing around Norfolk and Essex, sleeping in strange beds and eating at odd times, just left me feeling rather disconsolate. England suddenly seems so busy and noisy and aggressive. It's changed so much since we lived there. That car crash was just another piece of the puzzle."

"Perhaps England isn't that different since we lived there," Lesley suggested. "Maybe it's us that's changed."

"You know, you could be right." I smiled and patted my wife's knee. "We've been here eight years. Anyone exposed to the lovely people, the fresh air and the gentle pace of life in Ireland is bound to have changed – and not for the worse. After all, it is why we came here."

About two miles from Glenmadrie, Lesley slowed the car and pointed to a newbuild bungalow off to our right.

"I've made some new friends. Bill and Pat. They're a lovely English couple, both around our age."

"How did you meet?"

"In the best Irish tradition. I saw them in their garden, so I stopped the car and started to chat over the hedge. They're both keen gardeners too, so they invited me in for a cup of tea. We all got on like a house on fire."

"That's nice," I said. "I'm delighted you've made some more friends. Have they been here long?"

"They've just moved here. They're recently retired and looking to start a new life."

"Far away from the hustle and bustle of modern Britain?" I suggested.

"I think so," she replied.

"Well, they've certainly come to the right place!"

***

21

Although April brought a welcome improvement in the weather, there was hardly a hint of sun shining on the local economy. We kept hearing about the 'green shoots' of growth showing through, but nationally the unemployment rate was heading towards 15 per cent and in many rural communities it was probably closer to 25 per cent. My heart ached for those unfortunate people dragged into the mire of financial ruin by events far beyond their control. For sure there were some who invested unwisely, greedy for a quick buck, but the vast majority of the casualties from Ireland's economic crash were just regular everyday working folk. Thinking there was safety in numbers, they had followed the herd and exchanged a little financial wiggle-room for the illusion of a brighter future with a bigger house, a better car and more holidays. For me, hearing of doctors, solicitors, architects and bank staff joining taxi drivers, builders and nurses in the queue at the food banks, was proof the bubble had burst.

Personally, I could only measure the health of the local economy by the number of golf lessons I was doing. This wasn't necessarily a reliable indicator because the golf industry was changing. Although the top 100 superstars were earning genuinely obscene amounts of money, at club level the story was very different. Busy people don't have time to waste and they certainly can't easily justify taking a day off to whack a ball around a few hallowed acres, followed by lunch and drinks. Such an outing might be relaxing and fun, but it won't pay the bills. Much the same could be said for golf lessons, especially as there were now some 400 million free golf tips available on the internet.

As an industry, teaching golf would always be a niche sector of a niche sport; the last to make money and the first to lose out. Accordingly, although teaching golf was my first love, it was never my first choice for a career. When we arrived in Ireland, I had no real plans for how I would supplement our savings until my pensions began to kick in. Finding work as a golf coach was a real bonus. I had thoroughly enjoyed putting my skills to use again and I know I helped a lot of people to play a bit better. Although the raging river of lessons had slowed to a gentle trickle, all was not lost.

"With practically no business overheads, you may as well

keep your hand in," my accountant said.

"I suppose you're right," I replied. "As long as I manage my time correctly."

"Perhaps you could focus on teaching a couple of days a week," she suggested.

"Mondays and Tuesdays would be good." I nodded at the idea and smiled. "It would get me out of the house and I could do a little practice between lessons."

Fortunately, the renovations at Glenmadrie were complete and our strict no debt policy was paying off. Unburdened by ballast and with minimal expenditure, with some careful financial fettling, we were just managing to keep our heads above water. On the upside, I had a lot more time to write, chill out with the dogs and get under my wife's feet.

***

"Come and see," I said, dragging Lesley outside to the covered walkway which, combined with the wing and conservatory, borders three sides of our courtyard.

"What?" she groaned.

I pointed at the rafters supporting the roof. "It's working."

One and a half sides of the courtyard cover way have open arched windows and a couple of doorways. The section where we store our firewood has a corrugated steel roof supported by pine beams. During the winter, I had constructed several nesting platforms to help the swallows which spend their summers at and around Glenmadrie. The platforms were just short planks screwed to the underside of the roof beams, but they were proving popular. Three were already showing signs of active nest building.

"I haven't seen any swallows this year," Lesley said, "but they must be about."

As if to confirm her observation, at that moment a swallow arrived. Rather than entering through the arched window, with no more than a warning 'peep' it flashed through the doorway, along the corridor, turned a sharp left and flitted nimbly up to its construction site. In passing, this master of aerobatics expertly bisected the narrow gap between our heads and lightly brushed the tip of my nose with a wingtip. During that brief encounter, my brain recorded a fleeting image, an avian selfie of a slightly surprised face grinning at the ecstasy of flight – or perhaps I just imagined it.

Before long, our pond would be brimming with frogs; hundreds of amorous amphibians grumbling and purring like the sound of a distant motorbike engine. Then we would sight the first bats, ready to feast on the early insects; midges and mosquitos attracted by the warming sunshine and the humid air rolling in on the westerly winds. Their flittering twilight flights would be serenaded by the songs of a thousand birds, along with the ghostly mating calls of the tiny snipe, swooping and diving to attract a mate. All this is a harbinger of spring, a regular occurrence in the hills around Glenmadrie and as reliable as the finest timepiece.

***

Of course, Ireland is also known for another unusual breed, the hardy gardener. Even before the February snows have reluctantly melted in the warming spring rain, the gardeners will emerge from their winter hibernation. Blinking in the watery sunshine, clad in woolly hats and waxed jackets, they enter their greenhouses and polytunnels for the first time in months and begin the ritual of washing pots, mixing compost and planting seedlings.

As we live at altitude, subject to slightly more rain and generally cooler temperatures than the good folk down in the valley, the growing season at Glenmadrie is a little shorter than usual for Ireland. Consequently, Lesley has a lot to do in those early days of spring to ensure she's on track with her planting timetable – otherwise, there'll be no harvest in the autumn.

Unfortunately, this year my wife encountered some unanticipated obstacles to her horticultural schedule.

***

Lesley's mother had been taken ill again. Another bladder infection had left her confused and physically weak. Temporarily casting aside her gardening plans, my wife hopped on the next available flight to England – and not a moment too soon. Unable to get Muriel a doctor's appointment at the local surgery, Lesley took her directly to the hospital. She was admitted immediately and administered intravenous fluids and antibiotics. For a few days, her condition seemed grim, particularly when she was diagnosed with stage four heart failure. The prognosis seemed so hopeless Lesley began thinking of funeral arrangements. Two days later, Muriel was out of bed, strolling around the ward and chatting with the nurses.

"She's feeling much better," the young doctor said. "You can take her home tomorrow."

"What about her heart condition?" Lesley asked. "The consultant said she was in stage four heart failure."

"Heart failure?" The doctor flicked through Muriel's notes, shook his head and frowned. "There's no mention of heart failure here. You must be mistaken."

The mystery of the phantom diagnosis was never solved. Clear of her infection, Muriel was bright-eyed, clear-headed and keen to get home. Even her dementia seemed to have improved, at least temporarily. Apart from cleaning the house and making sure her mother had plenty of food in the cupboard, there was little else Lesley could do, so she took her scheduled flight back to Ireland. Just four weeks later, my wife was back at her mother's house again. Muriel had been in hospital for five days, recovering from a long-awaited bunion operation. Now she was home, Lesley was there to act as a temporary nursemaid until her mother could walk unaided. Knowing she was to be away for six days, my dear wife had worked tirelessly in the garden to catch up with the planting, then left me several pages of idiot-proof instructions on the care and maintenance of her vegetables and flowers. Unfortunately, Muriel's recovery was taking longer than anticipated.

"How long?" I exclaimed.

"Hang on…" Through the satellite crackle of the mobile phone, I could hear the rustle of my wife walking. The familiar sound of a door opening and closing, then the background of birdsong told me Lesley was now standing in Muriel's back garden. "Probably another week."

"A week?" Despite my best efforts, my voice had taken on a squeaky tone. I knew how keen Lesley was to get back to her gardening. Although I was diligently following the horticultural instructions she had provided, carefully watering plants, moving the less hardy specimens indoors if there was a risk of frost and opening or closing the greenhouse and polytunnel doors to maintain an even temperature, I was strictly forbidden from any planting or weeding activities. Given my history of incompetence in this area, I was wisely restricted to digging holes and mowing the lawn. Understandably, Lesley's vexation swung towards the health service.

"Nick, Mum can hardly walk and she's in a lot of pain. What with her age and bad circulation, the wound is proving very slow to heal. The hospital should never have sent her home, at least not until her stitches are out. I'm sorry, but I can't leave her like this."

"It's okay. I understand. You do what you have to. Muriel comes first."

"What about my flight home? Can you cancel it?"

"Don't worry about that, I'll sort it out," I said, raising a calming hand even though my wife was 900 kilometres away. "Once you're ready to come back, I'll book you another flight."

"Thank you," Lesley whispered.

Leaning back on the couch, I stared at the sitting room ceiling and sighed. Sensing my frustration, Lady nudged at my knee with her snout until I reached down and tickled her ear.

"Lady says 'Hi'," I said.

Lesley laughed. It was nice to know she was still capable of some good humour.

"How are the dogs?" she asked.

"They're fine. We had a lovely long walk up the forest logging trail this morning. Kia was chasing after the ball, then giving it to Amber so she could bring it back to me. I've got them well trained now, except for Lady." I gave my faithful Foxhound's ear a loving tug. "She stole the ball and hid it deep in the forest."

Lesley laughed again. "She only does that to prove her dominance."

"I only had one tennis ball in my pocket, so after that, we had to make do with a stick. Then Amber brought me this huge branch. It was four times her size, but somehow she insisted on trying to take it home."

"You should have taken it off her," Lesley suggested.

"I tried, but she wouldn't let go, even when I lifted her off

26

the ground. We ended up playing that game where she hangs onto the stick, wiggling like a fish and growling in delight."

"Typical Terrier!" she giggled. "How's Jack?"

"He's quite intelligent you know. His hips are still quite stiff and he doesn't want to walk very much, so he only comes as far as the forest gate. I guess he's figured out we have to come back that way, so he lays in the sun and waits for us to return."

"Clever boy!"

"We all miss you," I sighed.

"I miss you too," she replied. "I'm sure I'll be back next weekend."

"Fingers crossed."

***

Lesley's prediction proved to be prematurely optimistic.

"Another week?" I exclaimed.

"Sorry. The wound isn't healing well, even though I'm bathing it every day as directed. The district nurse says the stitches can't come out until next Monday at the earliest."

"Blimey! I'll be healed before then."

"Oh! I forgot." My wife tutted. "How did your operation go?"

A couple of years earlier I'd had a small cancerous lump removed from the bridge of my nose. Although it was fully excised and there was no need for any further treatment, as a precaution, every new lump and bump since then has been swiftly removed. On this occasion, the offending protuberance was just inside my left nostril. Lesley had jokingly suggested it was sun damage because I was always looking down my nose at people.

"It was fine. No worse than having a tooth filled. Except there was a surgeon and three trainees all trying to look up my nose at the same time," I explained. "He gave me a local anaesthetic, poked about with a scalpel, then cauterised the wound with a laser. Bish-bosh done. I was in and out in under 30 minutes."

"When will you get the biopsy results?"

"I already did. The surgeon gave me the all-clear. He looked at the lump under the microscope while I was there. I guess he wanted to check he'd got all of it, which he had."

"That's good," Lesley said. "I'm sorry I couldn't be there."

"Don't worry about it. I'd have probably gone on my own anyway. It was nothing. Like I said, no worse than having a tooth filled."

"Well, if you're sure…" My wife sounded subdued. Unsurprising, considering the circumstances.

"A funny thing happened after though."

"Do tell."

"I was heading out the hospital door and there was a young lady coming the other way, so I held the door open and gave her a big smile. You know how I like to be polite."

"I'm guessing she was rather pretty," Lesley suggested.

"I don't recall," I lied. "Anyway, instead of saying thank you, she looked at me in horror and almost ran away."

"How odd."

"Not so much," I replied. "It was only when I got into the car and looked in the mirror, I realised I had a huge blob of yellow antiseptic gel hanging from my nostril. As my nose and upper lip was still numb, I had no idea."

Lesley laughed so hard I think she cracked a rib.

***

"How's your mum?" I asked. It was a week later. My wife was still in England and seemingly no closer to coming home.

"The district nurse took the stitches out yesterday, but Mum still can't put any weight on her foot. She's got cream for the abscess."

"Oh dear. Give her my love."

"I won't be coming home yet," my wife whispered.

"Another week?" My question was rhetorical. "Don't worry. Sort your mum out first. We're managing here."

Lesley let out a long sigh. "Did you get your new phone?"

"Eventually!" I snorted a disapproving laugh. "The delivery guy couldn't find our house, so he just left the phone with some bloke at the garage. He was just a random customer buying petrol. Luckily, he was an honest chap and gave it to the lady behind the counter. She phoned me and kept it safe until I could drive down."

"Ha! Only in Ireland. If that had been over here, you'd have never seen the phone again."

"At least it got me out of the house," I joked.

"I take it you've been quiet at work?"

I grunted an admission. "Three golf lessons and plenty of time to write. Oh, and I had a hole-in-one."

"Another?" Lesley tutted teasingly. "How many does that make?"

"Err…It's my tenth. As far as I'm concerned, they're pretty meaningless events, pure luck really, but the young lad I was playing with went nuts. He was whooping and cheering. He was so excited he even did a cartwheel. It was really funny. Mind you, he is only ten."

"I guess you made his day," she said. I could hear the smile in her voice. It made me miss her all the more.

"Do you remember my client Betsy? The American woman who speaks 11 languages. You met her once when we went to the ballet."

"If you're referring to the tiny grey-haired lady who's about 75, we met at that Beatles tribute concert," my wife said.

"Not the ballet?" I shrugged. "Anyway, she's moving back to America. Apparently, she used to work for the CIA. Now she's been recalled from retirement to give evidence at some court case. It must be big because they're paying for her to relocate Stateside."

"Betsy! In the CIA?" Lesley exclaimed. "Are you sure she wasn't having you on?"

"I know she jokes a lot, that's why I like her so much, but in this case, she was deadly serious," I explained. "When I asked Betsy what she did in the CIA, she gave that, 'If I told you, I'd have to kill you,' answer – but behind the usual humorous twinkle, there was a glint of steely honesty in her eyes."

"Good grief!" Lesley laughed. "And most people would have dismissed her as an inconsequential old woman."

"I agree. It just proves you never can tell."

***

It was just over seven weeks since Lesley had 'popped over to help Mum for a few days', that she returned to Ireland. We had a long hug at the airport before setting off towards

Glenmadrie. She arrived at 11.30 am, after taking the morning flight from London Stansted. By the time she deplaned, negotiated passport control and collected her bags, it was nearing lunchtime. Once away from the mildly industrial surroundings of Shannon airport, we made good time on the narrow roads towards Glenmadrie. Lesley looked out of the side window, occasionally craning her neck to catch a glimpse of the passing countryside.

"I can't get over how quiet the roads are here," she sighed. "You really notice it when you've been away for a while."

"You've been away so long the dogs will have forgotten who you are!"

My joke fell flat.

"I'm sorry."

"Not at all," I tutted at myself for being so insensitive and reached over to hold my wife's hand. "Your mum needed your help. I wouldn't have it any other way."

Lesley squeezed my hand in silent thanks.

"Anyway, now you're back I can get this car booked into the garage," I added. "The brakes are getting hit-and-miss."

"Good to know," she sniggered.

For a few minutes, we drove in companionable silence. Each of us comfortable in our own thoughts. As we entered a series of bends on the narrow road near to the house, Lesley spoke again.

"Mum's getting worse. We may have to bring her over soon."

"I know," I replied. "I was thinkin–"

"LOOK OUT!" Lesley screamed.

Less than 30 yards ahead, a huge caterpillar-tracked bulldozer was coming around the corner. Driving without the usual forewarning of a lead car, this yellow monstrosity was so wide, the massive steel blade was brushing the hedges on both sides of the road. Fortunately, I was already slowing for the corner as the deadly wall of steel appeared, but as soon as I stomped the brake pedal, one wheel locked solid and the car slewed alarmingly on the muddy road. As my wife whimpered and put her hands on the dashboard, I frantically pumped the pedal, cadence braking until we stopped – just four inches short of a collision.

We both let out a sigh of relief. I locked eyes with the fresh-faced bulldozer driver. He smiled and gave us a friendly wave. I figured he was around a year younger than the underpants I was about to discard.

"You can open your eyes now," I groaned. "Welcome home!"

My wife didn't laugh.

3 – Unwelcome Visitors

Glenmadrie sits high in the hills at a thousand feet above sea level. This may not seem particularly significant or tall in the grand scheme of things, but looking west, our little hill is the highest point of land for 6,500 kilometres. Whatever weather the Atlantic Ocean may choose to throw at Ireland, be it rain, wind, sleet or snow, there is nothing to deflect its ferocity until it slides up the gentle west-facing slope of our hills. Such a position is only tenable because the house sits in a small depression, protected on three sides by slightly higher ground and the tall trees of our wood to the north. As well as being beautiful on the eye, the topography around our home can cause some interesting meteorological anomalies.

At sunrise, the hilltops to the west radiate glorious orange, whilst our land remains in shadow. In December, the low watery winter sunshine barely clears the hills to the east and south, leaving us in almost permanent shadow. Consequently, during cold spells, the frost and snow at Glenmadrie can last for weeks, even though the valley opposite looks green and lush. At some point almost every winter I can stand on my land, ankle-deep in snow, whilst watching someone a mile away cutting his grass. Conversely, in the summer months the setting sun can shine uphill, bathing Glenmadrie in gold whilst everyone else is already in the dark. This atmospheric peculiarity was particularly evident one summer evening when I was driving home at twilight.

After crossing the small bridge for Hell river, I had entered the flat plane of a long and wide valley floor. It was late in the evening and I was driving east, away from Ennis with the low setting sun glowing brilliant orange in my mirrors. Minutes later, with darkness falling, I was forced to switch my headlights on. Turning left to leave the main road, I began to head north on a narrow country lane. My route crossed several miles of darkened fields shrouded in the ghostly glow of knee-deep dewpoint mists. Ahead I could see the hills gently rising towards the still-blue sky. As the gradual ascent began, the road wound along hillsides and through narrow valleys. With the high hedges and overhanging trees blocking the last vestiges of the setting sun, I was soon driving in darkness, even though the sky above was still quite light.

As the climb continued, I passed several houses harshly illuminated by blindingly powerful garden floodlights. To my right, through gaps in the hedges, I could see the distant lights of Scariff and Taumgraney shining through the inky darkness of the flat valley floor. Three miles from home, the road passed through a final dark tunnel of tall trees before entering open ground. Suddenly the surrounding countryside is much lighter. As the hills to the west fall away, the surrounding moorland was bathed in the soft golden glow of the setting sun – as bright as mid-day and welcoming as a winter fire. Each time I have experienced this phenomenon, I've felt a warm sense of elation. Were my spirits uplifted by the bonus of this second twilight, or was it just because I'd returned to the peace and tranquillity of Glenmadrie once more?

Back home, I fussed the dogs and kissed my wife, before donning my scruffy jeans and sweatshirt then making Lesley and I a beverage. She was in the sitting room, busy knitting a cardigan as a gift for her mother.

"Lovely sunset," I said.

"I saw." She nodded towards the window. "It looked like the sky was on fire."

"There was an interesting piece on the radio as I was driving home. I was listening to that new Talk Radio station. They do a weekly farming journal. I thought it was quite amusing."

"An amusing farming journal?" She frowned. "Are you sure?"

"Oh yes," I grinned. "It was a sort of *Irish Farming for Beginners*. I thought it was very relevant for hereabouts."

My wife nodded and gave me a beckoning wave. "Do tell."

I chewed my lip and grimaced.

"As best I can recall, there were ten things they mentioned: first, farming is an around the clock job – 24/7 365 days a year."

"That makes sense," she said. "Just like gardening and owning chickens. I doubt old Tom or his son, Tiernan, ever take time off."

"Two: farmers eat a big breakfast and have dinner at 12.30, so they can '*Get a good run at the day*.'" Lesley winced at my attempted Irish accent. Undeterred, I had another go. "In the evening they might have *A bit of tea*. Just a small meal, perhaps some soup with bread. Three: the weather is never right. It's always too wet/dry/hot or cold."

"I can't disagree with that," Lesley laughed. "We're all gardeners of a sort."

"Four: farming people are hardy. They're out in all weathers," I said. "And five: they're tough. Do you remember when Jim broke his finger last year? It was bent backwards. I told him to see the doctor, but he said, *'Ah. Don't be soft – it'll be grand'.*"

"You're not very good at these Irish accents," my wife laughed.

"I do my best." I shrugged defensively and held up another finger. "Six: Irish farmers never go to the doctor."

"Well, they were certainly right about that," Lesley replied. "Remember last year when that mobile medical unit went to the livestock mart and got the farmers to take some basic health checks."

"Oh, yes." I nodded. "Half of the farmers were so unfit they were referred on for urgent treatment."

"And a couple had to go to A&E by ambulance, there and then," she added, tutting. "They may be a tough breed, but they're unhealthy too."

I laughed, albeit with some heavy irony.

"Now what else was there?" I clicked my fingers. "Oh, yes. EU grants are great! I guess the extra money is all that's keeping the farms hereabout from going under. They also said, farmers are endlessly resourceful. They can fix anything with a length of bailing twine."

"That's true," Lesley said. "Farmer Jim usually has his trousers held up with some orange string. I don't think they've discovered duct tape yet though."

"You could be right, but I did once see a farm gate held up with an old printer cable."

"That is resourceful." My wife smiled. "Anything else?"

"Yes. Don't organise anything during silage season, but I guess we already knew that one. Everyone is working around the clock and late into the night and racing from field to field, trying to get the grass cut and bailed before the rains return."

Lesley nodded. "And you'd better drive carefully and pull over–"

"Because they won't," I added, rolling my eyes. Over the years we'd both had some close calls dodging the huge harvesters and bailing machines. "They also said 'I have a cow calving' is an acceptable excuse for a farmer to get out of any social function."

"Good to know," Lesley exclaimed. "I'm guessing it doesn't apply to us. 'I have a chicken laying' hardly has the same gravitas. We may have to buy a cow."

"Good plan," I sniggered. "The last thing was that rural fields all have odd names. I know that's true because I once asked old Tom what his fields are called."

"You didn't mention it," Lesley said.

"I'd forgotten until now." I shrugged an apology.

"What were they?"

"As best as I can remember…" I pointed in the general direction of old Tom's various fields. "He has names like Mountainside, Stinky Field, Black Meadow and The Wet Bit. Although that last one isn't very specific – especially in Ireland."

"That's for sure," my wife laughed. "Did they mention that big farmer?"

"No." I frowned. "Where did you hear about him?"

"Last week, when I was having lunch with Christine." Lesley was referring to her diminutive but excitably energetic friend. She was a lovely lady, although inclined to ramble off track when well lubricated with alcohol. "One of her many friends stepped over to say hello and they began chatting. To be honest, I wasn't really paying attention, but Christine got rather angry about some big guy who was eating into all their farm profits. I got the impression he was some sort of local supplier who was overcharging."

"Oh dear," I tutted in sympathy. Like many farming families, Christine and her husband Peadar had to work long unforgiving hours just to make ends meet. "Life is tough enough without getting screwed over by a local supplier. Did you get a name?"

"No. She called him 'That big farmer'. She may have added an expletive. I presume it was someone at the livestock mart."

"I've seen a few of the farmers going into the mart, 'The Big Guy' hardly narrows it down!"

Lesley laughed and held up her hands in surrender. "It's all I can remember. I just thought I'd mention it, while we're on the subject."

"Here's a thought. Next time I see him, I'll ask Old Tom." I winked and tapped my nose. "He's bound to know."

***

One of the first things we liked about Ireland in general, and County Clare in particular, was the comparative lack of crime. When we first arrived on this green and inviting island, we were amazed to see unsupervised children safely playing in the streets and young lassies hitchhiking, sure in the knowledge they would arrive home unscathed. The risk of petty theft was so low, many shopkeepers were happy to display their unattended goods on racks outside their shops and homeowners routinely left their doors and garden sheds unlocked. Indeed, the local community was so trusting of strangers, even slightly eccentric English blow-ins like us, we had great difficulty convincing them to accept immediate payment for the thousands of Euros worth of building and gardening supplies we'd had delivered. The economic crash has changed much of this.

Ireland effectively went bankrupt when it entered the EU bailout programme in 2009. Since then, the government has operated under the strict financial guidance of the European Union, the European Central Bank and the International Monetary Fund. While this Troika is controlling the purse-strings, there has been almost no investment going into public services. High unemployment is draining the Social Welfare coffers and the total recruitment ban has devastated our hospitals. The overstretched Irish police force, *An Garda Síochána*, has struggled to keep up with the drug gangs, who seem to be awash with money and weapons. Consequently, resources have been moved to the cities, leaving many local communities unprotected and vulnerable. In rural areas, opportunist thefts, cattle rustling and violent home invasions are on the rise. Homeowners and farmers are taking previously unnecessary precautions by locking doors, chaining ladders and installing security lights and cameras. More than ever, we watch out for our friends and neighbours, and they look out for us.

"There's someone in the lane," Lesley shouted, trying to make herself heard over the barking of the dogs.

Frowning in confusion, I turned away from my computer screen and squinted out of the upstairs window. "I can't see

37

anyone," I shouted back. "It was probably just Jim on his tractor."

"I don't think so," my wife replied. "It was definitely a van. I saw a flash of white as it went by."

"A van?" I exclaimed. "That can't be right. The lane's barely passable. Why would a van come down?"

Around a century ago, the track at the rear of our property was a main thoroughfare, connecting Lough Graney with the villages in the valley to our south. At one time this narrow track would have been busy with horse-drawn carts laden with produce, farmers with livestock heading to market and smartly dressed people on their way to church. Before it was renovated by a succession of owners, Glenmadrie was a simple thatched cottage which faced this lane. In response to the needs of motorised vehicles, sometime around 1950, a tarmac road was laid. As this new road took a less arduous route a little further to the west, the original track fell into disrepair. Today it's no more than an over-grown muddy and half-flooded bridle path, used only by local farmers and a few hardy walkers. Deeply rutted by the churning wheels of Jim's tractor, with a raised central ridge of mud and grass, it's a slippery, ankle-twisting challenge for passing walkers and no place to be driving any road vehicle. Nonetheless, she-who-must-be-obeyed had spoken. Reasoning I'd earned a break from my current writing project, I saved my work and headed downstairs.

"I'm sure there's someone there," Lesley reaffirmed.

Amber, Lady and Kia were frantically scratching at the front door. Jack was whining at the exit leading to the courtyard, presumably because he was planning a pincer move to trap the intruders.

"I think you're wrong," I replied, bravely contradicting my wife. "But I'll go and have a look." I nodded at Jack. "Please let him out."

The instant I opened the front door, Amber pushed past my legs and bolted around the corner towards the lane, followed in quick succession by Lady, Kia and me. Immediately, I could see my wife had been correct. There in the lane, just past the old gate which had once been the entrance to Glenmadrie, was a small battered white van.

Above the cacophony of angry barking, I heard a man shout,

"Ah feck, they've got dogs." His voice was harsh, gravelly and overlaid with a thick Limerick accent. A second, younger voice added, "Gerroff!"

As I approached my gate, I shouted to bring the dogs to order. In reply, the dogs shouted back that they were rather busy dealing with two strange men and their car but would be with me in a moment.

"Hello?" I shouted, barely making myself heard above the incessant barking.

The two men circled around the front of their van and peered out warily. They both mumbled the stock Irish "Howyer" greeting, combined with a synchronised chicken-like chin thrust.

With identical wavy black hair dark eyes and square jaws, they could easily have been father and son. Both wore matching brown work boots, but the remainder of their clothing was a mish-mash of dirty and ill-fitting garments. The older man wore a black baseball cap, faded jeans, a blue polo shirt and a beige zip-up cardigan with a brown zig-zag pattern which hasn't been fashionable since 1968. The son had on a pair of brown corded trousers, which may have been older than he was, and a tightly zipped puffy black bomber-style jacket, with a rip on one arm where the white stuffing was bulging out. In rural Ireland such attire is commonplace and deemed suitable workwear for farmers, politicians, priests and so many other professions – therefore I was momentarily clueless as to the intent of our visitors.

"Can I help?" I asked.

"We're stuck," the younger man said. He kicked at the mud. "Dis road's a fecking disgrace."

"I'm not surprised you're stuck. This lane hasn't seen traffic for 70 years." I grimaced and pointed a thumb over my shoulder. "The main road's over there. Whatever made you come down here?"

"We saw da house and thought this was the way in."

I frowned. "Why?"

They shared a look and as if by some pre-arranged signal, the older man answered. "Errr…We wus wondering if youse wanted to sell yer car?"

I'm told I frequently miss social cues obvious to others. Nonetheless, on this occasion, a warning bell was ringing in my head and the dogs were making it clear they felt something was very off with these two. Their car shopping story seemed a little thin, particularly as neither of our cars were visible from the road or the lane.

"Which car were you interested in?" I asked.

The older man glanced over my shoulder. I saw his eyes flicker as he searched for an answer. His son interjected.

"Or barrels," he said.

"That's right," the father added gratefully. "We buy barrels too."

"Barrels?" I exclaimed. It seemed like an odd request.

Just then Jack came bounding down the lane, followed by Lesley. As he joined in the renewed cacophony of barking, I made eye contact with my wife and subtly nodded towards the house. For once she read my intent correctly, spun on her heel and headed back indoors. With a sharp whistle and a wave of my hand, I called the dogs into some semblance of order.

"Sorry lads, there's nothing for sale here," I said, firmly. "You'd best get on your way."

I noticed the younger man's eyes were never still. He avoided looking at me, preferring to spend his time examining the dozen or so pot plants and gardening implements Lesley kept at this side of the house. I got the impression he was constructing some sort of a mental shopping list.

"Where dus dis go?" The father asked, pointing down the lane.

"Just a muddy field, but there's no room to turn around." I cast my eyes back up the hill. "You'd best go that way."

"Can't." He kicked discontentedly at the rear wheel of the van. "We's stuck."

Fortunately, I'd had the foresight to slip on my wellies before leaving the house, so I opened the gate and walked through, making sure to casually close it behind me. Although both men were slightly taller and heavier than me, I had four dogs and the experience gained from several years as a karate instructor on my side of the scales. Feeling physically confident whilst remaining alert and wary, I walked to the front of the van to see the problem. For once the two men seemed to be telling the truth. Both front wheels were dangling in water-filled ruts and the underside of the van was firmly stuck on the high central ridge of mud. I was again struck by how determined, or perhaps desperate, these two lads must have been to drive some 300 yards downhill on this obviously impassable lane.

I whistled in disbelief.

"Wow. You certainly are stuck."

"Will you give us a shove?" the son asked.

I sucked my teeth and grimaced, but not necessarily in that order. "You'll need more than a shove to get out of this mess. Don't you have breakdown cover?"

"Breakdown cover? Pfft! Ya joking me!" The father laughed disdainfully. "We can't afford the likes of that."

"Can't you call a friend?" I asked, perhaps a little too flippantly.

His face showed a flash of dark anger and he took a hostile step forward, a moment later the son started to circle the van in an obvious pincer move. Clearly, the situation was about to take an ugly turn. I abhor violence and only learned karate as I thought it was an interesting sport and a great way to keep fit. Nonetheless, as the two men moved closer, I found myself automatically changing my posture and balance ready to react. Perhaps sensing the rising tension, the dogs began barking and making aggressive lunges. Both men paused and after a moment of contemplation, the father took a half-step backwards.

His face took on a scornful sneer and he hawked something from deep in his sinus and spat at the ground.

"We's a long ways from home and there's nobody who can come," he growled. "Anyways, it's your lane we's stuck in, so you'd better help or we can't get out."

"Dat's right," the son added.

He had a point, of sorts. They were stuck and unable to move. Although I wasn't feeling particularly charitable, I didn't want these two camping at the back of my house for one minute longer than necessary.

"Wait here," I sighed. "I'll see what I can do."

I herded the dogs indoors and grabbed my mobile phone. Luckily, old Tom's son Tiernan was quick to answer my call for help. In double-quick time he arrived in his enormous tractor and, after attaching a chain, unceremoniously dragged the offending vehicle back up the hill to the main road. As soon as their van was unshackled, and without a word of thanks or a friendly wave, our unwelcome guests drove off.

"Well," I huffed. "How do you like them apples?"

"Not very polite," Tiernan replied, his County Clare accent as strong as ever. "But it's about what I'd expect from them sorts. At least they've gone. That's the important bit like."

My foot nudged a muddy number plate laying in the road. "Perhaps they'll come back for this."

"Not likely," he laughed. "They probably robbed that van from someone yesterday."

I warmly thanked Tiernan for his timely assistance. His reply was typically gracious and he casually waved away my offer of payment. It made me feel warm inside to know we had such helpful and friendly neighbours.

Back indoors, I followed Tiernan's advice and called the Guards. As it turned out, they were rather interested in chatting with the two men in connection with several local robberies, including a violent cash theft from a shop the previous afternoon. Wishing I'd had the foresight to surreptitiously take a few photographs, I gave a description of the two men and read out the details of the number plate I was holding. Despite my help, the identity of our unwelcome guests remained a mystery. I heard no further news on the matter, so I presume they dumped the van or moved on to a different hunting ground.

On the upside, another mystery was solved that day. All was revealed as Lesley and I were eating dinner that evening.

"Aha." I clicked my fingers. "I asked Tiernan about that big farmer you mentioned."

"Oh yes?" Lesley's fork hung in the air, an inch from her mouth. "Did he know who it was?"

"Sort of…" I grinned, trying to find a suitable way of delivering the answer. "It took a minute, but then he figured it out."

"So Tiernan knew who it was?" she asked, before popping the food into her mouth.

"Oh yes," I replied. "He and his dad are getting ripped off too."

Lesley mumbled something which may have been, "*Who is it?*"

"Actually, it's not who, it's what."

She frowned threateningly and I sensed now would be a good

time to desist from milking the situation any further.

"The *big farmer* Christine was talking about is big *p-h-a-r-m-a*. She was complaining about the cost of veterinary medicines!"

I smiled triumphantly. "Mystery solved!"

For some reason, my dear wife didn't see the funny side of the misunderstanding.

4 – Welcome Visitors

A few days before Rebecca's wedding in Killarney, Joanne and Mark flew into Shannon airport on the early flight. This was our daughter's first trip to Ireland since her wedding and as County Clare was deeply embedded in the young couple's romantic history, they were both looking forward to the visit. As well as arranging our accommodation in Killarney, in preparation for their two day stay at Glenmadrie, my daughter and I had planned some local activities to keep us all entertained.

Once they'd unpacked and had a late breakfast, I took the dogs and our guests for a bracing 10-kilometre walk. The route took us up through the forest, across the high moor and down the hill overlooking Lough Graney before looping back up to the house.

"When are we going sailing?" Mark asked, throwing a tennis ball for the dogs. They sprinted off, excited as children at Christmas.

"Tomorrow," Joanne replied, "But we aren't sailing, we're boating."

Mark, already wise in the skills of being a husband, did well to hide his disappointment.

The day before their flight, Joanne had been active on the internet and rented a boat so Mark could see the mighty splendour of Lough Derg. Fancying himself a yachtsman, Mark had been in favour of hiring a small sailing skiff, but based largely on his inexperience in such a mode of transport, his new wife had overruled that idea and settled instead for a long fibreglass rowboat with an outboard motor.

"So, what are we doing today?" he asked.

"After this walk, we'll have some lunch and drive over to Craggaunowen. We can spend the afternoon there. It's a 16th-century castle and archaeological open-air museum."

My son-in-law looked at me as if I'd just confessed to being the love child of visiting space aliens.

"It'll be fun," I said, trying to attract some enthusiasm after my big reveal had fallen flat. "This walk has some wonderful views. I hope you've brought your camera."

"I guess 'fun' is a subjective thing here in Ireland," Mark commented, his voice dripping with irony. As an afterthought, he added a small smile to soften the blow.

"Don't forget Ireland invented fun." I jokingly added the passionate fist pump I'd learned at my last job as a way of stimulating enthusiasm in people who had just been made redundant. It didn't work then – or now.

"It's called craic," Mark replied. "But it's only fun because it includes alcohol and dancing."

"Good point," I conceded.

After barging Lady aside, Kia had recovered the ball and, after deftly dodging Mark's outstretched hand, our lovable black collie presented it to Joanne.

"Thank you, Kia," she said, somewhat insincerely. The ball was dripping with dog slob, so Joanne held it with her fingertips.

"Will there be alcohol and dancing tomorrow?" Mark asked with pleading eyes. "After all, we are on holiday."

"I guess you can take a beer on the boat," I replied, "but I'd avoid any enthusiastic dancing unless we're close to land."

"There'll be plenty of dancing and alcohol at the wedding," Joanne tutted, nudging Mark with her elbow. "A bit of fresh air will do you good and give you a chance to burn off a few calories before the festivities begin."

Realising he was outnumbered, Mark shrugged in defeat. "Have you got any fishing rods?"

"I have one you can use, but we'll have to dig up a few worms."

"Yay!" Joanne clapped her hands jokingly. "We're having fun already!"

"Yay…" Mark groaned expressively, then deftly dodged the tennis ball his wife had just thrown.

"What's the matter with Mummy?" my daughter whispered.

I watched Mark jog off after the ball, eagerly followed by the dogs.

"What do you mean?"

"Well, you've taken a few days off so we can go out together, but she's stuck indoors baking cakes for the market. What's that about? Have I upset her or something?"

"I don't think so. She hasn't said anything." I shrugged. "But you know what I'm like, unless she put up a big sign…"

"You wouldn't have noticed anyway," Joanne finished the thought for me. "I know you're hopeless at picking up on these things, but surely you must have realised it's odd for her to be working like this when you've guests staying at the house. Especially as it's us."

"Now you mention it, I guess it is a little odd," I conceded. "But…"

"But what?"

"Well, it's a busy bank holiday weekend and she's missing the market so she can go with us to Killarney," I explained. "A friend is running the stall, but your mum wanted to bake some extra cakes, That's why she's so busy today."

"That's what she told me," my daughter said. "But I sensed there was something else troubling her."

I shrugged. "Behind every angry woman, is a man who has no idea what he's done wrong!"

My daughter laughed and gave my arm a gentle squeeze.

"I think she's just tired," I added. "She's worried about her mother too. Even with the home help going in twice a day, Muriel is struggling to cope. We can't care for her from here, but she still refuses to move to Ireland – even though she acknowledges coming here is the best option."

"The apartment you've built is lovely. It's much nicer than her house and warmer too. It would be perfect for her to live in." Joanne sighed. "I guess she's just resistant to change and worried about losing her independence."

"I'm sure she is," I replied, "but she's asking a lot of her neighbours – and you. I know she's your grandmother and you want to help, but recently you've had to take a lot of days off work to attend to her. That isn't really a tenable situation, particularly as you've recently married and begun a new job."

"Mark's okay with it, but you're right about work. They take a dim view of me suddenly taking days off. The other day, when I had to take Muriel to the doctor, I missed an important client meeting. My boss wasn't shy about showing his dissatisfaction."

"Like I said, it's not a particularly tenable arrangement – and it's going to get worse." It was my turn to sigh. "I guess your mum is feeling disconnected and…a bit guilty. She misses you a lot."

Joanne chewed her lip and shrugged in grudging acceptance of my explanation. "Are you okay?"

"Pfft! I'm grand." I waved away her question. "Come on.

47

We'd better help Mark. He seems to have lost the ball."

***

The forest logging trail we were following was a 20-metre-wide gravel road which curved to the right as it gradually rose along the hillside. For the most part the incline wasn't severe and the hardpacked gravel surface made for easy walking. However, the towering pine trees surrounded us like the walls of an arboreal palace, permitting only tantalising glimpses of the surrounding countryside. Just after reaching the summit, as the road sloped steeply downhill, I turned left through a gap in the trees and led our party out of the forest and onto the high moor.

"It's a good job you know the way," Mark said. "I wouldn't have recognised this as a path to anywhere."

"There was a little finger sign nailed to a tree back there, but it was easy to miss." I pointed ahead. "Out on the moor, there are marker posts every hundred yards or so to guide us along the path. Before you pass by a post, always make sure you can see the next one."

Mark nodded sagely. "I expect it's easy to get disorientated up here."

"Especially when the weather is bad," I agreed. "Even in the summer, a sudden rain squall up here can be a life-threatening event, especially if you aren't properly dressed."

"This ground is a bit soggy," Joanne laughed. She had her arms out like a tightrope walker and her pink flowery wellies were already ankle deep in the tea-coloured water.

"Keep moving, or you'll sink!" I grabbed my daughter's outstretched hand and guided her forwards. "Much of this blanket bog is floating on water. That's why it feels rather bouncy. You'll be fine for as long as you keep moving, but if you stop, there's a fair chance you'll begin to sink."

"Good to know," she replied.

"The ground here is rock, overlaid with peat and a thick layer of Sphagnum moss."

"What's Sphagnum moss?" Mark asked.

Joanne sighed dramatically and gave her husband a loving thump on the shoulder. "What did you ask that for? Now we're going to get a lecture."

I ignored my daughter's jibe at my love for information.

"Actually, mosses would be more accurate. Most of the

plants are no larger than your finger, but they clump together like grass. I think there are around a dozen varieties of sphagnum mosses. I don't know the names, but if you look around you can see the different colours. Alongside the predominately flat pools of green, there's clumps of yellows, dark reds, pink, copper, orange and chocolate. Some of them are very pretty too."

"What are the white things that look like cotton?" Mark asked, pointing at an area where hundreds of white tufts were waving above the grass like small flags.

"It is cotton!" I laughed. "Well, actually it's called Bog Cotton. Although it doesn't grow in vast quantities, theoretically, you could use it to make clothes. It's certainly very effective at catching a spark if you ever need to start a fire. It's not immediately obvious, but there's all sorts of wildlife living up here and bogs are better at capturing carbon than the Amazon rainforest. But without sphagnum moss there would be no bogs. This place would look like the moon."

"You mean just bare rock, like the Burren?" Joanne was referring to the Burren National Park in the west of County Clare, where some 100 square miles of limestone rock has laid bare since the last glacier retreated around 10,000 years ago.

"Absolutely correct. Underneath this bog, the limestone and granite would look as barren as the Burren. The sphagnums built this bog. Without sphagnum mosses there would be no bogs in Ireland." I pushed at the moss with the sole of my boot. "The surface of this bog is made of an interlocking carpet of sphagnum mosses. This is floating on a layer of partly rotted plant material, which in turn is sitting on a deep layer of peat. The peat is created by the rotted plants being compressed over time – a bit like coal or oil. Anyway, it's all soaking wet, which is why it feels bouncy. Sphagnum moss is fantastic stuff. Watch this."

I dug my fingers into the moss and pulled out a handful, then squeezed. A torrent of water fell from my hands.

"Wow!" Joanne exclaimed.

"It's like a magic trick," Mark laughed.

"The mosses can hold up to 20 times their own weight in water. The ability of these plants to store water is what makes bogs such a viable habitat for so many bugs, amphibians and birds." Using my fingers, I gently teased a single plant from the clump. "Look closely and you'll see the plant has two types of branches. Some stick out and others hang down. The spreading branches give the plant structure and the hanging branches are pressed onto the stem and help to draw up water."

"Like capillary action?" Mark asked.

"I guess that's right." I nodded and carefully pushed the handful of moss back into the hole.

"Also, sphagnum moss has natural antiseptic, antifungal, antibacterial and antibiotic properties. During the First World War, it was dried and used for dressing wounds. It probably saved thousands of lives. These bogs may appear to be lifeless and uninteresting, but they have a desolate beauty as well as being a crucial environment for wildlife."

We walked on for around 20 minutes. Mark led the way, helpfully pointing to the next marker as we passed each guidepost. The path was no more than a muddy track, winding its way along the hillside and stretching across the flatter parts of the moor. If it wasn't for the marker posts and some rough wooden footbridges to help walkers cross the widest of the muddy ditches, it would have been easy to imagine we were the first humans to pass this way in generations. As we reached the highest part of the moor, the ground ahead began to fall away, revealing for the first time the landscape to the north. Far below, surrounded by green hills, we could see the waters of Lough Graney, glinting blue in the sunshine. Beyond those cool waters, the green land rose higher, turning brown and flattening where the high valleys contained the vast blanket bogs of Atorick and Slieve Aughty.

"Wow, what a view!" Joanne exclaimed.

"Not a boat in sight," Mark added. "Is that where we're going tomorrow?"

"No. That's Lough Graney, where Amber nearly drowned," I said. "Just behind that hill on the left there's this beautiful beach. Joanne and I were walking the dogs when Amber went for a swim and got out of her depth. I had to wade in and save her."

"Oh, that was so funny," Joanne added. "Dad was soaked through and had to drive home sitting on a plastic bag."

"I was very brave," I pointed out, but nobody rushed to support my position. "Tomorrow, we're heading south to Lough

Derg, it's on the River Shannon. Mind you, the river from this Lough feeds down to the Shannon via Lough O'Grady which flows through Scariff and Tuamgraney." I wiggled my eyebrows mischievously. "Perhaps you could swim."

"It's okay." Mark raised his palms in surrender. "We'll take the car."

"Your choice," I laughed. "Legend has it there was once a fair maiden called Graine who was out boating on the River Graney, but a storm blew up and she was thrown into the water. Apparently, she swam for a considerable distance before succumbing to the raging torrent. When she was found, Graine was still clutching a branch from where she'd unsuccessfully tried to pull herself out. She was buried under the rock of Tuamgraney, still clutching the stick. Over time that stick budded and grew up through the rock."

"You're making it up!" Joanne said.

"Not at all," I replied. "There's a famous poem about it by Brian Merriman." I pointed to the lake. "Just where the road crosses the river, there's a memorial stone carved with the poet's name."

"Shall we walk on?" Joanne asked.

"In a minute. Head over that way," I pointed to the left, "where those signs are."

A few yards away there was a small group of white information boards and a wooden bench. Sensing we were taking a short break, the dogs slumped down on the dry grass and did a little sunbathing, whilst we read the signs.

"Mass Rock," Joanne read. "Did people really come up here to celebrate mass?"

"So legend has it. I guess this rock dates back around 400 years to when the English outlawed Catholicism. People came to remote places like this to practice their faith." I shrugged. "It seems almost every hilltop in Ireland has its own Mass Rock."

"And every lake has a Holy Island," she added.

"True," I laughed.

"Look at this," Mark called. He was reading a sign about the remarkable geology of the area. "The rocks forming that cliff are from two different continents. The lower rocks are of shales which were deposited in the estuary of some mighty river more than 400 million years ago. Over time, upheavals in the earth's crust formed the shales into a mountain. The rock in the upper layer is sandstone. The type of pebbles within it and the angled layers, indicate this was once part of a dune on the edge of a desert south of the equator. This sandstone was formed around 370 million years ago."

"So all of this was once south of the equator?" Joanne exclaimed.

"That's why I wanted to show you these signs," I replied. "Over time, this very rock has moved some 10,000 miles. Fascinating, isn't it?"

"In some ways it's a shame Ireland isn't nearer to the equator," Mark said. "If it was, we'd probably visit more often!"

I winced at the barbed comment, but he had a point. A light drizzle was falling.

"Do we have far to go?" Joanne asked.

"About an hour."

My daughter grunted her disapproval and walked on.

The path ahead took a winding route down the steep hill and across some fields, before joining a single-track road in a long left-hand curve ending where it met a shallow river. There we would wade across the ford and begin the leg-aching 800-foot climb up the steep hill which led back to the house. Halfway through the downhill section, Lady disturbed a hare and enthusiastically gave chase.

"Oh no!" My heart sank.

I knew how single-minded Lady could be when she's in full-on hunting mode. With her nose down and tail up, she is deaf to the world – and the desperate calls of her master. Combined with her hopeless sense of direction, I was worried our hapless Foxhound would become completely lost. For 20 minutes we walked on whilst shouting her name. Occasionally, Joanne added a series of ear-splitting whistles, but to no avail. We could hear Lady's frantic yelping, a sure-fire indication she was hot on the trail of a hare, but the noise was becoming ever more distant.

"It sounds like she's heading for Galway," Mark commented.

My shoulders slumped. "We may never see her again."

There was nothing we could do but press on home and hope some kindly stranger would find the unruly hound and call the telephone number on her collar. But we need not have worried. Just as we reached Glenmadrie, Lady came trotting up the hill behind us. She was sopping wet, covered in mud, grinning broadly and panting like a racehorse.

"Lady's got more energy than me!" Joanne groaned.

As she bent to massage her aching calf muscles, I saw what was about to happen, but my shout of warning was too late. As if being vibrated by a mighty earthquake whilst enduring a sneezing fit, Lady enthusiastically shook herself, showering my daughter with copious amounts of muddy water.

"Lay-deee!" she squealed.

With a mighty effort, Mark and I resisted the urge to collapse in fits of laughter.

**

By the time we'd had some lunch and a chat, it was almost 3 pm. I was about to call time on our planned itinerary, when Lesley interjected.

"Craggaunowen Castle is only a half-hour drive away. You should still go. I haven't finished baking yet. If you stay here, you'll only get under my feet."

"It's a bit late in the day to be heading out again." I glanced at my watch and tapped the dial with my finger. "I think they shut at five."

My wife waved my objection away as if it were a troublesome fly. "Then you'd better get moving."

I glanced at Mark and Joanne for some moral support, but they both shrugged, indicating indifference, or a prudent unwillingness to get involved. So we decided to go ahead with the trip, even if it meant jogging around the attractions, which it did.

Craggaunowen Castle was built around 1550 by the MacNamara family, who also built the nearby Knappogue Castle, which is also a tower house. These structures are tall, blocky buildings. Although they have some battlements along the roofline, these were more for show as the buildings were intended to be secure residences rather than defensive positions against a determined attack. Like many similar properties, these castles fell into disrepair under the heel of Oliver Cromwell. Craggaunowen was eventually restored in the 1960s by John Hunt and, for a while it housed much of his large collection of antiquities.

"Nothing to see now?" Joanne asked, pointing at the almost empty room.

"Apparently not…" I frowned and flicked a page of the guide book. "It says most of the collection was moved to Limerick!" It took a few seconds before I made the connection. I rolled my eyes and slapped my forehead with an open palm. "D'oh! I've just realised they're referring to the Hunt Museum in Limerick city. It's a big grey building not far from King John's Castle, alongside the Shannon. As there is such a big following for everything horsey in Ireland, I'd always assumed the Hunt Museum was dedicated to fox hunting!"

Mark and Joanne both laughed.

"To be fair, there is a bronze statue of a horse at the front," I explained.

"Is there a fox too?" Mark grinned, clearly enjoying my embarrassment.

I looked to my daughter for some moral support, but she was already heading towards the next attraction.

As it was late in the day, we'd missed the displays of woodcrafts, but the ancient breed wild boar and Soay sheep were momentarily interesting, until the drizzle encouraged us to move along. The lakeside open-air museum has reconstructions of a megalithic tomb, a ringed fort and a crannog, which is a circular hut on a raised platform over the lake, like a crow's nest built on stilts hammered into the lakebed. Perhaps the most interesting attraction was a 36-foot long, two-masted currach boat. Hand built using traditional tools, it has a frame of Irish ash and oak covered in tanned ox hides, sealed with wool grease and lashed together with two miles of leather throngs.

"This boat was sailed from Ireland to America by the explorer Tim Severin in 1976 to prove his theory that the fabled Voyage of St. Brendan the Abbot actually took place," I explained. "Over several months, Severin and his crew sailed from Ireland all the way to Newfoundland. It was a journey of 4,500 miles and more-or-less proved St. Brendan had reached the Americas some 1,500 years ago."

"Wow!" Mark exclaimed. "That's incredible."

"The recreation was indeed incredible, but the original voyage was astonishing." Joanne added. "Such bravery."

"He wrote a bestselling book," I said.

"St. Brendan?" Mark quipped.

I tutted at the joke and rolled my eyes. "Tim Severin. We've got a copy at home." I tapped my watch. "Talking of which, we'd better get going."

***

We arrived back at Glenmadrie in good spirits and with growling stomachs, only to be confronted by my growling wife.

"There's no dinner and an oven-full of cakes are ruined," she moaned. "Just after you left, the flipping gas ran out!"

"Oh no!" I let out a groan of despair.

"Do you have to put money in a meter?" Mark asked, frowning in confusion.

"No," I replied. "We're too far out for mains gas. It's one of the joys of living here. Our cooker uses bottled gas."

"And I couldn't figure out how to change over to a fresh bottle." Lesley flapped her hands in obvious frustration.

"Sorry." I sighed and pulled my wife into a hug. I could see she'd been crying. "The cylinder valves are quite tricky to undo. You need a spanner and for some reason the nut turns in the wrong direction. I meant to fit a simple tap, so this wouldn't happen, but I forgot."

Lesley buried her face into my chest. "It's alright," she mumbled. "I'll just have to bake the remaining cakes tomorrow." My wife turned her wet eyes towards our daughter. "I'm so sorry but I can't come to the lake with you."

"It's okay, Mum, I understand," she said. "We could stay here and keep you company."

"Don't be silly. You'd only get under my feet." She gave a tight smile and a dismissive wave. "Go off and enjoy yourselves. You can take a packed lunch."

"Will there be cake?" I joked, before deftly dodging my wife's loving attempt to punch my lights out.

Despite Lesley's baking disaster, the day ended on a positive note. Once our gas supply was restored, I tapped my watch one final time.

"It's too late to start cooking now. Get your coats on, we'll go to that pub in Tuamgraney for a slap-up meal," I said. "My treat."

"At last some craic!" Mark cheered.

"Yay!" Joanne added.

5 – A Slow Boat to Nowhere

Despite the lack of dancing that night, we had all enjoyed an excellent meal and, as I was the designated driver, the newlyweds had taken the opportunity to relax, liberally lubricate their palettes with alcohol and enjoy the craic. By the time we left the pub, Mark and Joanne were clearly lacking the coordination required for dance but still happy to sing all the way home. Although our planned boating trip required an early start, the happy couple were surprisingly chipper over breakfast and even opted for a second portion of bacon.

"Did you sleep well?" Lesley asked.

"Uh-huh." Joanne nodded. We waited while she munched her mouthful of bacon butty and swallowed. "The fresh air here makes me so sleepy, I slept like a log."

Lesley laughed as she and I shared a look. "Fresh air? That would be it," she said, her voice tinged with a mother's irony. "So it had nothing to do with the booze?"

Joanne gave a small guilty grimace. "Well, perhaps it helped a bit…"

Once we'd made our packed lunch and cleared the breakfast dishes away, Mark and I went to my workshop to dig out my fishing kit.

"Is that all there is?" he asked, as I presented him with one rod and reel and a small paper bag containing two orange fishing floats, a selection of weights and a few rusty hooks.

"Yep." I shrugged, winced and scratched my chin. "I haven't fished since I was a teenager."

"But Joanne said you took her fishing a couple of years ago. I thought you'd have at least two rods."

I shook my head and pointed. "Just the one rod."

"So how did she fish?"

"Ask her," I grinned.

Lesley was still insistent we should continue with our boating trip, so we left her to the baking and set off towards Lough Derg.

"Mummy seemed happier this morning," Joanne observed.

I chewed my lip and tapped at the steering wheel.

"You don't seem convinced," Mark added from the space of the rear seat where he was relaxing.

"I suspect she's just putting on a brave face and keeping busy," I said, and left it at that. There didn't seem any benefit in ploughing the same field again. I grinned at my daughter. "Tell Mark about that day we went fishing."

She rolled her eyes and groaned at the memory. "It was a few years ago. We took my dad's fishing rod and went in search of a suitable lake. There are several fishing lakes around here, but that day they all seemed to be hosting fishing matches. Everywhere we tried was encircled with eager fishermen, each with tents, little chairs, keep nets and half-a-dozen rods. There was no way we were going to embarrass ourselves by using a discount store plastic fishing rod to dangle a garden worm in the water.

"Eventually we found this small lake with a little raised wooden jetty where we could sit and chat while we ate our sandwiches and pretended to fish. It was a very pretty lake and for a while I was happy to relax, soak in the sunshine and watch the ducks."

"But soon you wanted to fish too?" Mark suggested.

"I offered my rod, but Joanne wouldn't hear of it, so I made her one."

Before I could answer the scepticism in Mark's eyes, Joanne came to my rescue by explaining how she'd spotted several small fish swimming in the shadow of the jetty. At her request, I'd cut a short stick from a nearby tree and tied a line and hook to the end so she could entice the minnows with a small lump of cheese.

"Neither of us had any realistic chance of catching anything, but at least we were occupied," she said.

"For about 20 minutes, Joanne sat cross-legged at the edge of the jetty, holding her little fishing stick and looking for all the world like one of those garden gnomes."

Mark snorted a laugh at the image.

"Dad wasn't doing any better. He'd managed to catch a clump of weed and two trees, but no fish!" Joanne added. "Then this fellow came along. It was a local priest walking his dog around the lake. He didn't speak to me, but he stopped to chat with Dad."

"It was the usual thing, 'Have yea caught anything?' and 'Are yous on yer holidays?' so we chatted for a few minutes and he went on his way."

"Just before he left, the priest gently put his hand on my head and whispered, 'Bless you my child'. It was only after he'd gone, we realised he had seen me sitting there, crossed-legged and clutching my pathetic fishing stick and assumed I suffered from some dreadful mental deficiency!"

Mark laughed even louder when I added, "Her only deficiency that day was a hangover."

"That's for sure…" Joanne whispered. After a moment, she pulled a sheet of paper from her pocket. It was the booking form for the boat she'd hired. "Do you know where we're going?"

"Mountshannon, I presume." I pointed ahead. "It's where we rented the last boat."

My daughter sucked her teeth and squinted at the booking form. "That's not what it says here."

I waited patiently for all of 30 seconds before breaking the silence. "What does it say?"

"Dromineer."

"Where?"

"Dromineer. It's in County Tipperary," she added.

"County TIP!" I exclaimed.

"Isn't that where we are?" Joanne asked.

"No." I rolled my eyes. "We're in County Clare. I thought you'd booked a boat from Mountshannon. It's only about 25 kilometres away."

Joanne tapped the map on the booking form with her finger. "But it's says Dromineer is on Lough Derg."

"Lough Derg is huge," I explained, whilst pointing at the map myself. "And Dromineer is right over the other side. We'll have to drive all the way around to get there."

"Well I didn't know!" She folded her arms and stared belligerently out of the side window. Joanne was very much her mother's daughter.

"Will it take long to get there?" Mark asked, peering at the map over his wife's shoulder.

"About another hour," I replied, "but it's okay." I tried to defuse the building tension. "We'll take the lake road. It's a beautiful drive with some fantastic views."

Mark wasn't prepared to let it drop. "So, what you are trying to tell us is… It's a long way to Tipperary."

I finally got the joke he'd been setting up with its reference to the famous old song.

I groaned. Joanne tutted in exasperation and folded her arms a little tighter. Clearly, her mood wasn't going to be so easily broken.

Mark decided it was time to change the subject. "How's your book coming along?"

"The golf book is selling nicely and it's had some great reviews. The new cover photo you took really helps."

"I was referring to the other one. Your book about Ireland," he clarified. "How's that going?"

"It's grand," I lied. "Tipping along."

In truth, I'd finished writing my 'Irish Manuscript' a while ago. Since then it had been professionally edited, shared with several friends, rewritten and edited once more. In a moment of unrestrained optimism, I'd had several promotional copies printed, which now sat in a dusty box beneath my desk. Since then I'd sent out dozens of cover letters and synopses to prospective agents and publishers, all without success and often without the courtesy of a reply. Even when I did receive a response, the cold boilerplate rejection letters had done nothing to raise my flagging spirits. I wondered if I should give up, or continue lapping at the steadily receding waters of lake hope?

With exquisite irony, my manuscript became ready for publication at the worst possible time. The economic downturn resulting from the 2008 worldwide financial crash had caused many business sectors to review their approach to risk. Times were hard, particularly in the publishing world. Through my research and contacts, I knew many previously published authors were now struggling to find a taker for their latest works. And my heart had sunk when I watched an interview with an industry expert explaining how many traditional publishing houses were now being run by accountants, only prepared to back sure-fire winners, ghost-written for big name celebrities. If one of the most successful authors on the planet (whilst writing under a pseudonym) couldn't get a publisher without using her own very famous name, what hope was there for me? On the up-side, every cloud (allegedly) has a silver lining. The internet, coupled with the new technology of print-on-demand presses, which could produce a single book to order, was fuelling the rise of

Virtual Publishers. This new breed of business, unshackled from costly city offices, salaried editorial staff and secretaries, were hungry for the opportunities created by the changing market. Maybe I should give them a try?

Perhaps sensing my reluctance to discuss my book, Mark interrupted my train of thought with a change of subject. "And the golf. How's that going?"

"Quiet enough." I shrugged, noncommittally. "On the upside, I can easily make time for visitors."

"Unlike Mum," Joanne spoke to the side window.

I reached out and patted her hand. "She'll be with us in Killarney. You'll see plenty of her then."

"Pff." My daughter squeezed my hand and sighed. For the remainder of the journey I kept the conversation firmly edging towards safer ground. Both their jobs were going well but, fed-up with their rented accommodation, the newlyweds were busy house hunting every weekend. Unfortunately, their time was limited and so was the housing stock on offer.

"It's so frustrating when we give up a weekend to see a house and it's nothing like we expected," Joanne explained.

"Ha!" I laughed. "Been there, worn that t-shirt!"

"I know," she groaned. Both Mark and Joanne already owned properties which they were now renting out, but buying a house together was a new experience. "All the same," she continued, "it's so frustrating that we can't find something we both like."

"We haven't seen any that were even close to being suitable," Mark added.

Although they wouldn't admit it, I suspected part of the problem lay in their differing ideas of the perfect house. Mark wanted a fixer-upper with investment potential, whereas Joanne expected their first house together to be more of a readymade home.

"You could always buy a house here in Ireland," I suggested, albeit without any seriousness. "Since the collapse of the property boom, there are loads of houses going cheap."

"But no jobs," Joanne said.

"And it rains a lot," Mark added.

"You have a point," I conceded.

Despite Mark's dower warning, the weather for our boat trip

remained fine, partially because of the stiff wind blowing the clouds away. We found the boatyard quite easily by turning left from the main road and following the lane downhill until we reached the water. Once parked, Joanne led the way on the short walk past the yacht club to the rental boats. Mark and I followed, loaded down with fishing gear and our picnic bags. After our long drive, it was a relief to stretch our legs for a few minutes. The familiar harbour odours of warm fishy mud, spilled fuel oil and dying vegetation wafted by on the fresh breeze. To our right, the precisely moored lines of gleaming white sailboats bobbed unevenly in the gentle swell. The noise of a dozen lanyards tapping an irregular tinny rhythm against masts somehow found musical congruence with the sound of waves gently slapping at their hulls. As we passed, Mark looked lovingly at a sign advertising dinghies for rent.

I tapped him on the shoulder. "Eyes front!"

He aped disappointment and followed his wife. "I never get any fun," he whispered jokingly.

When we reached the boat rental office, Mark offered to complete the arrangements, but his well-meaning suggestion fell on stony ground.

"I'm doing it," Joanne snapped. "I'm quite capable! You two can stay out here."

"But I was only offering…" Mark wisely gave up.

As Joanne angrily strode into the office, Mark and I shared a look. When she came out again a few minutes later followed by a sheepish looking man, it was obvious the Irish tendency towards misogyny had fallen on stony ground. My daughter was in full angry-boss mode. We wisely stood back while she received instructions on which route to take once we were out on the lake and how to operate the boat. It was a simple 16-foot-long open rowboat, with a grubby white fibreglass hull and a small outboard motor. With the tour complete, the man handed Mark three orange life vests and mumbled, "She's all yours now," before gratefully heading back to the safety of his office.

I leaned towards my new son-in-law, pointed at his wife and whispered, "I'm afraid her warranty has expired. No returns permitted!" He stifled a laugh.

"What are you two grinning at?" Joanne asked.

"Nothing. Nothing," I replied.

"Well stop messing about," she ordered. "Bring that stuff down here so we can get going."

For some reason I offered to drive the boat, and mentally winced as soon as the words left my mouth. I winced once more as Joanne made it perfectly clear she was in charge for the duration of the outing and things would proceed far smoother if we two men would sit at the pointy end and mind our own beeswax.

Once her passengers and cargo were safely aboard, our self-appointed captain supervised the untying of ropes, expertly started the outboard motor and manoeuvred an almost collision free route through the dock, along a short river and out onto Lough Derg.

"Where shall we go?" I asked as the enormous stretch of open water was revealed.

"Corrikeen Islands." Joanne pointed ahead. "They showed me a map in the office. There's a couple of small islands about two kilometres away. That man said we'd have enough time to get there, do a little fishing and head back before it gets too late."

"Fine by me," I replied.

"You're the boss," Mark added.

Joanne pointed to the picnic hamper and made a beckoning gesture. "Beer."

Mark opened a can and handed it to his wife before opening a second for himself. As designated driver, a helped myself to half a sandwich and a bottle of juice.

"It's not a particularly fast boat, is it?" I observed.

"It won't go any faster," Joanne patted the outboard motor and shrugged.

"I think Mark was hoping to do some water-skiing."

They both grinned and toasted my joke with a swig of beer. I saluted back with my fruit juice. The sun was high in the sky and warming our backs, so despite the earlier indignation and animosity, we soon began to relax and enjoy the day.

With the stiff wind pushing from behind, we made sedate but steady progress putt-putting our way across the huge expanse of water. From our low vantage point, the view ahead was just a blanket of iron grey water merging to a distant horizon of pleasant green hills rising sharply towards the caerulean sky.

After some 40 minutes, just as we were beginning to doubt the very existence of our target, the two small islands came into view, gradually resolving themselves as being a little darker and more heavily vegetated than the background. They were slightly off our starboard bow, so Joanne elected to pass to the west and then make a clockwise circuit whilst we looked for a suitable landing spot. However, as we drew closer, a thick forest of two-metre tall rushes comprehensively blocked our view and it soon became apparent we were unlikely to make footfall on Corrikeen today. Eventually we found a sheltered spot between two banks of rushes on the southside of the smaller island, there we dropped anchor ate our picnic and failed completely to catch any fish. On the upside, by sitting quietly so low to the water, we were able to see several bird species. During an ad hoc game of avian bingo, we spotted Greylag Geese, a pair of Great Crested Grebe, several Moorhen, a Eurasian Coot, dozens of Common Tern and a fleeting iridescent flash of orange and blue which may well have been a Kingfisher. We'd hoped to see the recently reintroduced White-tailed sea eagles, but they were nesting near Mountshannon around 20 kilometres to the west and nowhere to be seen.

After a pleasant and relaxing two hours, we'd run out of food and beer.

"Perhaps we can send for supplies?" Mark suggested.

"Fat chance," Joanne replied. "We seem to be the only boat on the water today. It's remarkable that a lake so big and beautiful isn't heaving with pleasure craft."

"That's the beauty of unspoiled County Clare," I remarked.

"It certainly is quiet," Mark added. "Shall we head back?"

I checked my watch and nodded. "Otherwise our dinner will be in the dogs!"

Once the fishing rod was stowed, our captain started the motor and we began our journey back to dry land. Even after we'd remembered to pull up the anchor, our progress was painfully slow, but once we were away from the protection of Corrikeen islands and exposed to the full force of the wind, things became more serious. The previously gentle swell had been transformed into an endless succession of white-topped waves, angrily slapping the portside of the bow. Each collision rolled the boat from side-to-side and pushed the prow slightly to the right. By sighting a line from the banks of Corrikeen Island to the distant treeline of the shore, I could tell our forward progress was almost zero. Furthermore, the wind and waves hitting our left side were forcing the boat into a relentless clockwise circle, driving us away from the shelter and safety of the distant dock. At this rate we would soon run out of fuel, leaving us stranded and alone. More worrying was the amount of water slopping into the boat as the bow hit each wave. Although we all wore life vests, they were no protection against the chillingly cold water. If our boat floundered, the unintentional swim would quickly become a life-threatening event.

"We need to go faster," I said. "With the bow so low, we're shipping too much water."

"It's as fast as it will go," Joanne said, her face now stiff with concern.

Mark had been using his baseball cap to bail water, but he was losing the battle. "Turn into the waves," he suggested.

"I'm trying," she snapped.

"We should all sit as close to the stern as we can," I ordered. "It'll help keep the bow above the approaching waves."

For another ten minutes we soldiered on, battling the rising wind, slapping into the waves and bailing water.

"We're not getting any closer," Joanne groaned.

Mark held up his mobile phone. "No signal."

"I'm getting cold." My daughter nudged my knee. "Can you drive?"

"Sure."

Captain Joanne and her dad swapped places. Once settled, I put my hand on the tiller, pointed the bow into the waves and experimentally twisted the throttle. With a mighty roar the motor burst into life and the boat surged forwards. As the propeller thrashed the water to foam, our stern sank low in the water and the bow rose high above the approaching waves. In seconds we were skimming along with the island falling away behind and our destination coming ever closer. Whereas our downwind leg had lasted an hour, despite the stiffening wind, at this speed our return journey would be over in under 15 minutes. My daughter stared fixedly ahead, but Mark couldn't resist giving me a sly grin. As we entered the calmer waters of the dock, Joanne finally broke her silence.

"How did you do that?"

"There's a twist throttle on the tiller," I replied. "It's just like a motorbike." Trying not to gloat, I demonstrated how the throttle worked. "I'm guessing you didn't know."

She waved her hand dismissively towards the rental office. "That man just pointed towards the handle and told me it was the throttle. He never said how it worked."

Mark tutted expressively. "He probably thought you'd…"

Joanne glared at her husband and raised a warning hand. "Don't!"

"No harm done," I interjected, so saving my son-in-law from the risk of being hit by an oar and thrown overboard.

***

Back at Glenmadrie, things were looking up. Lesley's baking had been completed without further incident. Due to our later than planned return, she'd had enough time to have a nice relaxing bath and then deliver the cakes to her friend's house. Once I'd stored the fishing rod, unpacked our picnic hamper and washed my hands, I prepared a quick and easy meal of pizza, salad and chips. Despite feeling tired, Lesley was considerably happier and even laughed out loud when Joanne related how our boat had nearly been stranded on the lake, simply because she hadn't known how to work the controls. It was lovely to see mum and daughter happy once again.

6 – G-strings and Lycra

With our house sitter, Danni, safely installed, we fussed the dogs goodbye and set off towards Killarney. For a while everyone was quiet. They were probably all gritting their teeth as I threw our little car through my favourite series of bends, with all the exuberance of a downhill skier. However, once we entered a less serpentine section of road and everyone stopped sliding around on their seats, my daughter felt confident enough in her continued grasp on life to discontinue her silent prayers and break the silence.

"We'll be back on Monday…" She shook her head and grinned.

"Scuse me?" I asked, glancing at her in the rear-view mirror.

"As we left, you told the dogs we'd be back on Monday," she explained. "Do you think they understood?"

"Probably not," I conceded. "Afterall, dogs have no concept of time. Our lot get excited every time I come into the house, even if I've only been outside for a couple of minutes."

Joanne laughed. "Then why say it?"

I shrugged. "I guess it makes me feel better."

"Like the list of instructions you gave the house sitter?" she suggested.

"What do you mean?"

"There were four pages covering pretty much every eventuality," she tutted and grinned. "I think the only thing you missed off was what to do in the event of an invasion of alien spaceships."

I slapped my head dramatically. "Damn! Did I miss that off?"

Joanne laughed and shook her head again. "Seriously though, Dad, Danni seems quite capable. I'm sure she can cope. Anyway, giving her such comprehensive directions could make her feel like you don't trust her."

Lesley leaned forwards and gleefully poked me on the shoulder. "I told you so."

I frowned and rubbed my nose. "I'm just trying to be cautious…" My stout defence fizzled to a weak mumble.

"But four pages of instructions!" my daughter groaned. "It's kind of overkill."

Feeling like a tennis ball batted from mother to daughter, I whispered,"15 love!"

"They were laminated pages," my wife continued.

I looked to my son-in-law for some moral support, but Mark just smirked and gazed out of the side window, wisely avoiding eye contact.

"At least she'll know what to do in the event of an emergency," I countered."15 all."

It was a brave attempt, but this final plea for mercy fell on deaf ears. There was blood in the water and the sharks were circling.

"Danni still had the list from last time," Lesley added gleefully. "She was so worried, she brought it with her."

"You've used her BEFORE?" Joanne exclaimed dramatically.

"15/30," the umpire in my head intoned.

"Oh yes. She's the girl who looked after the dogs the last time Daddy and I went to Killarney, and when we came over for your wedding."

"NO! I thought she was new!"

"15/40." As the virtual tennis match continued, I looked pleadingly at Mark once more but he was pretending to be asleep.

"Danni's very capable and experienced," Lesley said. "And she loves dogs."

"But he still gave her one of his lists," Joanne declared.

"Match point," I whispered.

"He did." My wife poked my shoulder once more and delivered the winning shot. "All four pages."

"Game to Joanne and Lesley!" the umpire called. "New balls please."

Actually, my instructions were five pages long, but I kept that gem to myself.

***

We stopped in the beautiful village of Adare for a comfort break and a quick cup of tea, before pushing on towards our destination. Had we been on our own, Lesley and I would probably have spent an hour or so reacquainting ourselves with the most photographed village in Ireland, but Mark and Joanne wanted to reach Killarney and link-up with their friends whilst the day was young. Although we understood, Lesley and I still cast envious eyes towards the museum, the magnificent castle and Adare's picture-perfect rows of brightly coloured thatched cottages.

Perhaps conscious of our disappointment, Mark attempted to brighten the conversation.

"I must say, the renovations make your house look magnificent. You have a lovely home now."

"Thank you." I smiled.

"What do you plan to do next?" he asked.

"Well…" I sucked my teeth. "With the golf teaching being so quiet, my main focus will probably be writing."

"Yea, yea. I know that." He waved his hand dismissively. "What's your next project? Haven't you got some grand plan to do something else?" Mark has always been rather an irreverent tease. I sensed a twinkle of deliberate devilment in his eyes, but the enquiry also had an air of honesty.

I frowned. "What do you mean?"

Mark waved his arm expressively. "You're such a man of action, Nick, I can't imagine you'll be satisfied to sit on your laurels. Surely you must be planning to renovate another property, or perhaps buy a boat and circumnavigate the globe."

"Hardly." I smiled at the idea.

"But a boat would be nice…" he teased. "Or perhaps another property. With this recession, there must be plenty of investment opportunities here."

I could feel my wife's eyes burning into the back of my neck. "You're not getting a boat," she said firmly.

"Actually, our plans are very pedestrian," I explained. "We want to sit back and enjoy life."

"And see a little more of Ireland," Lesley added.

"…see a little more of Ireland," I repeated.

"After all you've done?" Mark nudged me with his elbow an whispered conspiratorially. "Surely you won't be happy doing nothing but sightseeing?"

"It's an interesting suggestion, Mark, and, at the risk of sounding a bit preachy, it speaks to the very reason we moved here in the first place. Before we left England, I had a great job, a flash car and a nice house, but we felt under pressure and dissatisfied. Our life was about having things and trying to pay for them. Material possessions are novelties that comfort and give a sense of optimism, but that sensation soon fades. Like with that old saying, 'Some people are so poor, all they have is money,' we found it was getting ever more difficult to distinguish what matters from what sparkles. Frustrated by being defined through our role as consumers, we rebelled and gave it up. That's why we moved to Ireland, so we could have the physical and financial space to thrive. Affluence isn't about what you earn or what you have, it's about lifestyle. Don't have what you want, want what you have."

"Yea, yea. I know," he groaned. "Nobody on their deathbed ever wished they'd worked harder. I know what you mean, but it all sounds a bit New Age to me."

I glanced at my son-in-law. He had a point. I tried a different explanation.

"Did you know, the happiest person I ever met was a child in Nigeria?"

"Not me?" Joanne asked, grinning. "Am I not the happiest?"

"You're a close second," I joked. "Or you were until you met Mark."

"That's true," she giggled. Mark rolled his eyes and tutted.

"Anyway," I continued. "All that little girl had to play with was a rusty bicycle wheel and a stick to push it along. To an outsider, wise in the ways of consumerism, she looked destitute, but I've never seen anyone smile so honestly."

"It still sounds a bit New Age to me." Mark frowned, but the teasing irreverence in his eyes was obvious. "Are you going to grow a ponytail and start wearing tie-dyed t-shirts?"

I laughed at his friendly dig. "Hardly. I've probably still got some of my old t-shirts somewhere, but the ponytail is definitely out."

My daughter snorted. "Particularly as these days your head has more skin than hair!"

"Thanks for that, Joanne." I chuckled ironically and rolled my eyes at Mark. "Look, I get what you're suggesting and I understand where you're coming from. You and Joanne are just starting out in married life. It's perfectly normal for you to have ambitious plans to buy nice things and want to build a successful career. I'd be surprised if you didn't, but don't let that ambition

70

blind you to what matters."

"Which is?"

"Err…the short answer is being happy. The how, is another matter." I scratched my cheek and grimaced. "I guess that brings us back to your original question. Will I be happy sightseeing and doing nothing?"

"And will you?" he asked.

"I'd like to think so, but…" I paused as I tried to collect my thoughts.

"You don't sound confident," Mark observed.

"It's not that…" I chewed my lip. "I've always been driven and focused, particularly at work. Although I wasn't obsessed by money, for a long while I was strongly motivated by a desire to be seen to do things well. For much of my life it was how I measured myself and that's a very dangerous trait. Anyone calculating their self-worth based on their performance at work, the opinions of others, how much money they have acquired, their last golf score, or any number of inconsequential things, is always going to remain dissatisfied. You're right by suggesting I could never be content being idle. Now the renovations are finished I will have to find a new distraction. Perhaps it will be my writing," I shrugged, "but whatever it is, I'll make sure I enjoy it. That's what the last few years have taught me – taking pride in the little things, that's what makes me happy."

"So you're not getting a boat then," Mark joked.

"No boat," my wife replied sternly.

***

At the hotel, we checked into our rooms and headed back to the lobby to meet up before heading into town. At least that was the plan. When Lesley and I exited the elevator, we found Joanne in an animated discussion with several women of around her age. She briefly smiled and waved, before returning to the conversation. Mark was standing to one side, looking slightly out of place.

"What's going on here then?" I asked.

"Old friends," he replied. "They're all part of the wedding party. I'm afraid it's an impromptu school reunion."

"I don't recognise any of the faces," Lesley said.

"Me neither," I added. "I guess it's been a while."

Mark leaned in and whispered. "Apparently, they're all going horse riding." He grimaced. "It's not really my thing, but there you go."

The group was edging towards the exit.

"It's not my thing either," Lesley added. "We're probably heading into town. Tell Joanne we'll see you later."

"Enjoy the ride. I hope it doesn't rain too much." I grinned.

Mark groaned and reluctantly shuffled after his wife. At the door, he glanced pleadingly over his shoulder.

I made the phone sign with a fist and two fingers. "Call me," I shouted, theatrically. "We'll do lunch."

Lesley nudged me with her elbow. "Leave him alone! Poor lad."

"I'm sure they'll have fun."

Left to our own devices, we decided to go for a drive.

I started the car and looked at my wife. "Where to?"

She smiled and, with all the drama of a magician revealing an overfed white rabbit, produced a leaflet.

"The Kerry Bog Village," she said, pointing north. "Head thataway for a bit then follow the signs for the Ring of Kerry."

I tugged my non-existent forelock and gave my best English chauffeur impression. "Yes, m'lady."

The Ring of Kerry is a 111 mile long scenic drive around the Iveragh Peninsula. As it winds its way through the rural seaside villages, the circular route provides spectacular views of the lush mountains and rocky coastal landscapes. With such awe-inspiring vistas freely available, it is no surprise the Ring is one of the must do items for most visitors to Ireland. Even though the numerous tour buses all circumnavigate the route in a counter clockwise direction to help minimise delays, the road is still routinely clogged with traffic.

As it was a pleasant day, almost windless, with a warm sun shining through a scattering of fluffy clouds, the tourists were out in force. Although our drive to the Bog Village would only cover around 15 miles of the Ring, we were travelling in a counter clockwise direction and found ourselves following a long line of coaches. With the steady stream of oncoming traffic – a mixture of airport rental cars, weaving dangerously as their tourist drivers rubbernecked the scenery, and packs of leather-clad motorcyclists relishing the winding roads – we found our progress to be particularly slow. There was nothing for it but to sit back and enjoy the scenery.

"This is our second trip to Kerry and we still haven't driven this entire route," Lesley said.

"The drive is supposed to take around four hours..." I checked my watch. "But at this pace it'll likely take all day. Perhaps next time we come we can make a day of it."

"That would be nice."

I tapped the steering wheel and tried to peer past the coach ahead. "Why are they going so slowly?"

Lesley patted my hand. "There's no rush."

I sat back in my seat and for a few minutes entertained myself by accepting an invitation to engage in a face-pulling battle with a child in the coach ahead. Whereas I had the flabby jowls and mouth flexibility necessary for competitive gurning, she had clearly been practising for several days and, with both hands available, was the worthy winner.

My wife looked to her left. "Wow, look at those mountains."

"Those are called the MacGillycuddy Reeks. I read about them last time we were here. They're Ireland's highest mountain range. The tallest one in the middle is called Carrauntoohil. I think it's over 1,000 metres high."

"Very impressive."

"Not as impressive as that." I pointed through the windscreen to where the cause of our slow progress was finally revealed. It was a man on a bicycle, but this was no ordinary man and it was no ordinary bicycle.

Before I proceed with this story, I want to ask for some temporary latitude.

Even before the world embroiled itself in a complex mire of political correctness, I had always done my utmost to avoid judging people because of their features, age, religion, ethnicity, body type, skin colour and presence (or lack of) hair. In part this is because, as a slightly chunky balding old coot, I am an easy target for retribution, but also because I have a terrible memory for names. Inadvertently drop a silent fart in a crowded elevator and you may plead innocence by wrinkling your nose and tutting loudly, but there is no acceptable excuse for the social faux pas of forgetting a name. I don't know why it happens, but names just fall out of my head like coins through a worn trouser pocket.

After many embarrassing episodes, I eventually learned the solution was to mentally associate names with a strong visual image of similar sounding objects or physical features. However, I am genuinely wracked with guilt when I remember Bobby's name because he has distinctive man-boobies, or Hailey through noticing her hay-like hair. Worse still, was the day I inadvertently called the lovely Donna L'ampleur, Doughnut Lampshade! So, given my own sensitivity to these matters, I hope you'll forgive me for colouring outside the lines of political correctness for a few minutes. Which brings me back to the particularly noticeable gentleman on the bicycle.

A few years ago, we saw a man on an aged pushbike wobbling along a quiet country lane in County Clare with a settee strapped to his back like a wide rucksack. How he even managed to stand under the weight of this huge sofa was a mystery and made his ability to ride a bicycle at the same time all the more impressive. What we were witnessing now was even more remarkable.

Lesley squinted through the windscreen. "Is the circus in town?"

It was a genuine question and an understandable error. The body in question was so huge it could conceivably have been a much thinner person wearing one of those inflatable Sumo wrestler suits. That he was slowly riding a ridiculously undersized pink bicycle along the busiest road in Killarney only added to the possibility he was advertising some local attraction. Like a clown demonstrating a humorous circus trick, his bike suddenly wobbled across the road, narrowly avoiding a collision.

"Good grief!" Lesley exclaimed.

"Well, you have to admire his willpower."

"But not his fashion sense." My wife winced involuntarily as I closed the gap and our quarry came into focus.

Coming from someone who spends most of her waking hours wearing ancient paint-speckled jeans, faded t-shirts, holey-knitwear and muddy wellington boots, the comment may have seemed rather harsh, but she had good reason to be critical. The gentleman in question had somehow squeezed his 50 inch wide posterior into black cycle leggings, thereby stretching the sweat soaked Lycra to the point where it had become translucent. Unwary motorists had a shockingly unrestricted view of his dimpled buttocks attempting to devour the white G-string he had inexplicably chosen to wear that morning. That a man so large could ride a bike obviously designed for a female child was impressive, but his incredibly slow forward progress was a triumph of determination and balance over the laws of physics – so much so tourists were ignoring the magnificent Killarney countryside and slowing their vehicles to take his picture.

"He seems to be rather a tourist attraction," Lesley observed.

I laughed. "Well he's remarkably stoic, even with all the attention he's getting."

Unfortunately, his tolerance soon dissipated. When it became my turn to pass, I was suddenly confronted with a seemingly endless stream of oncoming traffic.

"Where did all these cars suddenly come from?" I mumbled.

Unable to safely overtake on the twisting road, I had no choice but to crawl along, waiting for a gap and watching the component parts of his gluteus maximus hypnotically dancing in time to the pedals. Three minutes later, convinced I had exceeded my allotted photography time, the red-faced cyclist scowled and waved for us to come by. In reply, I mimed a combination of silent words and hand gestures indicating my unwillingness to risk his life by making such a perilous manoeuvre when a safer opportunity would surely present, if only we could all be a little patient. My meaning was lost on the poor fellow and several of the drivers behind, who obviously felt I was deliberately hogging the entertainment and indicated thus by tooting their horns.

"I can't get by," I groaned.

The cyclist glared at me again, shouted something unintelligible and waved his fist in anger. After a second half-hearted attempt to apologise failed, I slumped into my seat, stared glumly ahead and wondered how I had suddenly become the target for derision. When a half-gap finally appeared, I grabbed my chance and overtook. One glance in the rear-view mirror at his purple face and angry bulging eyes was enough to chill my heart and encourage me to accelerate away so quickly I almost missed the turning we'd been looking for.

Lesley and I spent a couple of hours wandering happily around the Kerry Bog Village. It is a meticulous reconstruction of a small Irish hamlet, with several pretty thatched cottages displaying antique furniture and figurines, so as to convey the living conditions through the Irish famine. Scattered around outdoor were displays of period equipment used by turf cutters and farmers. After a look at the tiny Kerry Bog ponies, we said hello to a huge but friendly Irish Wolfhound – the world's tallest dog – had a quick tour of the giftshop and took afternoon tea. Although the Kerry Bog Village was one of the smaller attractions we'd visited, the attention to detail made it a worthwhile stop.

"That was nice," Lesley said, as we headed back towards Killarney. "I thought it was charming."

"For such a small museum, it was certainly worth a visit," I nodded in agreement. "I wonder if they've got a horse called Dog and a dog called Horse."

Lesley laughed. "Those Wolfhounds are certainly big enough to be called Horse."

"That cake was nice."

"I hope you left room for dinner."

"Of course. Anyway, we'll be eating alone. Joanne sent a text earlier. They're off out with her friends."

"Oh." Lesley looked momentarily disappointed, but her face quickly broke into a smile. She pointed ahead. "Look."

The massive cyclist was also heading back to town. I groaned as the familiar pink bicycle and rotating bum cheeks once again blocked our view ahead. Somehow, the winds of outrageous fortune had conspired to repeat our earlier encounter. For an excruciatingly long four minutes we were trapped immediately behind the angry cyclist. Despite the obvious stream of oncoming tourist coaches and motorbikes blocking my attempts to overtake, he continued to gesticulate and glare in our direction.

Lesley put her face into her hands and mumbled, "This is too much of a coincidence. The poor man must think we're stalking him."

"It's not safe to push by," I explained. "Especially with the way he's wobbling around."

The man gesticulated, veered and shouted.

"Perhaps he's upset you haven't taken his picture," I suggested.

My wife shook her head in silent reply. At last there was a

gap wide enough for me to safely overtake. My good intentions had once again been misunderstood. As we passed, the sweating cyclist shook his fist and bellowed an expletive.

"I know the economic crash has taken its toll here," I said, "but calling me a banker seems a bit over the top."

Lesley chuckled. "I don't think that's what he said…"

7 – Drunk and Disorderly

As Joanne and Mark were out with their friends for the night, Lesley and I decided to check out the hotel leisure facilities. Despite the hotel being full with wedding guests and tourists, we had the place to ourselves. After opening our pores for 20 minutes in the sauna, we took a long swim then headed back to our room to shower and change.

"It's a shame we haven't got a pool nearer to the house," Lesley said, as she was drying her hair. "I used to enjoy swimming when we lived in England."

"How about joining the leisure club at the golf course?" I suggested. "They've got a lovely pool. We could go together."

"I know. It's a nice idea, but being so far away, it would be…" She gave a small grimace.

"Inconvenient?" I finished her sentence.

Lesley nodded. I began flipping through the hotel welcome pack.

"There's a pool in Ennis," I said. "Didn't you go there with Christine?"

"A couple of times." Her voice lacked any real enthusiasm. "Driving all the way there and back for a half hour of swimming seemed like too much trouble. When we lived in Braintree, I could walk to the pool in five minutes."

I understood what she meant. Country living has many benefits and a few drawbacks; being a long way away from modern conveniences like doctors, dentists, shops and swimming pools, to name but a few.

"There's a swimming club down at Lough Derg," I suggested half-heartedly.

Lesley snorted a laugh. "Is the lake heated?"

"Or you could try paddling around in our pond."

"In amongst the ducks and tadpoles." She smiled. "Anyway, our pond is a bit smelly."

"Well the frogs don't seem to mind," I replied, my voice heavy with mock disapproval. "There's no pleasing some people."

My dear wife threw her towel at me.

I defended myself with the hotel welcome pack. "Shall we eat in the bar? They have a pretty good menu."

"Sure. Perhaps afterwards we can walk into town and do some window shopping."

"Okay." My reply wasn't terribly enthusiastic. I'm not a fan of any shopping, be it window, internet or the type which involves lists, crowds, queues and the exchange of money for things I didn't know I wanted. However, the prospect of spending the evening sitting in a noisy bar or watching a pay-per-view movie whilst squirming uncomfortably on the hotel bed, didn't appeal either. So window shopping it was, or at least that was our plan.

Unlike our home town of Ennis, where most retailers have shut by six o'clock, Killarney caters to huge numbers of tourists, so the majority of shops stay open until 9pm when the consumers of baubles and trinkets finally give way to those seeking refreshment and sustenance.

"I'd forgotten how busy this place gets," Lesley grinned. "It's so vibrant."

"Given how hard the recession has hit the shops in Ennis and Limerick, it's great to see so many people out spending their money. I only wish they'd splash a little cash up our way too." I looked around at the teeming crowds and smiled. "Maybe there's hope for Ennis yet."

We were thoroughly enjoying our slow walk, aimlessly exploring the town centre and a few interesting looking side alleys. Although the streets were crowded, there was no hint of undue bustle or any irritated tutting whenever the pavement was blocked by groups of tourists, or friends who had stopped to chat. Everyone we passed seemed to smile and nod, happy to make eye contact and give a friendly wave. On this warm evening, the sense of bonhomie was infectious and we soon found ourselves exchanging pleasantries with the other tourists. A tanned, middle-aged couple from California stopped and asked us for directions to a particular pub. Fortunately, we had passed it earlier, so I was able to point them in approximately the right direction. Both their accents had a breathless drawl with a hint of vocal fry, as if they were recovering from laryngitis. They were part of a group taking a whistle-stop coach tour attempting to visit all the main attractions of England, Scotland and Ireland in just three weeks.

"Wow. That's a lot of sightseeing in a short time," I

exclaimed. "You must be exhausted."

The lady nodded. "We've enjoyed the trip, but we sure are looking forward to heading home at the end of this week."

Her husband smiled and added, "After three weeks sharing an intercity bus with the same people, we've made a lot of friends." He leaned closer and whispered. "And a few enemies."

Lesley sniggered. "I can imagine. After three weeks on a bus, my husband would have shot someone."

"Only if you hadn't shot me first," I added, hoping for a laugh, but being disappointed.

"Is this your first visit to Ireland?" the lady asked.

"Actually we live here, well, up in County Clare to be precise," Lesley explained. "We're only in Killarney for a wedding."

"Oh gee," the lady exclaimed excitedly. She looked over my shoulder and waved at someone. "Hey, Jenny! Come over here. These English people actually live in Ireland."

In moments we were surrounded by a large circle of their coach party. They lovingly pestered us with questions about how we came to live on the emerald isle and what life here was really like. Our audience listened with rapt attention to our answers and oohed and aahed like children at a magic show when I described Glenmadrie and the surrounding countryside of East Clare. After ten minutes, we parted ways like old friends, with much handshaking and smiles.

Once we turned the corner, Lesley laughed out loud. "Well that was odd. Nice but odd. It was like we were rock stars just because we moved to Ireland."

"I know what you mean. One fellow asked me for my autograph."

"Really?"

"I may have mentioned I'd written a book." I gave an embarrassed grimace.

Continuing our random meandering, we turned into a narrow side street. At the back of yet another pub, we had to squeeze sideways to pass an aged car being loaded with beer. The front seat and wheel well were stacked with crates and seven aluminium beer kegs lined the back seat. Whereas the Guinness barrels were carefully tied down with blue rope, the four ginger-haired children were not. As we passed, their father angrily banged his palm on the car roof and shouted. "I'm after telling ya twice, get orf them kegs afore yea break summit!"

Hand-in-hand, Lesley and I walked on through the town taking in the sights and enjoying the unaccustomed activity and affluence. The air was thick with the mingled smell of warm concrete, mixed with the scent of beer, chips, garlic and chargrilled meat. Ahead, we spotted a young man weaving his way along the pavement on the short journey between two pubs. Despite being on crutches, he moved with all the determination of someone desperate for a drink – or a pee. With both of his legs twisted and withered, he was clearly disabled, yet somehow he balanced sufficiently well enough he could gleefully give every third person a stout whack on the shin with his crutches. He dived through the pub door, leaving several unfortunate pedestrians hobbling in his wake.

"That poor fellow," I whispered. "Well at least he seems happy."

After browsing for books, looking around an antique shop and buying several bags of sticky treats in a retro sweet shop, we made one final stop before heading back towards the hotel. The gift shop was a standard affair, with a typical range of tourist gifts advertising Ireland, Killarney or Guinness. There was also a small display of Waterford crystal, which is what had caught Lesley's eye. When we entered the shop I said hello to the lady behind the counter, who I assumed was the owner or manager, and she smiled sweetly in return. After a few minutes, bored with watching the back of my wife's head while she looked at the crystal, I tried to engage the manageress in some sociable conversation.

"Working late tonight," I commented. "You must be looking forward to having your tea."

The grey-haired manageress was around 60 years old, but slim, with a healthy pink complexion and smoky eyes. She slowly turned her head in my direction, as if noticing me for the first time. As she spoke her eyes looked a little out of focus, as though she was looking at something very far away and a long time ago.

"I had me tay already," she said, breathing a wall of peppermint and alcohol in my direction.

"Have you been at work all day?" I asked, speculating she

may have been called away from a party to cover for a sick member of staff. "You must be tired."

"No, I only started at six," she replied, trying to focus on me, but missing with both eyes.

"Oh, right then," I said uncertainly. "Well, I'd better be getting back to my wife."

Perhaps surprised she had failed to notice a second customer, the lady quickly turned her head. As her eyes bounced around in their sockets and her legs wobbled uncontrollably, she grabbed the counter for support.

"Yesh," she slurred carefully and gave me a stiff smile. "Happy to help."

When I turned away, she was valiantly trying to prop her bottom onto a stool behind the counter. I slowly walked over to Lesley, who was holding up an ornament and squinting, in an attempt to make out the price without the aid of her glasses.

I whispered in her ear, "I think the woman behind the counter is drunk."

"Really?" she asked, still squinting at the tag. "How much is this?" She held the ornament up for me to see. "I wanted to get something for Christine."

"Jesus Christ, it's €80! You're not going to buy it are you?" I hissed.

My wife sighed and mumbled something to herself.

"She's completely sloshed," I whispered, trying not to laugh. "It looks like she can hardly stand up!"

Lesley put the ornament back on the shelf and looked at me for the first time. "Who is?"

"That woman behind the counter," I whispered, surreptitiously pointing over my shoulder. "She stank of booze and mints."

Lesley looked towards the front of the shop. "What woman?" The counter was unmanned.

"Perhaps she went out the back," I offered.

"Who did?" Lesley asked in a distracted voice as she drifted towards the exit.

"The woman who was behind the counter. You know – the drunk one?"

"I can't believe she'd be drunk and at work," my wife insisted, striding towards the door. "You probably just imagined it."

Meekly, I followed behind, suitably chastised for my overactive imagination, but grateful we had avoided an unnecessarily extravagant purchase. In passing, I glanced over the counter. There, laid on the floor, soundly sleeping in a visible fog of brandy fumes, was the manageress.

As we were walking back towards our hotel alongside the busy Muckross road, I spied a curious vehicle sitting in the traffic. It was a mobility scooter, but not one of those modern sleek black battery-powered machines, permitted on pavements and in supermarkets, this was a very different offering. Taller than it was long, wrapped in a beige canvas cover with yellowed plastic windows, this ancient invalid carriage had a noisy two-stroke engine and a familiar passenger. It was the same young man we'd seen earlier, deliberately whacking a few shins and ankles with his crutches as he made his way between two pubs. Just as I mentioned this to Lesley, the driver shouted something unintelligible at the car ahead and waved his fist so vigorously he momentarily lost his balance. There were traffic lights ahead and the road was gridlocked with standing traffic, so his forward progress was slower than our walking pace. As we drew level, the driver glared at me with unfocused eyes, belched loudly then flicked us the bird.

"He seems well lubricated," Lesley giggled.

Although it was dark, the mobility scooter wasn't displaying any lights. I mentioned it to Lesley.

"Perhaps I should tell him," I suggested.

"Best not." My wife took my hand and firmly pulled me forward. "I recall he was pretty handy with those crutches."

We lengthened our stride towards the hotel.

Behind I heard the squeaky toot of the buggy's horn, followed by an angry shout, "Wake up yea lazy feckers, get a move-on!"

"The alcohol certainly hasn't dispelled his belligerent attitude," I joked.

The traffic edged forward hopefully, but stopped all too soon as the lights turned red once again.

"Hey, look!" I pointed ahead.

Finally giving in to alcohol-fuelled anger and impatience, the aged invalid carriage was driving up the centre of the road and weaving unpredictably through the slow moving traffic. As we watched in disbelief, the driver approached a red light with suicidal determination. With only the sound of his diminutive horn as a warning, he drove straight through the intersection at an alarming speed, scattering several cars and their startled drivers in his wake. The little vehicle continued off into the darkness of the Muckross road, detectable only by the lights of the swerving cars and their tooting horns. Some two hundred yards later, the buggy suddenly turned sideways to the oncoming traffic and lurched to an abrupt stop. In the amber glow of the street lights, we saw the sozzled occupant slowly slip out of his vehicle and onto the road. Several cars stopped and we could just make out the concerned motorists attempting to help the young lad back onto his seat. I could almost sense their disbelief, when clinging desperately to the steering wheel for support, he performed a ragged K turn, gave them a merry toot from his horn, and set off uncertainly towards home.

"Perhaps he isn't disabled after all," I speculated. "Just very drunk."

***

The wedding ceremony was a delightful affair, punctuated with the traditional smiles, tears and a chorus of noses honking loudly into tissues. It was lovely to see another of Joanne's friends starting out on a new phase of her life. Even though we hadn't seen much of Becky since our move to Ireland, we were honoured with the wedding invitation and more than a little tearful when the rings were exchanged. The ceremonial room was perfectly prepared for the event. All the chairs and tables were draped with gleaming white covers and the walls and flower stands were decorated with yards of red silk ribbon. Despite the beauty of the bride and her maids, my eyes were relentlessly drawn to the enormous picture windows and the breathtaking view across Lough Leane to the distant shoreline where the glowering MacGillycuddy Reeks were perfectly mirrored on the glassy surface. Ireland at its best.

As soon as the new bride and groom had finished their first kiss, they stepped into a side office to complete the legal formalities. Whilst the signing and witnessing progressed, the guests were asked to take their seats in the dining area. This was a magnificent and airy room with a bar, the same lake view, a balcony, a dance floor and a dozen tables surrounding a centrepiece with a cheese dip and a huge chocolate fountain. For a while the guests waited patiently, getting acquainted with our tablemates, discussing the wedding and generally putting the world to rights. After an hour, people began to notice the absence of our hosts. Eyebrows were raised. Questions were being asked, the most common being, "When are we going to eat?" It had been nine hours since breakfast and the rumbling of stomachs around the room could easily have been mistaken for a distant pond of mating frogs. Soon the rumours began to circulate. The bride and groom have had a big row. They've been abducted by space aliens. Someone has been taken ill. Or, they've forsaken their guests and made an early start on their honeymoon. The truth was the wedding photos were taking much longer than planned. After taking some pictures by the lakeside, the happy couple had set off with their families and close friends in a fleet of carriages in search of something more memorable for the wedding album. They were currently a few kilometres away, balancing precariously on the slippery rocks at the bottom of the spectacular Torc waterfall.

Over the next hour the guests waited with polite but diminishing patience. As if this was part of a carefully planned practical joke, twice a procession of smartly dressed serving staff marched into the dining area like parading penguins, only to be ushered out again. For those of us who eat on a schedule more precise than a German railway timetable, seeing our starters pass so enticingly close by, made the smells wafting from the restaurant seem all the more enticing.

"I nearly had it that time," someone shouted.

"Food!" laughed another. "Bring food!"

A gruff Essex voice added, "Shall I send out for pizza, luv?"

Perhaps fearing an extremely polite and well-ordered riot would result in the early demolition of the wedding cake, several trays of bread rolls were distributed to keep the slavering hordes at bay. These were quickly consumed and a second batch was delivered, along with the warning, "Don't fill yerself up with bread or yeh won't eat yer dinner." Whilst the adults had remained relatively acquiescent during this difficult period of food rationing, the children became ever more wayward and rebellious, circling the chocolate fountain like hyenas stalking a wildebeest. Finally, one particularly valiant little girl pleaded so enticingly, the glowering maître d's heart melted and he showed her how to dip an outrageously large strawberry into the chocolate. With the floodgates finally open, the children crowded in, all keen to sample the delicious offering.

"Right," came the gruff Essex voice again. "I'm having me some of that!"

In a surge likely to scatter the children, the adults marched towards the middle table. Within minutes the strawberries had vanished and the remaining bread rolls were consumed, leaving behind only some splatters of chocolate and a few smears of melted cheese. When the wedding party finally returned, the welcoming cheer from the serving staff was almost as loud as that of the wedding guests. With the meal and speeches completed, the festivities finally got under way.

Two hours later, feeling bloated and a little queasy from eating too much cheesy bread and chocolate coated strawberries, Lesley and I elected to take a stroll. After the noisy fug of the dancefloor, stepping into the cool night air brought me a wonderful sensation of peace. In the absence of clouds and light pollution, the sky to the west was a glorious vista of twinkling stars. As my eyes adjusted to the unfamiliar gloom, I was easily able to identify several constellations and planets, set against the gentle glow of the Milky Way. The path we were following was barely discernible in the inky darkness; it led down a gentle incline towards a gravel beach. In the still night air, the glassy waters of Lough Leane mirrored the sky so perfectly it seemed the starfield stretched from below our feet to behind our heads and was only interrupted where the mountains of the MacGillycuddy Reeks blocked our view.

Hand in hand my wife and I stood in companionable silence and watched the bats flitting overhead in search of moths and midges. Several times we gasped like children at a fireworks display as meteors silently streaked across the sky. With the distant throbbing beat of dance music from the hotel as an auditory backdrop, the area surrounding the lake seemed eerily silent, but it was only when the ghostly form of an owl passed close overhead without even disturbing the air, I realised what true silence was. As someone who dislikes crowds and loud music, it took a huge effort to turn my back on such a moment of nirvana and return to the hotel.

With the guests fortified with equal measures of wedding bliss and alcohol, it was no surprise the dancefloor was packed. During the hour we had been outside, jackets had been removed, bow ties undone and perfectly coiffed hair let down. Freeze framed in the flash of the strobe lights, what were once smartly dressed wedding guests now resembled a group of refugees who had just stumbled into a Hieronymus Bosch painting. The heaving mass of sweaty bodies writhed, twisted and bounced in enthusiastic delight to the chest pounding rhythm of the music. Any thoughts I may have had of joining the throng were dispelled when a spilt pint of beer proved to be too much lubrication and several dancers slipped laughing to the floor.

My wife nudged me with her elbow, grinned and pointed to the far end of the hall. There my daughter was teaching a group of around 20 children some ad hoc dance moves. How typical, I thought, with all this merriment going on, it's Joanne who takes the time to make sure the children are entertained.

To be heard above the deafening music, Lesley leaned closer and shouted in my ear.

"One day, she's going to be a great mum."

I smiled and nodded, proud of Joanne and delighted to see Lesley's earlier emotional fug had dissipated.

***

In the hungover silence during the early-morning drive home, I speculated as to why Lesley had recently been so unusually down in the mouth. Discounting for the moment the very real possibility I was the cause of her angst, I was left with only three possibilities: either she was unwell, missing Joanne, or worried about her mother. Optimistically excluding the first on the basis she'd already had enough bad luck on that front, I could only conclude the problem lay in a combination of the other two.

Even though we still thought of Joanne as our daughter, she was now Mark's wife and seeing them together again reminded us our little girl was now very much a grown woman, forging her own life, with a bright future ahead. After several months apart, such an observation only reinforced the feeling our lives were now on different tracks. Conversely, Lesley's 77 year old mother, Muriel, was spiralling towards the inevitability of full-time care.

At the best of times, dementia is a difficult disease to identify, but with the British health service so overburdened and underfunded, Muriel had yet to see a specialist to receive a definitive diagnosis. Pragmatism can easily be mistaken for callousness, particularly when a GP shrugs and says, "What's the point of a diagnosis? She's old and there is no cure." Muriel had been prescribed tablets which could delay the symptoms, she had Meals on Wheels and a home help to make sure she was dressed each morning, what else could they do? Lesley and I had spoken on several occasions of bringing Muriel to live with us in Ireland, but those discussions had always been largely theoretical. In any event, neither Lesley or her mother were particularly keen on the idea. Whereas I thought moving Muriel to live with us was a practical solution and a duty due to a family member who had always been there for us, both Lesley and Muriel were unenthusiastic about the idea and generally unwilling to take the discussion further. However, the obvious decline in Muriel's mental and physical faculties was bringing that conversation depressingly closer. For now, we could only watch and wait.

**

Overall, Mark and Joanne's visit and our trip to Killarney had been a thoroughly enjoyable event. We were delighted to see Becky looking so happy. Without once referring to my copious instructions, Danni had done a magnificent job of keeping the dogs healthy, our home safe, and the garden watered. We were grateful to everyone for the time we'd had together.

"It was fun," Mark said. "Even the bit where we almost died boating on Lough Derg."

"You may be joking," I replied, "but listen to this." I read from the local paper Danni had left behind. "This weekend, Lough Derg was at the centre of two major rescue operations in less than 24 hours. The coastguard was called out when 22 school children got into difficulties while kayaking this morning. It follows yesterday evening's incident when 35 people were rescued after as many as eight rowing boats capsized during an international event.

"The sailors were taking part in the week-long FISA World Tour hosted by Limerick's St Michael's Rowing Club and ran into difficulties due to deteriorating weather conditions."

Clearly shocked by the news, Mark turned to his wife.

"Listen to this Joanne," he called. "Over the weekend, 57 people were rescued from Lough Derg after they were caught out by sudden bad weather."

"But I got us back safely."

I nodded, wisely unwilling to mention it was me who brought the boat back to the harbour.

My daughter smiled and mimed polishing her nails on her lapel.

"So my boating skills weren't too bad after all!"

8 – Paths and Palpitations

Lesley leaned on the long wooden handle of her garden hoe, stretched her aching back and watched with curious eyes as I approached the hallowed grounds of her vegetable garden. I was returning from my morning dog-walking excursion and she had been alerted to my presence by said dogs running on ahead. In an effort to protect her cabbages, potatoes, carrots, sweetcorn and the like from scrapping chickens, hungry hares and the feet of our clumsy canines, I'd previously erected a stout chicken wire fence along the length of the adjacent path. Although it frustrated Lady, Amber and Jack in their urgent efforts to get to their mum, Kia was made of sterner stuff. Barely breaking stride, she jammed her snout under the bottom edge of the wire and pushed through.

"Kia! You bad dog!" Lesley wailed, before reaching down to give the devoted pooch an ear rub. Mixed messages. The other three moved to the first available sunbeam and slumped gratefully to the ground.

"How goes the weeding?" I asked.

"Slowly." She waved her hand dismissively at the soil. "I only did this bit a couple of weeks ago. The weeds grow so fast here, particularly when the weather is this nice."

Ireland had already enjoyed several weeks of warm and dry weather and the outlook remained positive throughout September. Even in the dark depths of a recession, the uncommon sight of sunshine and cloudless blue skies had done much to raise our collective spirits. A proper summer!

"I guess it's why they call it the Emerald Isle." I joked.

Like a sniper looking through a telescopic lens, my wife fixed me with a stare of rebuke and disapproval. Bad backs and insensitive witticisms aren't happy bedfellows. I held up a calming hand and grinned in what I hoped was a disarming fashion.

"Only kidding."

"It's alright." She dismissed her momentary anger with a flick of her hand and a sigh. Her cool blue eyes softened. "You were a long time."

"Uh-huh." I nodded excitedly. "I've started a new project." I waved the long handled loppers I was holding. "I'm cutting some paths up in the forest."

"What's wrong with the logging road?"

"Nothing really." I scrunched my nose as I searched for a suitable explanation for what was a spur of the moment idea. "It just gets a bit boring walking up and down the same track all the time. I like to head off into the forest, but it can be hard going because of all the low branches. So I decided to cut some new paths."

"And you thought it would be a good idea to use my new loppers because…?" The hanging question and her best mummy stare were making me feel as if I should rush off to do my homework or tidy my bedroom.

"Ah…" I shuffled my feet in embarrassment. Garden tools were as personal and important to Lesley as my golf clubs or fountain pen were to me, but she'd had the loppers for six months so I'd figured they were no longer off limits – even though they were still in the original packaging. On the other hand, they were a birthday gift, so perhaps I should have taken that into consideration. "Well, with the telescopic handles and the hooked blade, they're perfect for cutting branches…" My excuse drifted off uncertainly. I was busted and I knew it.

"I'll give them a good clean," I added.

My wife was smiling. Her face showing more sympathy than gloat. "It's okay. They needed to come out. It sounds like an awfully big job. Where are you cutting the paths?"

"To start with, up there." I pointed to the hill behind our house and land. Like most of Ireland, the pine forests around Glenmadrie were owned and managed by Coillte, the Irish Forestry Service. They own more than 1,000,000 acres of forest, most of which is largely accessible to the public without charge. For some time I'd been irritated by my forest excursions being limited to the logging roads or slow half-crawls as I explored through the tangled branches and undergrowth. But that was about to change. "Do you remember last week when we could hear someone up in the forest?"

"You mean when we heard the sound of a couple of chainsaws drifting up and down?"

I nodded. "That's it. We couldn't figure out where they were, or why."

"I remember," Lesley added. "We decided it was probably

someone stealing some firewood."

"Well…" I held up a finger. "Mystery solved. It was forestry workers cutting access paths so the inspectors can get in to do whatever it is they do."

"I think the inspectors measure the trees to assess how well they're growing," Lesley said, keen to dispense some more of her encyclopaedic knowledge of all things green. "They probably need to check for Pine Weevil damage too. It's quite common around here and can easily kill a tree."

"Well, that explains it then." I nodded.

"Can't you use the paths they've cut?"

"I will," I nodded again, "but their paths are only around 50 metres long. They go into the forest like exploratory fingers, but they don't join up. Well, not yet anyway."

My wife tipped her head to one side and squinted suspiciously. "Are you allowed to make new paths?"

"Ah, it'll be grand." I'd answered using my best Irish accent whilst dismissing her question with a nonchalant flick of my hand. "Anyway, Jim's cattle have already done most of the work for me."

"Jim's cattle?" Lesley frowned in obvious confusion. "What have they got to do with it?"

"Whenever they escape from his field, they climb up into the forest where they push through the branches like bulldozers and end up all the way up here. There's probably miles of tracks in there, albeit rather low ones. I've followed a few of them by crouching or half crawling, but that's a bit hard on the back." I grinned. "If I was half my height, I wouldn't need to do any cutting at all." I pointed towards the hill again. "Anyway, the lower branches on these trees are all dead. They're so dry, most of them will snap off quite easily. It's only the thickest ones that need the loppers. Even so, there's still a lot to cut to make a safe passage. It takes around an hour to cover 30 yards, but if I do a little bit every time I walk the dogs, it won't be too much of a chore."

"Well it's up to you. Just be careful with my loppers."

I doffed my hat. "Yes, dear."

"And while you're at it, you'd better clear that path down to the river." My wife was referring to the hiking trail which, as a part of a long looped walk, came up past our land. It was one of our favourite dog walking routes, but recently it had become so overgrown as to be almost impassable. "The Council used to send out a team of workers each spring," she continued, "but that seems to have stopped."

"I guess with the recession, they're having to compromise." I pointed west, towards the distant moor. "Remember last year, they closed this section of the East Clare way and took down all the signs, even though it was a very popular walking trail for the tourists and hikers." I grimaced. "It's probably the same story for this path too."

"That seems like a false economy," Lesley sighed. "Especially after they spent all that money on building that footbridge across the river."

She was right. The saving gained by closing these popular walking routes were surely going to be overshadowed by the loss of tourist dollars. Furthermore, once these rural paths were overgrown, it was unlikely they would ever reopen. It made maintaining our stretch all the more important.

"I'll begin work on clearing the path down to the river at the weekend. I suspect it will take a while, but it'll be worth it." I raised an inquisitive eyebrow. "You can help if you like. It'll be much quicker with two of us."

"No thanks!" Lesley smiled and thumped the soil with her hoe. "Take the dogs. They can mooch around while you work."

I looked at our gang of canine miscreants, asleep and unmoving, like lizards warming in the sun – except for Lady. She whimpered softly in her sleep, her back leg slowly cycling as she chased a dream hare.

"Oh good…" I sighed ironically. "They'll be a great help!"

***

As luck would have it, while I was clearing the track heading down to the river, I discovered someone was doing the same thing in the opposite direction.

"Ahoy there!" I shouted.

"'Ellow?" The accent was clearly not locally cultivated. "Ben jij ook aan het werk?" I guessed it might be German, but I could be wrong.

"Um…" I scratched my head. "Do you speak English?" I pleaded.

"Yah," came the jolly reply. "Ve are closing."

I breathed a sigh of relief. Through lack of use, I have long forgotten the small bit of French and German I learned at school and, not wishing to rely on the standard English system of speaking loudly to foreigners and randomly adding 'ski' at the end of words, my only recourse would have been elaborate mime.

By standing on tiptoes and peering over the dense foliage, I could see my fellow path-clearers were a tall man and a considerably shorter woman. I presumed they were husband and wife and likely to be a little older than Lesley and me. They were kitted out with matching top quality hiking jackets, trousers and boots. It was far more appropriate workwear for clearing bramble, with its wickedly sharp thorns, than my thin and slightly bloodstained t-shirt, wellington boots and jeans. The man led the way, attacking the vegetation with fearsome swipes from a billhook, like a pirate storming a ship. The woman followed close behind, delivering a constant narrative of instructions and using a pair of work-wearied loppers to further widen the path.

Like engineers tunnelling under the English Channel, we communicated with shouts of encouragement until our paths met and we broke through with a celebratory cheer and a formal shaking of hands. The tall man greeted me with a genuine and jolly smile. His magnificent white beard and straggly hair were decorated with accidentally acquired twigs and leaves. The lady had her long grey hair sensibly platted into a ponytail and tied with a pink ribbon. She nodded politely from behind her husband and gave a shy smile, her twinkling blue eyes barely visible under the wide brim of her floppy green Stetson hat.

As this intrepid couple had done almost half of my work, I felt it was only fair to invite them back to the house for tea and scones. By now Lesley had become accustomed to me returning from my walks, leading waifs and strays and demanding sustenance. She welcomed such diversions as a fact of rural life, which gave her a welcome break from the gardening and led to many new friendships.

Levi and Eva were a Dutch couple who lived around 6 miles away. Practical, pragmatic and delightfully energetic, they had moved to Ireland from Germany in 2009 to spend their retirement hiking and riding their horses. Unfortunately, their timing couldn't have been worse. They'd bought their house at the peak of the property boom, just a few months before the financial crash sent prices tumbling. Now with rock bottom exchange rates, Levi's pension was barely covering their costs. Furthermore, in short order, they'd become grandparents twice over, but as their children all lived in and around London, Levi and Eva's visits were expensive and infrequent. Although they both professed to love living in County Clare, I quickly got the impression they'd already set their hearts on moving to England as soon as possible.

We had a pleasant afternoon sharing our respective stories, chatting about chickens and putting the world to rights. Even though we didn't ride horses and they were uncomfortable around dogs, we hit it off splendidly. Of course, as soon as it became clear our guests were cat people who viewed dogs with the same ambivalence and distrust as their feline charges, our dogs made every effort to convert them to our cause.

"Perhaps if you just said you loved dogs, they'd leave you alone," Lesley suggested.

"Ees okay," Eva laughed, brushing the dog hair from her mud-encrusted jeans. "Ower cats would be ze same with you."

As we waved them on their way with promises to meet again, I couldn't help delighting in the many new friends we'd met since moving to Ireland.

***

The summer rolled on and a week later the sun was still shining from a clear blue sky, further extending our run of pleasant weather. Although it was never going to rival the climate of California or southern France, Ireland's long run of 'not so wet and dreary as usual' weather was very welcome and had done a lot to lift the spirits of those less fortunate than us. Many people in Ireland were really suffering financially as the recession dragged on. Food was expensive, taxes were up, unemployment was high, debts were rising and with many people trapped in negative equity, mortgage arrears were soaring. In amongst the depressing stories of dole queues, food banks, loan sharks, business failures and home repossessions, the news media struggled to find anything uplifting to report. Fortunately, there were still a few laughs to be had if you knew where to look.

"Listen to this." My wife was reading from the local paper. "Clare County Council have decided it will be too expensive to normalise and correct the proper names and spellings of some tourist attractions. Apparently, the official historical spellings are often at odds with the spelling used by the locals, and that disagrees with the spelling on new road signs erected by the National Roads Authority. For example, Ennistymon was changed to Ennistmon, Lahinch to Lehinch and Miltown Malbay to Milltown Malbay."

"Perhaps the National Roads Authority is conspiring with Kerry County Council to ensure no tourists can ever leave Killarney."

Lesley laughed. "If they are, they're doing a cracking job. Killarney was packed with tourists when we were there."

I clicked my fingers.

"That reminds me, while we're on the subject of spelling. One of my golf clients is a teacher. He told me a funny story the other day."

"Go on. I could do with a laugh."

"Let me get this right…" I closed my eyes and scratched my chin whilst trying to remember the correct details. "Sally had been off sick and her mother sent a note to the school. It said young Sally had missed class the previous week because she had suffered an attack of diarrhoea. As if things weren't bad enough for the unfortunate Sally, the mother had spelled the illness Dire-rear – which can only translate into terrible bottom!"

My wife choked on her coffee. Happy days.

***

"I'm going outside to shoot some new pictures for my golf column."

Lesley looked up from the cardigan she was knitting.

"I thought you were giving that up." She frowned with genuine confusion. "You said writing for the paper wasn't really worth your time anymore."

I shrugged and added a half-smile in an attempt to cover my embarrassment. My wife was right. Writing my golf tips instructional column for the local rag had once been a lucrative venture. It gave me professional kudos and a lot of local exposure, but more recently the effort involved in producing 1,000 words of humorous but informative instruction each week, far outweighed the returns. Recycling the same tips over and over had become a depressing chore. Golf is simple and yet endlessly complicated, but the complicated parts don't sell golf lessons and there are only so many ways you can write about the simple bits. Upon review, I'd come to the conclusion my underlying apathy had seeped into my writing and may have contributed in some part to the decline in bookings for lessons.

"I thought I'd give it one more go," I said, brightly. "Perhaps with a change to the layout, different pictures and some new ideas, it might rekindle the interest I had before."

"But surely you'll still be saying the same things?"

"Ah yes…" I tipped my head and held up a cautionary finger, "but in a new and exciting way."

Lesley didn't answer. She fixed her eyes firmly on her knitting. For a moment I thought her catatonic silence was driven by suppressed anger or some inner conflict, but the microscopic movements of her lips told me she was counting stitches. I waited patiently for her to finish her calculation. Fully 30 seconds later, she gave a sharp nod to confirm her count was in order before fixing me with her best, on-your-own-head-be-it stare.

"It's up to you."

I smiled and headed towards the door. Her sotto voce parting shot was more warning than observation. "At least you'll be making some use of that new camera you bought."

Lesley had a point, well, half a point. Purchasing the camera was good, it was just the timing that was bad. Anyway, I needed the camera – I wanted the camera. It was my new toy.

To accurately film a golf swing requires specialist digital video equipment, capable of capturing 100 frames per second. Costing around €30,000, such a camera was an expense well beyond the means of a lowly golf coach. However, I'd recently heard about an inexpensive digital camera, designed for holiday snaps, which could capture stunningly clear images at 250 frames a second. I felt like I'd progressed from stone tablets to a word processor overnight. What's more it cost just €299. The camera was a perfect teaching aid to help clients understand their swing errors. Furthermore, I could video my demonstration swings, load them onto my computer and copy the specific image I wanted for my newspaper column in a matter of minutes. For once, a picture really was worth a thousand words.

There was no need to drive all the way to the golf course. I set the camera tripod on our front lawn. With a background of tall pine trees, short grass underfoot and my catch net just out of frame, it would appear as if I were hitting shots on the fairway. For 30 minutes, I messed around, changing settings on the camera and filming demonstration golf swings. It was a humid and windless morning. The sun was shining from a clear blue sky, promising another glorious day. Flanked by forests and vast tracks of moorlands, serenaded by birdsong, the gentle fluttering of butterflies and the drone of bees, I couldn't have asked for a better place to be. The Irish recession was almost over, we had money in the bank, our bills were paid, my Irish manuscript was ready to publish and, with a reinvigorated newspaper column and perhaps a website, there was hope yet for my golf teaching business. Life was good and I felt relaxed and happy, which made what happened next all the more surprising.

Just as I stepped forward to review the previous golf swing on the camera, I was struck with a sensation somewhere between the negative G-force of a bumpy aircraft ride and my blood pressure dropping like bathwater down a plughole. Sparkles danced in front of my eyes and my head swam. As my vision blurred to grey, I went down on one knee, rested my head on the cool grass and desperately tried to regulate my racing heartbeat.

The symptoms were disturbingly familiar to that day eight years previously, which triggered a sequence of events culminating in our move to Ireland. The words of my then doctor roared above the pounding blood in my ears, "Carry on like this and you'll be dead in six months." But that was back when I was living under immense pressure and burning the candle at both ends – and in the middle too. Now things were different. My life was incalculably better. It couldn't be happening again.

After a few deep breaths, things settled a little and my vision gradually came back into focus. As quickly as it occurred, the strange feeling passed. With my head no longer swimming, I carefully stood upright and stiffly marched my rubber legs across to the house where I could lean against the wall. Although I no longer felt faint, my heart was jumping in my chest in a violent and irregular rhythm, like a frightened rat attempting to escape from a cage. After several long shallow breaths, the rat had been replaced by a couple of excitable hamsters and I felt sufficiently in control of my faculties to head indoors.

"What's the matter? You look like a ghost," Lesley exclaimed, before I'd uttered a word.

As rare as it was to receive some unsolicited concern from my wife, I really didn't want her to fuss.

"I'm grand," I lied, trying not to puff too noticeably. "I just had a funny turn...probably stood up too quickly...I'll be okay after a cup of tea."

For once Lesley wasn't so easily diverted by the casual wave of my hand or my blasé attitude. And my heart wasn't helping much either. Even after I'd sat quietly on the couch for fifteen minutes, it was still rumbling, jumping and bouncing in my chest like a defective diesel engine. In the hope she'd stop fussing unnecessarily about a little panting, sweating, wincing and chest grabbing, I agreed she could drive me to the doctor.

My pasty face got me fast-tracked to the front of the queue and five minutes later I was sitting with my doctor. He was similarly unsympathetic to my protestations. After taking my pulse and blood pressure, he attached an electrocardiogram machine, frowned, fiddled with the leads, frowned even more, tutted seriously and sent me directly to the local hospital.

9 – Jogging in Pyjamas

"This is ridiculous!" We were ten minutes from the hospital and I was trying a final desperate plea for mercy. "There's nothing wrong with me, I probably stood up too quickly or something."

"That's the third time you've said that…" Lesley drummed her fingers on the steering wheel. The tone of her voice indicated I had already exceeded my daily moaning allowance. "Stop fussing. Doctor Mark said it's only a precautionary check-up. You'll probably be done in an hour."

"Yes but–"

"But nothing!" she snapped. "You'll go in and that's the end of it."

I resisted the temptation to say, "Yes, Mum."

"Anyway, Doctor Mark said you need to go to A&E, if only to get into the system. Remember?"

I shook my head. "I must have missed that bit."

She rolled her eyes and sighed. "You never listen."

"Sorry? What were you saying?" My joke fell a little flat.

"Doctor Mark said, with the health service being so underfunded and overburdened, he's routinely sending people directly to A&E so as to bypass the waiting lists. That's why you're going to the hospital. A little inconvenience today will save months of waiting to see a consultant and get tested for…" she waved her hand vaguely, "whatever it is."

"But there's nothing wrong!" Once again, I bravely risked my wife's wrath and a tongue-lashing which would have required hospital treatment anyway.

"What about this random tiredness?" Lesley challenged. "You told Doctor Mark, some days you feel you could run two marathons and the next you're so exhausted you can hardly stand."

"I guess that is a trifle odd…"

"Odd? Of course it's odd," she growled. "How long has that been going on?"

"Only a few months…" I mumbled.

"A few months!"

"Definitely less than a year," I added quickly.

"Less than a…When were you going to TELL ME THAT?" My wife was so red-faced, I could feel her blood pressure rising.

Fortunately, for her and me, we had reached the hospital. I put my hand on her arm.

"Let's get this over as quickly as possible." I squeezed her hand. "On the way back home, we'll stop at the shops and buy something nice for dinner. Perhaps we'll get one of those pizzas we like, the one with the goat cheese and caramelised onions."

"Okay." She held up her crossed fingers. "In and out and back home for dinner."

I copied the gesture. "That sounds like a workable plan."

But it was not to be.

As soon as we entered the building, it felt as if we'd been transported to a third world hospital. The waiting area was packed, all the seats were taken and several people were standing. Along the corridor, I counted a dozen patients laid on hospital trollies; presumably they were waiting for beds to vacate up on the wards. From the grim, tired faces of the hospital staff, it was obvious they were all having a bad day. I put this to the receptionist and added my best smile, just to be on the safe side.

"Bad day, bad week, bad month..." she groaned, shaking her head. "Bad year."

"I'd heard the Irish Health Service was struggling and under resourced, but I didn't realise it was so bad."

As I wasn't bringing anything new to the discussion, our conversation fizzled and for a minute she silently tapped away at her computer keyboard, entering my details. After checking everything was in order, she hit the enter key one final time and I was formally admitted into the system. Her tired eyes brightened a little as she handed back my doctor's letter.

"You'll be alright. Hearts come first." She gave me a gentle smile. "You won't have long to wait."

She was right. We were still trying to figure out how the beverage machine worked when I heard a nurse call my name. I waved and followed her into the treatment area, all the time trying to avoid making eye contact with all the numerous bruised, bloodied and obviously unwell patients I had just jumped ahead of. I felt awful, but what could I say? "I'm sorry you have to wait even longer to have your broken foot or split head attended to, but I felt a little dizzy earlier and that comes first." I seriously considered throwing myself on the floor and faking a seizure, just so I wouldn't feel so guilty.

"In and out," I whispered to Lesley. "We'll be home in no time."

But my hopes were soon dashed. The treatment and assessment area was made up of two rooms, each around 20 by 30 feet. There was a row of windows on the right, which looked out onto the carpark. The blank wall on the left was painted institutional beige. The first room had four curtained cubicles on the right and a couple of computer desks on the left, which were piled high with charts and the remains of several half-eaten meals. The second room was accessible through a wide double doorway, it contained eight further cubicles. I counted twelve patients, including me. As there were doors at either end of the treatment area, there was a constant flow of foot traffic, mostly tired looking nurses and busy hospital porters.

The nurse asked me to wait in the first cubicle on the right. Lesley took the seat and I perched on the hospital trolley so I could look out of the window. Two minutes later a different nurse came over clutching my chart. She pulled the curtain shut and proceeded to repeat the exact same questions I'd answered at the reception desk just ten minutes earlier. I guessed she was double checking they had recorded my information correctly, which was fine by me and infinitely preferable to having a leg sawn off in error, just because someone put a tick in the wrong box.

Whereas the efficiency of the administration department was impressive, along with their ability to generate huge quantities of paper, the medical staff's belief that a half-closed flimsy curtain provided any privacy was suspect. I winced internally, imagining my fellow patients taking copious notes while the nurse interrogated me loudly and in excruciating detail about my address, place of work, the golf column I wrote (she'd recognised my name from the paper), my general health, which body parts had been operated on, when I last ate and the regularity of my bowel movements. With the admin over, we progressed to the examination phase. With swift and reassuring efficiency, the nurse checked my temperature, blood pressure, oxygen levels, took blood for various tests and did another electrocardiogram reading. That 20 minutes of hectic activity was followed by a lot of waiting around for something to happen.

I'd arrived at the hospital on a Thursday afternoon of the hottest week of the year. Although I now felt fine and the doctors could find nothing wrong, within a couple of hours they decided I should wait to be admitted to the cardiac ward. This precautionary move was openly discussed as a way to circumvent the waiting lists.

"If I discharge you now," one doctor told me, "you'll be waiting for months to see a consultant."

"But I'm perfectly fine," I exclaimed. "Yet I'm taking up valuable space whilst those poor people out there are waiting to be seen."

He shrugged and patted my arm. "You're here now and I have a responsibility to treat you to the best of my ability. You presented with symptoms suggestive of a cardiac issue. That is not something to be taken lightly. Please be patient, I'm sure a bed will open up by tomorrow."

"Tomorrow?" I gasped. "You mean I have to stay here overnight?"

"I'm afraid so…" He grimaced sympathetically. "We'll have to move you into a side room so we can treat some other patients. At least it will be a little quieter in there."

"Okay," I sighed. "Whatever you think is best."

Lesley went home to feed the dogs and check on the chickens before returning briefly to bring me a couple of books, my phone charger, some clothes and toiletries. For the next 108 hours, I laid on a trolley in a windowless side-room parking area, trapped between a painfully thin elderly man who slept all the time and a belligerent and restless drug addict, slowly coming around from an overdose. The room was unpleasantly hot and airless and so noisy I found it impossible to sleep. On the one occasion I did nod off, I was woken a short while later when the cleaner turned on the lights and began mopping and polishing the floor. My only respite from this cruel torture was when I was called to the cardiac lab for a stress test. This involved me being wired to another ECG machine and jogging for 15 minutes on an inclined treadmill whilst wearing my ill-fitting pyjamas and fluffy slippers. Despite my unusual attire, the need to repeatedly tuck my genitals back out of view and the oppressive heat in the room, my heart refused to reach the targeted number of beats per minute.

"You're very fit," the nurse said, looking away as bits of me once again escaped through the slot in the front of my pyjamas. "Do you run a lot?"

"I used to," I panted, "but these days I prefer hiking up through the forest. It's a really good workout."

She tapped the readout and smiled ironically. "Nothing to see here."

"Oh good," I sighed. "Can I go home now?"

"It's not up to me." She shrugged.

"But I'm just taking up space here and for no good reason. It's like I can't be discharged until someone has taken my temperature, but there isn't a spare thermometer, so I'm occupying a valuable bed while somebody really ill has to wait." I closed my eyes and took a deep calming breath. "I'm sorry. I know it isn't your fault…"

She smiled and leaned closer to whisper. "Sadly, your analogy isn't far from the truth. With all the cuts, the health service is running on empty."

She was right. At that moment, more than 400 patients around Ireland were on trolleys, waiting for a hospital bed. Feeling guilty to be using up such scarce resources when I was obviously well enough to be at home, I decided enough was enough. Late on Sunday night, I managed to corner one of the doctors while he was eating a sandwich and updating charts. By the light of his desk lamp, we had one of those, "Don't quote me but…" whispered conversations. I made my case and he made his. It was all very amicable. In the end, I acknowledged his dire warning, signed the forms and discharged myself. Back home, I fussed the dogs, had a shower, a hot milky drink, gratefully climbed into my bed and slept like a dead man.

***

Perhaps the health service admin failed, or worked perfectly, or the late-night shift doctor didn't rat me out for discharging myself against his advice, but a week later I had an appointment to see the cardiologist. After my blood pressure was checked, I was given an echocardiogram and led through to see the great man. I had anticipated the cardiologist would be an overweight and overworked man with few social skills and a name I couldn't spell or pronounce. I couldn't have been more wrong.

For someone at the pinnacle of his profession, he was young, fit and maddingly handsome. With thick wavy blond hair, sparkling blue eyes, perfect teeth and an athletic physique, he could easily have been the poster boy for Olympic rowing. Although Dr Brendan Hennessy was decidedly Irish, his accent was 98% Oxford English with just a hint of County Cork. He stepped out from behind his desk and greeted me with a warm smile and a genuinely welcoming handshake. The only things on his mahogany leather topped desk were a gold fountain pen, a telephone and my chart.

Once I was seated, Brendan perched casually on the edge of his desk, calmed me with a gentle smile and lightly patted my chart with his hand.

"Your heart is fine," he began without preamble. "You're probably fitter than me."

"Thank you. That's good to know." I suspected he'd easily beat me in a 100-metre dash, but it was a nice thing to say.

A smile flicked momentarily across his face, before he folded his arms and leaned forward. Back to business.

"But we still need to get to the bottom of what is going on." He fixed me with a steady gaze, searching for the truth. "You've had a few of these episodes, haven't you?"

"Several," I admitted. "Most were when we lived in England, but not so much since we moved here. They've mostly been little flutters, like you'd feel if you suddenly realised you'd forgotten your wife's birthday."

He laughed.

I added. "Those events were certainly nothing like what happened the other week."

"How long have you been coughing at night?"

"Good grief!" I exclaimed. "How did you know about that?"

Brendan casually waved towards the wall. "The guy who sold me those diplomas told me about it." He added a smile so I knew he was only joking.

I got his point. "Well, you certainly know your stuff. The coughing wakes me up most nights. It's so frequent, I'd almost forgotten."

He nodded again, pulling the clues together in his mind.

"I'm going to refer you to a friend of mine. He's a gastroenterologist."

"Tummies?" I frowned in surprise. "You think I may have a stomach problem?"

He nodded. "He'll have to do some tests, but I suspect you've had a hiatal hernia for some time." He raised his fist and pushed it through his other hand like an obscene gesture. "It's where the stomach pushes up into the diaphragm. I've seen these symptoms several times before. There's only a few clinical studies which make the link to a hernia, but lots of valuable observations from patients." He grimaced a shrug and stood. "That's if the internet chat rooms are to be believed."

"So, I'll hear from him?" I asked, as I stood too.

"You shouldn't have to wait long. In the meantime, raise the head of your bed by six inches and try to sleep on your left side..." He scribbled a prescription and handed it to me. "And take these tablets twice a day."

***

Brendan was true to his word and I received an appointment letter in record time. His advice on changing my sleeping position and sloping the bed, combined with the stomach-acid suppressing tablets, had worked miracles. By the time of my first visit to the gastroenterology clinic, I was feeling in grand form. Like a new man. I didn't meet Brendan's friend, but the gastroenterologist I saw agreed with the diagnosis.

"We'll have to do an endoscopic examination for confirmation. It's where we put a camera down into your stomach." He opened his mouth and pointed a finger down his throat like a trainee sword swallower.

"It sounds delightful," I croaked.

He waved dismissively. "Don't worry, we'll put you to sleep. You won't feel a thing."

"Good to know." I smiled and relaxed, but only until he spoke again.

"Given your age, while we've got you under, we'll start with a colonoscopy." He sipped his coffee and smiled reassuringly. "Just to check everything down there is okay."

"That's fine with me." I returned his smile. "Just be sure to wipe the camera before you put it in my mouth."

I swear coffee came out of his nose.

***

With Lesley going to England for ten days to visit friends and family, I would be in charge of Glenmadrie, the dogs, chickens and her garden. The day before her flight, she took me on a lengthy tour of the plants in the garden, greenhouse, polytunnel, vegetable patches and around a dozen windowsills in the house, giving me precise instructions on what to water, how much to administer and which watering techniques I should use. It was early October and Ireland was basking in the final throws of our summer, but wet, cold and foggy weather was forecast to arrive within a few days.

"Remember to open the polytunnel and greenhouse if it gets hot," she said.

I nodded dutifully.

"And close them if it gets cold."

I nodded again. "Don't worry. This isn't my first rodeo."

Lesley ignored me, or didn't hear my jibe.

"And don't forget to pick the strawberries every day, or the wasps will get to them," she added.

"What about the peaches?" I asked, adding notes to my list of instructions.

"Them too, but only if they're ripe. But don't leave them too long, or they'll fall off and get damaged."

"That's very helpful." I wrote, 'Pick peaches – or not.'

"Don't forget to talk to the leeks and the tomatoes. It encourages them to grow."

"Really?" I asked suspiciously.

"It's an experiment. Prince Charles does it too."

I frowned at the thought. "First I've heard of this. What do I say?"

"It doesn't matter what you say." She waved my question away dismissively. "Just do it – please."

"Should I talk to the cabbages?" I asked.

"Don't be ridiculous." Lesley rolled her eyes. "Cabbages are stupid."

I wrote, 'Talk to leeks and tomatoes, but nothing else.'

"I suppose you can manage the chickens?"

"I already do." All things considered, I did well to avoid any obvious tutting. "But don't worry. I won't let them out unless I'm going to be here all day, which will only be on the weekends."

"You've got golf lessons?" she asked, surprised.

"Not very many, but I've got one or two booked on most days." I smiled. "It'll keep me out of trouble while you're away."

"I'd better show you how to feed the dogs."

"But I know how to feed the dogs!" I did some obvious tutting.

"You always give them too much. They get fat whenever I'm away."

I put my arm on her sleeve. "I can cope you know. Stop fussing."

"I know…" She nodded. "I'm just worried…"

"About your mum?" I completed the thought.

Lesley nodded.

"I'm sure she'll be fine. Anyway, this is a good opportunity for you to check things out."

She nodded again.

"And have a nice rest," I added.

***

On what turned out to be the last day of our summer, I walked the dogs early then drove my trusty little Toyota to the golf course. It was a gorgeous day. With the windows down and a warm breeze blowing through the car, I felt wonderfully happy and relaxed enough to risk singing along with the radio. Although it is often confused with the sound of a donkey being castrated and is known to frighten small children and birds, my singing brings me pleasure. On this occasion, when the music stopped, the song continued and I found myself humming, 'Ain't no sunshine when she's gone,' for the rest of the day.

With exquisitely cruel timing, my first lesson cancelled while I was driving, so I didn't see his text message until I arrived. By then it was too late to return home and with just two hours until my final client of the day, I shouldered my clubs and headed out of the carpark. On the far side of the course, in a quiet corner where the base of a steep hill met the edge of the lake, was a short par-3 hole where I could do a little practice. An hour later I took a break, sat at the water's edge and hummed that song while I ate a sandwich I'd prepared. It gave me a chance to think.

During the weeks since my appointment with the gastroenterologist, I'd had time to read the leaflets he'd given me and do some follow-up research on the internet. I now understood a little of why the condition can burn the oesophagus, causing persistent sore throats and night-time coughing. I also knew it could irritate the vagus nerve and mimic a stress attack. While I'd been reassured to discover the symptoms we'd discussed, along with several we hadn't, could all be attributed to a hiatal hernia, a few things troubled me. To begin with, as hiatal hernias are notoriously difficult to repair successfully, they are usually managed through a lifetime of diet and medication. Whereas I was irritated to discover I had something which probably couldn't be fixed, much like my oafish stupidity, I would learn to live with it. Also, all the recommended actions in the leaflets were things I was already doing. I didn't smoke or eat spicy foods; I took regular exercise, watched my weight and avoided eating late night meals. Although I didn't drink much, even Guinness upset my stomach, so around a year previously, I'd given up alcohol completely. Now I was taking the tablets and sleeping on my left side with my head higher than my feet, I felt great again. Despite all the positives, there was one thing which irked me.

Our move to Ireland was predicated by a series of these half-fainting palpitation events. At the time they were diagnosed as stress attacks and my doctor had delivered a dire warning about my need to change my lifestyle. Admittedly, back then I was under a huge amount of stress – both financially and at work, but I felt I was coping. What if he was wrong and I wasn't buckling under the stress and about to drop dead, just suffering the early symptoms of the hernia? Had we known, perhaps Lesley would never have suggested the move. Was our decision to begin a new life in Ireland really based on false data? Perhaps it was just fortuitus timing. In any event, it has led us to a better life.

Sitting on the lakeside in the warm sunshine, without a care in the world and with nothing to do but share my sandwich with some ducks and watch a grey heron feed, I decided I wouldn't change a thing. However we got here, Ireland was now our home. Life was good and I loved it.

10 – The Good the Bad and the Angry

"I think I shall sell the Toyota," I said to Lesley.

"Why?" she asked.

"It's 20 years old," I replied. "The time is right."

I'd just arrived home from playing golf with my professional colleague, Andrew Rich. I didn't tell my wife that a few minutes earlier, I'd terrified myself and the driver of an oncoming logging lorry on the narrow lane which transverses the Slieve Aughty mountains. I'd driven for long enough on Ireland's narrow rural lanes to develop the sort of foolhardy complacency which could lead to soiled underwear or death. Stupid me. Although that road cuts through rolling hills with thousands of acres of beautiful pine forest, it has many long straight stretches with great visibility. As a regular traveller, I'd inadvertently slipped into driving these sections with rather more rapidity than was wise for someone in an aged car, without the benefits of a crash helmet, roll cage or adequate maintenance. Flying along without a care in the world, with the windows down and the wind blowing through both of my hairs, I rounded a slight bend in the otherwise straight road and was shocked to see a huge lorry, completely blocking my passage. Whereas I was always on the lookout for deer, hikers and cyclists, on this road lorries are obvious enough to be spotted from several miles away. My first thought upon seeing this massive articulated vehicle was, "Where the hell did he come from?"

Bright yellow and overloaded with tons of tree trunks, this rolling roadblock was probably visible from space without the aid of a telescope – and yet it had somehow appeared from nowhere. During the nanosecond it took for my right foot to travel from the accelerator to the brake pedal, I surmised this magic trick had been achieved by hiding the lorry up one of the many logging side roads. Laden down and travelling slightly uphill, the lorry driver had friction and gravity on his side and was able to stop his vehicle in short order. I was less fortunate. Heading downhill, with the wind on my back and bereft of swanky braking technology, my plucky little Toyota Starlet shut its eyes, locked its wheels and skidded along the road, squealing like a schoolgirl on a rollercoaster. At that point, I became an unwilling passenger, sliding uncontrollably towards the scene of the accident. The life which flashed before my eyes was a little disappointing and so short I had enough time to watch a rerun, before my car shuddered to a stop just inches from the lorry.

My heart had just recommenced its primary task, when it almost stopped beating again. Without warning, the world around me suddenly disappeared. Blown on the tailwind, the cloud of acrid thick grey tyre smoke I had created momentarily enveloped the car like an illusion from a Las Vegas magic show. The lorry driver was so impressed when my car suddenly reappeared, he gave me a round of applause and followed with another hand gesture which was impolite, but more merited. The skid marks I had just made on this less-travelled road were 60 metres long and remained visible for six months. At that moment I vowed to drive a little slower, sell my Toyota and buy something with better brakes.

"Will you be able to sell it?" Lesley asked, frowning. "I mean. Who would want such an old banger?"

Her comment wasn't unreasonable. For many people, buying a car is no more noteworthy than booking a regular skiing trip, but for us such transactions are significant and important. I'd bought my trusty Toyota several years earlier from the roadside. The sign said low mileage and one lady owner, a young trainee hairdresser. Back then, the black Mercedes saloon had become the transport of choice for almost everyone in Ireland, even hairdressers. That particular young woman had been pleased to exchange her first car for a small handful of Euros and in return I was delighted to have acquired an economical little runabout at such a reasonable price. Several years and 60,000 miles later, the gleaming red paint had faded to pink and the bodywork wore more dents and scratches than a battle wearied tank. Even so, I felt there was still some hope.

"I was looking on that DoneDeal website," I explained. "Andrew said it's like Ireland's version of eBay. Apparently, it's a great place for buying and selling almost anything."

"And?" Lesley rolled her wrist in a come hither gesture.

"Oh…" I realised I'd forgotten to make my point. "There were a few Starlets on there, older than mine and with higher mileage, but they still seem to be selling. I guess now times are hard, people are looking for more economical cars. With any luck, we can trade up without being noticeably out of pocket."

Lesley shrugged. "Well, you know more about cars than me. It's up to you."

That afternoon, I washed the car, cleaned the inside, took some nice pictures and placed the advert. Just ten minutes later I'd sold my Toyota.

"There's a fellow called Naill driving down from somewhere north of Galway," I said.

"Phew! That's a long way to come for a little car."

"He's very keen. Didn't argue the price or anything."

Lesley looked sceptical. "That seems rather odd. You were asking more for it than you paid for the car in the first place."

"He saw the picture and I have a full service history." I shrugged. "He runs a garage. Apparently he wanted something cheap and bombproof for his customers to borrow. That car certainly fits the bill."

It was dark long before Naill arrived. As Glenmadrie was so remote, I had directed him to an easy to find village a little way north of our house. I drove out to wait on the village shop forecourt. He and one of his garage mechanics arrived in a white works van. In short order, they checked the car over and drove me home, where we completed the deal. True to his word, Naill paid the full asking price without complaint. Although they had a long drive ahead, the two men joined us for tea and biscuits before setting off. Naill was particularly interested in our story and the renovations we had done to the house and garden.

"I'm really sorry I can't stay longer," he said, checking his watch. "I'd like to have heard more. Your story is fascinating and I so love old buildings like this. You've done a lovely job and should be very proud."

"Thank you very much," I replied, shaking his hand.

I was delighted to sell my little car to such an honest and likeable person. More so when I discovered I'd inadvertently left my new mobile phone on the dashboard. Although he was already 30 miles away when my error was discovered, Naill had no hesitation in turning around and bringing my phone back to me. I couldn't have been more grateful.

If only all my car trades had gone so well.

***

Buoyed by my newfound talents as a successful wheeler-dealer and confident I could easily outsmart the gullible public and the motor trade, a week later I set out on my quest to buy another car. Had I worn a sandwich board emblazoned with the sign 'gullible and keen to part with cash,' I couldn't have done much worse.

I'd set a reasonable budget, done my research and found what seemed like a good buy. It was a British-built Rover. While not a sexy brand, the parts were cheap and the car was known to be quite reliable, except for one thing. These models were originally fitted with substandard head gaskets, an important engine component which was cheap to buy but expensive to replace. It was a well-known fault any would-be buyer would do well to check. Which I did, when I met the seller and his younger assistant at his garage near Athlone.

"Oh yes. It's had a full service and the head gasket was changed." Seamus nodded towards the workshop doors. It was a Sunday, so everything was locked up. "We did it here, a couple of weeks ago. Isn't that right, Junior?"

"Yep." Junior nodded, hawked something unmentionable from deep in his sinus and spat it into the gravel. I was pleased Lesley was still sitting in our car. "Couple of weeks ago, to be sure we did."

"What about the water pump?" I asked, averting my eyes from what Junior had just expectorated.

"Of course." Seamus tutted dismissively and rolled his eyes dramatically. "You wouldn't change the head gasket without changing the water pump, now would you?"

"Not if yous doing the gasket you wouldn't," Junior added.

"The carpet seems a little damp in the back," I suggested. "I hope there isn't a leak."

"Tsk. Don't fuss about a little water. It'll soon dry out. Junior left the window open is all," Seamus said. "Didn't yea?"

"Aye. That I did." He smiled widely, revealing all five of his teeth.

Seamus leaned in and whispered. "Stupid fecker, don't know his arse from his elbow some days. He's me sister's kid." He tapped a grubby finger on the side of his nose. "You know how it is?"

I nodded politely and left it at that.

After a short, trouble-free test drive and some negotiations, the deal was done for slightly more than I had made by selling my trusty Toyota. Feeling rather proud of myself, I followed Lesley back to Glenmadrie.

It was a pleasant autumn afternoon, but cool, despite the sunshine. Our route home took us south, through the town of Gort and on through some glorious countryside. I was thoroughly enjoying the journey, gradually getting used to my new steed. The nippy little engine was purring along merrily and the car appeared to be almost fault free, except for a few things. There was an annoying tendency for the car to pull to the left, coupled with an increasingly noticeable shudder under braking. As well as the irritating wind-whistle from the driver's window, the radio refused to work and the heater seemed to be stuck on the cool setting. I'd twiddled with the controls for a bit, but gave up when the knob fell off and disappeared under my seat. Hey ho. These were all just little faults, insignificant in the grand scheme of things and easily rectified at my local garage, where I'd already booked the car in for a quick check over. As it turned out, my snagging list was just the tip of a very large iceberg.

The repair shop report made for depressing reading. Apart from the faulty radio, broken heater, misaligned suspension, dangerous steering, defective brakes and leaky door seals, they also noted the water pump and head gasket had never been changed and were both faulty.

"He lied to my face," I complained to Lesley, a week later. "That Seamus fellow looked me in the eye and lied."

"Perhaps you just misunderstood him," she replied, doing her best to see good in everyone.

"Uh-uh." I shook my head and waved the fault report. "Seamus clearly said they had replaced the head gasket the previous week. He said they'd done it in their own workshop!"

In a fit of anger, earlier I'd phoned the garage to demand a refund.

"And what did the garage owner say?" Lesley asked.

"He said he'd never seen the car and didn't know anyone called Seamus or Junior." I chewed my lip and shuffled my feet. "It would appear they were using the forecourt as a ruse."

My wife tutted sympathetically and gently patted my shoulder.

"Well, my dear, it would appear some unscrupulous person

has once again taken advantage of your good nature."

I sighed. "That seems to happen a lot."

Despite the jaw-droppingly long fault report list, all was not lost. Our marvellous local garage took charge of the decrepit Rover and their crack team of Polish mechanics quickly got to work. They did an excellent job and three days later my car was returned to me in tiptop condition. With the silver paintwork gleaming, it had a working heater, dry carpets, repaired suspension, better brakes and an engine purring like a contented kitten. I was delighted with the results, but with the garage bill topping out at slightly more than I paid for the car, it was clear my short career as a wheeler and dealer in the motor trade had drawn to a close. Perhaps it was time to think more seriously about writing.

***

The year drew to a close in typical Glenmadrie style. In what had become a festive tradition, Lesley and I once again failed to decorate the house and refused to buy each other gifts. We both preferred to spend that money doing random acts of kindness for others less fortunate than ourselves, not just at Christmas, but whenever we had a little to spare. Of course we still sent gifts to both of our mothers and our daughter too. A few days before Christmas, we invited Bob and Pamela up for lunch. They were gardening friends of Lesley's, so the conversation circled around various horticultural subjects for the majority of the afternoon. They even endured the cold sleety rain to have a tour of our garden and greenhouses. For once I was happy to do the dishes, as long as it kept me in the warm and dry. Pamela was a retired nurse and Bob used to teach music and art at primary school. They'd moved to Ireland from their native Yorkshire and had met Lesley at a local garden centre. To thank them for their friendship, Lesley had bought Pamela a crystal vase. They reciprocated by unveiling a beautiful oil colour painting of a finch sitting on a holly bush. Bob had painted it himself earlier that year and had it framed ready for Christmas. It was a lovely and thoughtful surprise. The painting now hangs in pride of place on our living room wall.

***

This was Joanne and Mark's second Christmas as a married couple, but the first where they were hosting a family dinner. We chatted on the phone that morning. Our conversation was brief as Joanne was busy preparing the turkey and trimmings. It was lovely to hear our daughter so happy. A couple of days later, we received an email with a mass of attachments. Lesley and I sat together at my computer and looked through a pictorial history of their day.

"It seems they had a wonderful time," I said.

"Joanne looks tired," Lesley remarked. "Happy, but tired."

"She's been working hard. What with the new job…" I pointed at the picture showing a food laden table, "and making this lot too."

"She didn't even have a drink. Apparently she was the designated driver. Poor thing."

I opened another picture, it showed Muriel with a small plate of food and a glass of her favourite tipple. Although she was smiling, some of the sparkle had gone from her eyes. The progress of her dementia was becoming more noticeable. Believing this was the last Christmas Muriel would spend in England, Joanne had made a special effort to make it a memorable day.

"Your mum looks like she was enjoying herself," I said.

Lesley smiled but remained silent. Perhaps, like me, she was thinking back to my recent stay in hospital. Seeing the decrepit state of the Irish health system at first hand had been a shock for both of us and raised many concerns about what support we could hope for when Muriel eventually came to live with us.

***

Whereas Lesley is always grumpy in the morning, particularly before her first cup of coffee, I am insufferably bright and breezy. Our daughter takes after her mother.

"Do you know what time it is?" she growled, rather loudly.

I moved the phone away from my ear and checked my watch. As I'd already had my breakfast, walked the dogs, fed and cleaned out the chickens, phoned my mother, hoovered the house and had a shower, I'd lost track of time.

"It's half past ten," I replied, cautiously.

"Why on earth are you phoning so early?" she groaned.

"We're still in bed."

"To wish you a happy New Year?" I suggested, a little weakly. In what was fast becoming another Glenmadrie tradition, Lesley and I had seen the New Year in by being fast asleep, two hours before midnight. In retrospect, I should have considered how others might have celebrated the dawning of another year.

My daughter blew a raspberry and hung up. When she phoned back an hour later, Joanne was clearly feeling a little more spritely.

"I'm sorry for hanging up," she said. "I wasn't feeling very well."

"It's okay," I laughed. "I expect you've got a hangover."

"I wasn't drinking last night."

"Designated driver again?" I suggested.

She ignored my quip. "Is Mummy there?"

"Yes. She's sitting next to me on the couch. Hang on, I'll put you on speaker." I clicked the button. "Go ahead. She's here."

There was a pause, long enough to make me think we'd dropped the connection. Just as I was squinting at the phone, Joanne and Mark spoke together.

"We're having a baby!"

11 – Fur Coats and Soft Rushes

The baby was due towards the end of July.

"We didn't want to say anything, until we were sure the pregnancy was progressing correctly," Joanne explained. "But everything is fine."

"Well, we're delighted for you both," Lesley said.

"Even though we're a bit young to be grandparents," I quipped. "It's really going to damage our street cred."

My wife hissed and nudged me with her elbow. "How are you feeling?"

"A lot of morning sickness," Joanne groaned, "but otherwise I'm okay."

That explained why she hadn't been drinking for a while.

"Mark must be over the moon," I added, knowing our son-in-law had always been keen to start a family.

"He's got morning sickness too," Joanne laughed, "but that's because he drank too much last night."

"Things are going to be very different for you next year," Lesley warned, in a kind motherly voice.

"Different, but a good different," I added.

"Have you told Muriel yet?" Lesley asked.

"We're going over to see her this afternoon," Joanne replied. "I thought it would be best to do it in person. You know how she is on the phone."

"She'll be over the moon to be a great grandmother," Lesley said. "Give her an extra hug for us."

"Will do."

Lesley and I both had trips to the UK planned for May and June. At Joanne's insistence, we held back from the natural impulsion to book additional flights.

"Please wait until after the baby is born and the fuss has died down," she suggested. "I'm sure I'll really appreciate an extra pair of hands in September or October."

Of course our daughter was right, but I could see the pain of separation writ large on Lesley's face. For now, all she could do was knit baby clothes, talk regularly with Joanne on the phone and occasionally look wistfully towards the east. With Muriel and Joanne so far away, we were again feeling the miles tugging at our heartstrings. Ireland was a beautiful place to be and we had a wonderful lifestyle, but there were times when we wished ourselves back in our old home – if only for a few days.

***

During the previous year I'd sent out 20 or so enquires to publishers and received more than a dozen rejection letters. Despite being rather a wimp when it comes to criticism, I'd refused to allow those emotionless boilerplate denunciations of my work get me down. Afterall, the editing had gone well and the feedback from friends and family was good. When another rejection letter arrived at the end of January, I decided it was time for action. My Irish manuscript had been gathering dust for too long.

"If I can't find a publisher, then I'm going it alone," I declared.

"About time too," Lesley replied. "It would be a shame to waste all that work."

She was in the kitchen kneading some dough for scones. A lock of hair had escaped from the hair net she wore for baking, it hung over her right eye. She puffed at it twice and shook her head, but it quickly flopped back into place. With a grunt of dissatisfaction, she wiped it away with her forearm, leaving a smudge of flour on her nose. I came to her rescue, gently pushing the unruly hair back into place and wiping the flour away.

"Your golf book did well. Are you going to use the same platform?" she asked.

I nodded. "Probably. I've some research to do first, but I think so."

"Research?" She frowned in confusion.

"It's a fast changing market," I explained. "There's a lot of new businesses popping up. They've all got their own ideas and different offerings, but not all of them are going to work. It's a big job, preparing the manuscript to meet their particular requirements. I just want to be sure I've chosen the right company."

"Okay," she smiled. "I'm sure you'll figure it out."

With exquisitely ironic timing, the following week I received a publishing offer from a company in London. Two days later, I got an acceptance letter from a publisher in Essex and a day later

120

one more from another publisher in Cambridge.

"Nothing for months and then three offers come all at once," Lesley laughed. "They're like buses!"

I smiled back. Whenever Lesley got excited, her Birmingham accent became stronger. In this case she'd pronounced bus by replacing the S with a strong Z.

Naturally, I was delighted with this sudden interest in my writing, but my euphoria was short-lived. Although it seemed my quest to get a publishing deal was a success, Lesley insisted we took some time to cool our heels and think.

"Much as I want your publishing dream to come true, we have to be sure we're doing the right thing," she said.

On Saturday I did a load of internet research, checking the writers' message boards, looking for company reviews and searching for complaints. Over breakfast the following morning, we carefully studied each of the contracts, making notes and occasionally swapping papers. It reminded me of my parents reading the Sunday editorials.

"If I'm reading this right…" I tapped one contract with my pen, "they won't share any sales data for a year and I won't get any royalties for 18 months."

"That won't do at all. This one is asking you for money." Lesley dismissively tossed the second offering onto the table. "They want to publish your book as-is."

"I wouldn't pay them money, that goes without saying," I shook my head and frowned, "but isn't it a good thing, them wanting the book as-is?"

Lesley patted my hand. "Much as I'm a fan of your writing, do you seriously think every paragraph, sentence, phrase, comma and full stop is correct?"

She had a point. My spelling was notoriously bad, especially when it came to homophones. On many occasions, my computer simply gave up trying to figure out which word I was failing to spell. Sometimes, with heavy digital irony, it asked if I wanted to try using a different language. With that in mind, it was inconceivable any reputable company would choose to print my work without any alterations whatsoever.

By Sunday night, our honest evaluation of the three offers was a disappointing no. We decided I would push on with plan A, publishing through the same platform I'd used for my golf book.

"Better the devil you know," Lesley said.

I replied with a quote. "Publish or perish."

***

The months dragged on, delivering a succession of dull wintery days and long frosty nights. Some days there was a hint of snow in the air, but it didn't amount to much more than a light dusting. I was up to date with most of the urgent DIY tasks and as the weather was stubbornly unpleasant, I confined myself to preparing a snagging list of maintenance I'd need to do in the spring. Living in such a remote spot, cabin fever is a genuine risk, so we made a point of travelling to town at least once a fortnight, if only to have a meal or do a little shopping. There were a couple of bright and reasonably mild days during February, so I took the opportunity to meet with Andrew and play a little golf. Sloshing about in the mud wasn't much fun, but me being out of the house for six hours gave Lesley a welcome break. When I got home, she had a surprise for me.

"Come up to the chicken run." She smiled and beckoned me with her hand. "There's something I want you to see."

"I'd better put my wellies on," I replied. "It's muddier up there than the golf course."

With our three raggedy old chickens no longer laying eggs with any reliability, we'd recently added a trio of Rhode Island Red hybrids to our little flock. This breed are enthusiastic diggers, efficiently using their large claws to search for bugs and tasty worms. Although their pen was large enough for 30 birds, their constant scrapping, combined with the winter weather, had quickly transformed the grassy soil into a quagmire of smelly mud. A few days earlier, I'd laid some boards for us to walk on and shovelled in a ton of chipped bark I'd stolen from Lesley's stock of gardening mulch. Even so, the muddy pen still resembled a twilight scene from the trenches of World War One. As we slipped and slithered our way across the boards, I politely enquired what was so flipping important that it couldn't be shared verbally over a nice cup of tea.

My wife replied with a stern glare and stopped any further impertinent questions by holding a finger to her lips.

"Just before you got back," she whispered, "I put the

chickens to bed and checked for eggs. Look what I found."

She cautiously lifted the lid to the nesting box and nodded for me to look inside.

I squinted into the twilight. "What?" I mimed.

She nodded her head more firmly.

I looked again. Six red chickens and one little black one. Nothing to see here. Then it hit me. We don't have a black chicken.

"Did someone give us a black chicken?" I whispered.

"No! she hissed. "Look again."

With my eyes now accustomed to the gloom, I could see the imposter wasn't a chicken at all. It had sleek black fur. The sort once favoured on extravagantly expensive coats. Incredibly, a full-grown mink was fast asleep, curled up in amongst the chickens. Somehow this notoriously vicious killer had broken into the coop, feasted on chicken feed and snuggled down for the night. Lesley slowly lowered the lid of the nesting box and used a finger to gently close my mouth.

"Talk about strange bed fellows!" I exclaimed.

The next morning, we watched in amazement as the mink followed the chickens around the pen as if he'd lived there for years. They seemed unperturbed to share their space, food and bed with this wily assassin and in return, he didn't kill them. Four days later, he disappeared as mysteriously as he'd arrived. He was just another wandering wonder of country living.

***

As winter rolled into spring, nothing much happened in our lives. The next day, nothing much happened again. We get a lot of days like that. However, it would be a mistake to imagine the absence of sensational melodrama as being somehow tedious. There is a natural rhythm to rural life, the passage of time marked by the calendar of changing weather, the phases of the moon and varying length of the days. Each season has its own special music, as easily recognised as a favourite tune and as anticipated as the gentle chime of a much-loved grandfather clock. But of all the seasons, it is spring which has the most activity.

Many times spring comes to Glenmadrie gradually. Wobbling on uncertain legs, it steps cautiously around the slushy remnants of winter, always ready to run and hide should the cold weather suddenly return. But this year, spring strode confidently into the room with all the ebullience of an eccentric aunt arriving for tea. Marching around the house, she discards her umbrella, removes her tweed coat, ruffles her hair, throws open the doors, bursts into the garden and invites us all to come for a walk. After weeks of dreary cold drizzle and iron grey overcast sky, the weather finally broke. Late in the evening, the setting sun parted the clouds, turning the last vestiges of the day into a pallet of colour. As the gold bled to orange, blue, and then black, I saw the first stars in a month. Above I could see the distinctive triple dots on Orion's belt and to the south, just peeking above the horizon, Sirius, the dog star. It is by far the brightest star in the night sky, but sitting so low on the horizon causes its light to pass through the warming layers of the atmosphere. Most stars appear to twinkle, but during spring in Ireland, Sirius pulses in a steady rotation of blue, white and red which is often mistaken for the mechanical flashing of aircraft safety lights.

Eight hours later, daybreak was announced by the songs of a thousand joyfully exuberant birds, all searching for a mate. In the garden, daffodils were gratefully turning their yellow trumpets towards the warming sun. And up in the forest, where my hand-cut paths were gradually lengthening, the ferns were beginning to unfurl. Below their arching fronds was a carpet of tiny white flowers, poking above the triple green leaves of shamrocks, Ireland's most recognisable plant.

In quick succession, we mark the first appearance of frogs, bats, swallows, the disorderly calling of cuckoos and the ghostly twilight boomings of a dozen snipes displaying for their mates. These tiny birds swoop and dive across the moorlands, using their tail feathers to create the distinctive sound, which was once a puzzle to me, but now brings warmth to my heart.

A less joyful sound of spring occurs when the calves are first separated from their mothers. This usually occurs in May and is a necessary action if the cows are to continue providing milk for sale. Although the plaintive moans of the lonely calves echoing through the morning mist and the anxious answering bellows of their mothers, may sound like something from a dinosaur park, there is a despairing sadness in their voices, which tugs at the heartstrings. This lonely serenade goes on around the clock and can last for a week, by which time it tugs on the nerves too.

***

Our friends, Sally and Bruce, had decided to move to Dubai. They arrived in Ireland joyfully surfing the Celtic Tiger waves, but were now finding the still waters of the recession less inviting. They were unhappy to be leaving Ireland, but pleased to be heading somewhere with warm sand and plentiful money for those with the right job skills. Sally and Bruce were an exuberantly effervescent couple, the sort who lit up any room and were the heart and soul of every party. In many ways they were our antithesis. Perhaps that is why we got along so well. We were sad to see them leave.

The weekend before their flight, we invited Sally and Bruce up to Glenmadrie for a final meal. With guests coming, I set about cleaning the house – a task we'd scrimped on for a week in favour of catching up in the garden. Whilst Lesley carried on weeding and pruning, I cleaned the windows, scrubbed the bathrooms, polished the furniture, vacuumed the house, mopped the floors and laid the table. By the time Sally and Bruce arrived, our home was gleaming like a new penny and smelling sweeter than roses. Everyone was delighted to greet our guests, except Lady, who had been a little off colour all day. After a couple of minutes, she stirred and grudgingly left her bed to enquire what all the fuss was about. As the other dogs parted the way, Her Royal Highness trotted over to where our visitors were standing and explosively puked her dinner across our new living room floor mat. Fortunately, Sally and Bruce were dog owners too and they got the joke. Trust Lady to be the centre of attention.

***

May rolled into June and the sun shone on Ireland, albeit periodically and without much enthusiasm. Nonetheless, it was a good excuse to be outside. With my golf lesson bookings still sporadic and no new writing projects underway, I could devote a little time to some home maintenance and DIY. Although my snagging list was quite long, the first two jobs came with the compliments of Sally and Bruce.

They were planning to rent their Irish home and had gifted us two unwanted items from the garden, for which we were most grateful. They were a small greenhouse and a large lawnmower. It took half a day to remove and transport the greenhouse glass up the hill to Glenmadrie and the entire afternoon to dismantle the aluminium frame. Some of the parts fitted in our car, but the remainder had to be wrapped in old blankets and strapped to the roof. Although it was tiny when compared to our own greenhouse and polytunnel, Lesley felt this greenhouse would work well for potting-on her plants. I had no idea what potting-on was and didn't really want to ask, just in case it involved growing something illegal. However, like any dutiful husband, I was happy to reconstruct the greenhouse on the spot she chose.

Although I'd taken dozens of photographs and videos during the dismantling phase, when it came to the reconstruction, I soon realised I couldn't make head nor tail of the jumbled pile of aluminium parts. Fortunately, the internet came to my rescue. In under 30 minutes, I was able to locate and download the assembly instructions for that exact model. With a parts list and instructions in hand, it was then a relatively simple process to build and level the base, construct the frame and fit the windows. A day later, Lesley's new greenhouse was sitting proudly in a sunny spot, which was far enough from prying eyes that whatever nefarious potting activities she undertook would remain private.

The mower was so heavy it had required two people to lift it into the back of our estate car. It was an unwieldy beast, with a powerful petrol engine, a 20 inch blade and a weighty steel roller. My first thought was to sell it and donate the money to a local charity for battered women, but once I'd done a service and given it a run, I had a different idea.

"I'll give some money to the charity, but keep the mower," I told Lesley.

"Why?" she asked.

"Our old mower is all but clapped out. It's literally falling apart. This way, we get a better mower and the charity gets some quick cash." I didn't mention our old mower's decrepit state was caused by me sawing a chunk out of the backplate to permit Ireland's devilishly thick grass better egress from beneath the machine.

"It's up to you," she replied.

"And…" I continued, "with this more powerful machine, I

can make much better progress clearing that top meadow."

Lesley smiled and waved dismissively. "Work away."

Whereas my dear wife was largely ambivalent when it came to lawns, as a golfer, I adored large open green spaces and the sweet smell of fresh cut grass. Furthermore, it irritated me that fully two thirds of our land was so overgrown as to be almost inaccessible. With the benefit of regular cutting, our front lawn no longer looked like a cow pasture, but much of our land still did. Although I'd made some progress by clearing a small area from the chicken run up to the pond, this 50 by 20 metre stretch was tiny in comparison to what remained to be done. It had been hard going, partly because the thick knee-high meadow grass was so resistant to cutting, but mostly because of the rushes.

The soft rush is the scourge of grasslands in Ireland, particularly when the land has been overgrazed by cattle. Until recently, a local farmer had used our meadows to graze a few of his cows. In wet conditions, cattle will wreck the grass and destabilise the soil like industrial versions of our chickens. Furthermore, unlike native goats, the cattle will only eat the lush grass, leaving the rushes to thrive. These fibrous clumps are as tough as old leather and can grow to the size of a man. Without competition from other plants, soft rushes will quickly spread. Every clump of rushes has around 500 shoots, each capable of producing 8,500 seeds. With the surrounding grass chewed down to the roots by the cattle and the soil exposed, there is nothing to stop the rushes from spreading. Repeat the process for a few years and any meadow will be totally overrun with rushes. They are fireproof and impossible to dig up, so the only solution was to laboriously spray every clump with coloured weed killer and encourage the grass to regrow. For two years I'd fought the good fight and with the majority of the rushes gone, it was a perfect opportunity to cultivate the grass.

The following day I began cutting a large south-facing slope at the southern end of our land. It was laborious work. As the grass was so thick, I had to raise the blades by making the mower do a wheelie on its heavy drum. Even so, every five minutes or so, the engine ground to a stop and I had to clear the trapped grass by hand. Just as I was about to give up the whole job as a bad idea, our neighbour came to the rescue.

"Hello there!"

The distant shout caught my attention. I looked up from pulling yet another clump of grass from under the mower.

"Hello?"

"Hello there!"

The second shout got me looking in the right direction. Old Tom's son, Tiernan, was leaning over the fence down by the road. He gave me a friendly wave. I waved back and trudged through the grass until I was within reasonable shouting distance.

"Hi, Tiernan," I said, pointing unnecessarily over my shoulder. "I'm cutting the grass."

"Aye, that you are." He nodded stoically. "That used to be a fine meadow. It'll be grand to see it right again."

I puffed and wiped my brow with my sleeve. "It's hard going."

He squinted over my shoulder and frowned. "You'd do it quicker with a big mower."

"That's the biggest I've got," I said.

"Or a tractor…"

I grimaced. "We haven't got a tractor."

"I do." Tiernan smiled and pointed a grubby thumb at his huge yellow tractor.

"Could you cut it?" I asked, suddenly getting his drift. "I'd be ever so grateful and happy to pay."

He casually waved away my offer of payment.

"Ack, it won't take but a few minutes to cut with this."

I pulled out three fence posts and lowered the wire so Tiernan could get his tractor onto the land. Once the yellow monster had circumnavigated the pond, Tiernan twisted in his seat and beckoned for me to climb up. Fully ten feet above the ground, I stood on the footplate and held on for dear life as the young lad roared around following my shouted directions. The high powered mower attachment made short work of the grass and remaining rushes. In under half an hour, he'd cut all of the accessible areas of our land. I was delighted. With the worst chopped down, cutting the grass would be a considerably less Herculean task.

Once the tractor was back on the road, I shook Tiernan's hand and again offered to pay for his time. He smiled and once more shook his head.

"You're most welcome," Tiernan said. "It's what folk do for each other in these parts."

You've got to love Ireland.

12 – Rules and Rulers

Rules, rules, rules! Harry Day, the World War One fighter ace, was reputed to have said, "Rules are for the obedience of fools and the guidance of wise men," although I'm sure he wasn't thinking of that foul edict, the health and safety regulations.

"There's something wrong with the gas oven," Lesley shouted. She was in the kitchen dishing up our evening meal.

I leaned forward on the couch and squinted through the doorway. "What do you mean?"

"These pies aren't cooked." She waved her hand in exasperation. "They've been in there for an hour and they're hardly defrosted."

"That doesn't sound right," I sighed and stood up. "I'd better have a look at it."

During the process of renovating our kitchen, we'd bought a gas cooker. We already had an oil fired Rayburn cooking range, but it was old, smelly and cumbersome to use – much like me. Lesley felt gas would be a better option than electricity, but as we were many miles from the mains, we'd ordered a model which used bottled gas. With workmen so hard to find, I'd done the installation myself. Using the standard orange rubber pipes, I had connected the cooker to two large gas cylinders which were positioned discretely outside the kitchen window. Everything had worked splendidly for several years, until now.

I fiddled with the controls for a couple of minutes and experimented with some settings, before coming to the conclusion the thermostat for the oven wasn't working.

"It's lit, but the flame isn't coming on correctly," I observed. "So the oven won't get hot enough to cook."

"Can it be fixed?" she asked.

"Oh sure." I nodded. "It's just a case of swapping out the sensor. I'd do it myself, but there's no need. We took out the extended warranty. I'll phone them in the morning."

"Oh good. They can do a service at the same time."

Inevitably the cooker warranty had run out just a month earlier.

"I swear they send out a coded message as soon as the warranty expires!" I exclaimed.

Although I located the correct part online, it was fiendishly expensive. Fortunately, my luck was in. The manufacturer offered to service and repair the cooker for almost the same price, but we'd have to wait a week until the engineer was in our area. Although the gas hob was still working, Lesley had to bring the Rayburn oven out of hibernation for her baking. There was much cleaning required before it was ready to use, along with a good bit of unladylike swearing while she got used to its arcane temperature controls.

I happened to be in town on the day the engineer arrived – which was inevitable, given I was at home on both of the previous days when he didn't turn up. However, when I arrived home that evening, hungry for supper, not only was the cooker still broken, but it was also disconnected from the gas supply and proudly displaying a large red sticker emblazoned with the words, "Unsafe, do not use."

Apparently, running the rubber hose from the gas bottle to the cooker by just poking it through the wall does not comply with health and safety legislation. If the hose had split, or been chewed by an inquisitive mouse, the gas would have leaked into the wall and other spaces, turning the house into a huge bomb. To protect against this, the rubber pipe should run inside a copper tube, which is sealed to protect against leaks. It cost me a couple of hundred Euros to hire another gas engineer to correctly install the still faulty cooker, and certify it as safe, before the original repair man would even agree to replace the defective part. This time I was on hand when he arrived, as were our dogs. I trotted outside to apologise for the incessant barking, but I needn't have worried, Gerry seemed at ease with our pooches. Once they realised he wasn't an unauthorised intruder, and was unlikely to give them a biscuit, they all wandered off to resume their afternoon naps. As we approached the two gas bottles at the rear of our property, Gerry stopped and sniffed.

"Gas leak?" he asked, his face darkly suspicious.

"No!" I laughed and waved my hand under my nose. "It's muck spreading season. I'm guessing you don't get into the countryside very often."

"Aye. That's right." He nodded stoically. "I do most of my jobs around the city. I'm only here 'cos the regular guy took ill."

After a cup of tea and several of our best biscuits, Gerry got to work.

"This health and safety legislation has turned the world mad," I said, tutting dramatically.

"Indeed, indeed." Gerry smiled sympathetically.

The new part was fitted in minutes. I watched as he carefully removed the red warning sticker from the cooker.

"You do know, it's all just a moneymaking con?" I added, rhetorically.

He turned a kind ear to my complaint and nodded sagely.

In irritation, I waved my hand at the cooker. "I could have done that."

"I'm sure you could." His voice was a marvellous example of controlled politeness, but I detected a hint of sarcasm when he added, "After all, it's only gas – what could possibly go wrong?"

***

As I'd failed miserably in my quest to accidentally blow up our house, I set to work destroying other things.

Lesley's spring tidying in the garden had created several huge mounds of horticultural waste. Added to this were 30 or so hefty branches, which I'd lopped from damaged trees over the winter months. This dry detritus was perfectly suitable for burning, so my wife appointed me chief arsonist and gave me a work order.

"You can get this lot burned," she said, "but not here."

"Not here?" I snorted a laugh. "Where shall I burn it then, Florida?

Lesley sighed expressively and looked at me as if I were a truculent child – which isn't far from the truth.

"I meant don't burn it down here." She waved an arm towards one of her many flower beds. "It will make a mess and damage my plants. You can burn it up in the quarry."

"You're kidding!" I exclaimed. Our quarry was around an acre in size, almost circular, with 50 foot high rock walls and a wide base of gravel. It had been excavated more than a hundred years ago, to extract the valuable limestone. As it was no longer in use, we had deliberately left this secluded area untended as a sanctuary for wild flowers, insects and any animals seeking a secure home. If it hadn't been a couple of hundred yards away and up a steep hill, it would have been a perfect place for a bonfire.

"It's the only clear space we've got," Lesley explained. "The meadow you've cut is just as far and I can't imagine you'd want a big burned patch in the middle of your lovely grass."

She was right. Furthermore, as we'd had several weeks without any substantial rain, the grass in the untended areas of our fields was tinder dry. Starting a fire anywhere else on our land would be hazardous in the extreme. I grimaced a shrug and nodded my acceptance.

"But how on earth am I going to shift this lot up to the quarry?"

"I guess you can either carry it up there, or load the estate car and drive round – assuming you can find the key to the quarry gate." My wife smiled. "Anyway, it's your problem now. I've got gardening to get on with."

"Thanks…" I inwardly groaned.

As it seemed the least labour intensive method of shifting the garden waste, I began by using the estate car. With the rear seats removed and the tailgate up, there would be enough room to take a third of the stuff Lesley wanted me to burn. Once loaded, it would be a simple matter of coming out onto the main road and driving the short distance up the hill to our quarry. At least that was the theory. In practice, it was a different matter. Despite my most enthusiastic stuffing and stamping, most of the branches and twigs refused to fit in the car with anything approaching the efficient use of space. At best, the first load probably weighed just ten pounds and amounted to a fraction of what I needed to shift.

Up at the quarry, the rusted lock yielded, after several squirts of oil and a bit of profanity, but once the gate was open, it was obvious I wasn't driving any further. After being unattended for a couple of years, the flat gravel base, which once resembled a huge parking lot, was now overgrown with tall grass and dotted with dozens of scrubby bushes. Dragging my first load into the quarry, I decided the best spot for a bonfire was at the base of the south facing cliff. By happy coincidence, this was directly below the spot where I would be dropping the remainder of the garden waste, once I'd humped it up the meadow by hand. With the car empty, I closed the gate and drove back to the house.

Just as I was bracing myself to make dozens of trips, dragging branches by hand across the meadow and up to the quarry edge, I had an epiphany. The problem with shifting this quantity of detritus wasn't the weight, it was the unwieldy bulk. If I could somehow squeeze the branches into a smaller space, they'd be much easier to move. With a 20 foot length of rope from my shed looped under the largest pile, I tied a slip knot and gradually began to pull the loop closed. After a bit of stamping and tugging, the ten foot wide stack of branches and twigs was squeezed down to a tidy bale just 18 inches across. With my fingers slipped under the rope, the bundle was no harder to carry than a cumbersome suitcase. The trip up the hill took just ten minutes. Once I'd reached the edge of the quarry, it was a simple matter to untie the rope and push the bundle over the edge. Three trips later and part A of the job was done. Now it was time to light the fire.

With a petrol can, an old newspaper and some matches in hand, I trudged up to the quarry again. Once I'd massaged the huge heap of branches and twigs into a manageable shape, I moved to the upwind side and kicked a hole large enough to take the scrunched up newspaper. Although the wood was pretty dry, as a final touch, I sloshed the top and sides of the pile with a couple of pints of petrol. There was only a slight breeze on my back, but the combination of old matches and slightly damp newspaper made the fire difficult to light. Twice, I got the paper burning, only to see it fizzle out at the first puff of wind. Thinking the petrol had probably evaporated by this time, I gave the branches a second christening and dripped a teaspoonful of fuel onto the damp paper. I only had two matches left. With hunched shoulders and my back to the breeze, I cupped the flame in my hand and cautiously offered it to the newspaper. The petrol ignited with a sound like an oak door in a cathedral slamming shut on the wind. A wall of yellow flame momentarily engulfed me as I was pushed backwards by a wave of hot gas. With my ears ringing, I lay on my back laughing and watched in fascination as a cloud of burning paper circled upwards like a murmuration of fiery starlings.

An hour later, with the remains of the fire burning safely in a small controlled heap, I walked back to the house for dinner. My timing was perfect, Lesley was preparing to dish up the pasta.

"The fire is burning nicely," I reported. "I'll pop back and check it again in an hour."

Lesley frowned and peered at me. "What the hell happened

133

to your eyebrows?"

"What do you mean?"

"They've gone!"

I laughed and shrugged. "I got a bit overenthusiastic with the petrol."

"Twit!" She shook her head.

I grinned like the village idiot.

"Phew. You stink of smoke!" My wife wrinkled her nose and waved her hand in front of her face. "Have a quick shower and change your clothes for goodness' sake."

"But I'm going out again shortly," I pleaded.

"Or you can sit outside…"

During my walk back to the house, I'd noticed several swarms of biting midges circling hungrily in the still evening warmth. They are the scourge of rural Ireland. I didn't much fancy feeding bugs whilst I ate.

"Alright," I groaned. "I'll go and have a shower."

"Leave those stinky clothes in the porch," she ordered, "and be quick about it."

After we'd eaten and had a cup of tea, I donned my smelly clothes once more and headed back to the quarry. I wanted to check the fire was out before Lesley and I settled in for the night. As I reached the top of the cliff, the sight before me was surprising. The entire quarry was soot-black and devoid of grass.

"I reckon the wind got up while I was eating dinner," I explained to Lesley a little later. "It probably swirled around the quarry, dragging the flames with it."

"We're very lucky the fire didn't make its way onto the meadow."

She was right. For a while the entire quarry must have been alight, but miraculously, the flames had stopped at the top of the cliffs. Had the fire breached that invisible barrier, there would have been nothing to stop it burning all the way to the house. Lucky us.

***

Encouraged by another burst of half decent weather, I cracked on with my DIY list.

Cautious but confident, I did the high work first. As I didn't fall, my theory Lesley would let me off the remainder of the list if I tumbled to my death, remained unproven. First, I removed and refitted several sections of sagging guttering, which had begun to drip and overflow whenever it rained. Once everything was secure and sloping at the required angle, I was able to clear any blockages. Living as we do, in an area surrounded with trees and with such clean air, our guttering regularly fills with a combination of moss washed from the roof and pine needles. This sticky tar-like black gunk is a perfect growing medium for any wind-blown seeds. If I didn't clear the guttering at least twice a year, we'd quickly have a forest of bonsai trees growing along our roofline.

Despite my best efforts, the traditional lead flashing I'd installed over our coverway hadn't done much to stop the rainwater getting between the clearlite edge and the wall. Even though the coverway is outside, it's designed to be a dry area, so the constant rivulets of rainwater running down the wall had been an irritation all winter. Fortunately, I managed to source a stick-on alternative flashing designed especially for us technically challenged home renovators. Once I'd cleaned the wall and added a coat of bitumen primer, it was a simple matter of not falling through the roof while I pressed the new flashing into place. It worked perfectly, as did another of my fixes.

Even before I'd rewired our living room, we'd noticed when our compact fluorescent lightbulbs were turned off, they had a peculiar habit of flashing. This anomaly was only visible in a dark room, and as all the other appliances in the house worked perfectly, I assumed it was a peculiarity of Irish eco bulbs, or perhaps fairies. I hadn't realised the true cause of the flashing lights was cowboy builders, the name we'd assigned to those responsible for any bodged jobs left to us by the previous owners of Glenmadrie.

"When I rewired the house, I connected the new consumer unit to the existing mains cables where they came through the wall," I explained to Lesley.

"A bit like you did when you copied the old central heating layout?" she suggested.

"That's right," I said brightly.

"But the old central heating layout was wrong," she reminded me.

"That's right." I frowned at the memory. I'd forgotten the

135

problems we'd had with cold radiators before I changed the plumbing.

"Was the old wiring wrong too?" Lesley asked.

"That's right," I said, once again.

"Can you fix it?"

I grinned proudly. "I already did."

The electrical cables in domestic wiring are colour coded, black for neutral and red for live. This system is largely idiot proof, even for idiots like me. Even though our new electrics worked perfectly, apart from the odd flashing lights, I bought a clever little computerised circuit tester. It immediately identified the problem. The colour coded wires entering the house were back-to-front. The fix was a simple matter of swapping two wires and running the circuit test again. It all checked out and the mystery of the flashing lights was finally solved. However, not for the first time, I wondered what other surprises the cowboy builders had left for me to find.

***

My final tasks during this burst of DIY activity, were to repaint the outside of the house and tidy our driveway.

With rain showers occasionally stopping play and so many tricky areas to reach, it took around a week to give the exterior walls two coats of quality paint. With such harsh weather conditions through the winter, it wasn't worth skimping on a cheaper brand. Even so, I knew I'd probably need to paint again the following year.

Our driveway is more than 80 yards long. Forming a gentle crescent, with two turning areas, it runs from the road to the house and terminates at a large square area where we hang our washing. The driveway had been untouched since we'd bought the house. It was only by looking back at those early photographs I realised by how much it had deteriorated. The constant rain of pine needles, combined with dead leaves and the ever present moss, had gradually turned the once pristine gravel into something resembling a farm track. Once I'd scraped away the worst of the muddy top coat, I tried to source some gravel. Our local hardware store only kept gravel in 20 kg bags, but they kindly gave me the number of a commercial quarry that would do large domestic deliveries. Before making the call, I carefully measured the driveway, turning areas and a few additional paths, to calculate the total surface area we needed to cover.

From the deafening background noises, I imagined the quarry man was standing close to where they were loading the lorries.

"What d'ya want?" came the harsh voice.

Trying not to shout, I explained I was hoping to buy some gravel and told him the surface area I needed to cover.

"What type d'ya want?" he shouted.

"I don't know," I replied. "What would you recommend?"

"Dat's up ta yea," he bellowed.

I groaned inwardly. "Well, what have you got?"

Like an overworked and underpaid waiter reading from the daily specials, he rattled off a list of more than 20 products. Many had mysterious and exotic names like, 20 mil clean, clause 810 wet, clause 804 and, two down – which may have been some sort of gravel, or a reference to a crossword clue. I'm always puzzled and frustrated when I encounter such seemingly unnecessary overuse of technical terms, but this wasn't my area of expertise, so I bit my lip and politely confessed my ignorance. After a few questions, and a pause while a particularly loud lorry went past, the kindly gent yelled his advice.

"I'd say you'll need a full load of ¾ down."

"Thank you," I replied. "That'll do nicely."

Apparently, ¾ down referred to graded quarry stone, crushed to chips no larger than ¾ of an inch. It was reasonably priced and perfect for the job. A huge lorry arrived the following morning. After failing three times to reverse around the bend to the area I'd indicated, the driver unceremoniously dumped his load about halfway up our driveway, gave a friendly wave and drove off. With both of our cars now trapped behind a grey mountain of stone chippings, my plan to gradually redistribute the gravel along the driveway over the next few weeks was now in tatters. Lesley and I both grabbed a shovel, a rake and wheelbarrow and got stuck in. It took three days of backbreaking work, but the end result looked considerably smarter.

As a finishing touch, I bought a lockable post box and attached it to a stake at the entrance to the driveway. It looked nice and would save our postman from the time consuming task of leaving his van to open the gate and trudge up the driveway to the house. He was so thrilled with this modern convenience, he left us a thank you card, which we thought was a nice touch and a typically Irish gesture.

***

With all my DIY tasks up to date, the rain lashing down and Lesley away in England for a few days, I could get down to the important business of watching a little golf on television. As a player, I find televised golf to be dreadfully tedious and time consuming, so I usually watch a recording and skip to the best bits – which in this case was the prize presentation at the end of the tournament.

After much political to-ing and fro-ing, Mr Enda Kenny had been elected as Taoiseach of Ireland. He was delighted to win this top political job, particularly after serving a nine-year stretch as leader of the opposition. Once he had been sworn in, taken the seal of office, formed his cabinet, and received his briefing on the truth about space aliens, how much debt the country was in, and which space aliens we owe the money to, Mr. Kenny got down to work.

As a keen golfer Enda was thrilled with the invite to present the winner's trophy at the Irish Open. After four days of hanging around, sloshing through muddy puddles, and being interviewed to fill the gaps created by rain delays, the time finally arrived for the Taoiseach to present the prize to the winning golfer. However, with the comedic excellence that only dyslexic secretaries and computers with spellcheck can deliver, the autocue was changed. And so, to a television audience numbered in the millions, the Sky sports presenter introduced the new leader of Ireland as Edna. I almost fell off the couch.

There was a pregnant pause. Through my tears of laughter, I could see Mr. Kenny desperately wanting to say, "It's Enda, not Edna... My name is ENDA!", but he didn't. With all the elegance and self-control that befits his lofty position, and wearing a stiff smile like someone suffering with terminal haemorrhoids, he congratulated the winner on his achievement and presented the cup. Bless him.

A few days later, there was another pregnant pause. Mark sent me a text message, "Joanne has gone into labour. We're off to the hospital."

13 – And then they were Four

It was early morning. I was buttering some toast when the text arrived.

"Which hospital has she gone to?" Lesley demanded.

I shrugged and nodded towards the phone with my chin. "He doesn't say."

My wife groaned and rolled her eyes in frustration. "Well ask him!"

I did. There was no reply. Lesley sat still and waited calmly – for about 30 seconds.

"Perhaps I should get a flight," she said, jumping up. My wife grabbed her purse, walked a tight circle and sat down again.

I reached over and gently patted her hand. "I know it's frustrating, but there's nothing we can do but wait."

"But…"

"Even if you were in England, you probably wouldn't be allowed in with her," I suggested. "Anyway, Mark's there. He's quite capable."

"But…"

I kissed the top of my wife's head and gave her a calming hug.

"I share your frustration, but there's nothing we can do but wait."

Three hours later, I got another text. "Everything is going normally."

"There!" I showed Lesley the text. "Nothing to worry about."

"I'm still concerned," she said. "What with her being late…"

I laughed. "Joanne is late for everything, so it's no big surprise she's a couple of weeks overdue giving birth."

"Last time we spoke, she said the doctors were considering a caesarean section."

"I know," I nodded. "So it's a good thing she's gone into labour."

Head down, Lesley mumbled into her chest, "I guess…"

Two hours later we received another message. As concise or abrupt as the first – depending on your level of anxiety – it simply said, "Nothing is happening yet."

Conscious all this sitting about and worrying wasn't helping anyone, I suggested Lesley came outside and helped me complete a DIY task.

"It won't take long," I explained. "I just need you to hold the ladder while I go up the chimney and finish repairing the concrete around the pot."

She sighed. "Can't you do it without me? I might miss her call."

"Not really. The chimney is really high and I'll have to stand at the top of the ladder. I'd be much more comfortable knowing you're there." I added a little smile to encourage her acceptance. "I'll keep my phone handy, in case Mark calls."

"Okay," she said, without any real enthusiasm.

I was worried about Joanne too and I understood Lesley's reluctance. Frankly, I wasn't particularly keen to go up the ladder either. Our chimney was high enough to get my full attention – particularly as I'd dropped my ladder last year and it now resembled an aluminium banana.

It didn't take long to change into my overalls, mix a little mortar and get the ladder correctly positioned. With my assistant in place, I left my phone on a nearby windowsill and began to climb. As I was holding a bucket containing some tools and the mortar in one hand, I had to let go of the ladder as I moved up the rungs. Nearer to the top, I gripped the side rail and slid my hand upwards between each step. My grasp was fairly secure, but given the height and the ladder's inclination to flex and slip, I was pleased Lesley was holding the base tightly in place. Reaching the top, I began to fill the cracks in the concrete chimney cap.

"I can see my house from here!" I joked.

"Very funny," Lesley shouted back. She didn't sound amused.

"Actually, it's odd being able to see over the house," I replied.

I worked quietly for a while, focusing my eyes on the task ahead, trying not to look down, but doing my best to remember I was perched precariously at the top of a ladder.

"I'm nearly finished up here," I reported, breaking the silence.

"Okay." Lesley's voice sounded distant. I guess she was thinking about Joanne too.

"I'm sure everything is going well," I shouted.

"I wonder what she'll have." It took an effort to avoid looking down whenever she spoke.

"Hopefully, a baby," I quipped.

"You know what I mean," Lesley called.

"I think Mark's secretly hoping for a girl," I shouted, "but I'm sure they'll be happy either way."

Lesley didn't reply.

The last crack I needed to fill was hidden from view on the opposite side of the chimney pot, an arm's length away. As I needed to let go of the ladder to reach so far, it was going to be a tricky balancing act. I took a deep breath, put one hand on top of the chimney capping and stretched out. Working entirely by feel, I began massaging mortar into the crack with my fingers. Just as I'd finished the repair, the ladder gave a shudder and slipped a couple of inches lower. With a yelp of fear, I grabbed the chimney and hugged it like a long lost friend.

"The ladder's slipping," I called. "Keep a tight hold."

Silence.

"The ladder's slipping!" I shouted.

"What?"

Lesley's voice seemed unusually distant. Keeping a tight grip on the chimney, I risked a downwards glance. My wife was nowhere to be seen. I called her name and, with the assistance of some audio triangulation, I tracked her response to some bushes around forty yards away. I still couldn't see Lesley, but there was some suspicious horticultural movement in a flower bed behind the shrubs. Surely, my chief ladder holder hadn't abdicated responsibility for keeping her devoted husband alive, in favour of a little light weeding?

"What are you doing?" I demanded.

"Just clearing up a bit," she replied casually. "I would still hear your phone from here."

In a tight voice, and with the aid of a few motivational profanities, I directed my dear wife to swiftly resume her position at the base of the ladder. Once I'd reached the safety of terra firma, I was surprised the expected apology was not forthcoming.

"There's no need to swear!" she snapped.

Suddenly on the defensive, I carefully reviewed the events of the last few minutes. Unable to find myself at fault, I bravely pressed ahead.

"I almost fell," I growled through gritted teeth. "You were supposed to be holding the ladder."

My wife's blue eyes widened at this apparently new piece of information.

"You mean, while you were up it?" she asked in all innocence.

"Ye–" I took a deep calming breath and made an effort to stop my hands clenching. "Of course. What did you think I wanted?"

"Oh." My wife smiled innocently. "You said to hold the ladder while you went up. If you wanted me to hold it while you were up there, you should have said."

"Of all the stupi–" My answer was cut short as my phone pinged to announce the arrival of an incoming message. Unfortunately, it did not announce the arrival of a grandchild.

Mark's message was consistent in its brevity. "They've taken her down."

"Down where?" Lesley demanded.

"I don't know!"

"Quick!" My wife jabbed her finger towards the phone. "Call him and find out what's happening."

Yet again, there was no answer. I tried calling Mark's parents, in the hope they would have some more information, but my call went to answerphone.

I sighed. "I guess we'll just have to wait."

"She's in the right place," Lesley sighed. Her comment seemed like an attempt to reassure herself as much as me.

Once I'd cleaned up and put the ladder away, we headed back indoors. With our minds swirling, we abandoned our attempts to read in favour of mindlessly staring at the television. The call finally came at 8pm.

"It's a boy!" Mark exclaimed. His voice was tired and thick with emotion.

Lesley and I hugged each other and shouted our joyful congratulations.

"He's healthy and hearty," the proud dad said. "Seven pounds and six ounces. Born by caesarean section."

Mark had to rush back to his wife, but in the morning, he sent us the first picture of David, our handsome grandson, with his beautiful mum. We couldn't have been happier.

It wasn't until a few days later, we discovered what had gone on behind the scenes.

In keeping with birthing tradition, after going into labour in the early hours of the morning, Joanne was rushed to the hospital by car. She remained serenely calm, despite being terrified by the erratic driving of her panicking husband. Once his wife was safely checked into the maternity ward, Mark tried to let everyone know what was going on. Unfortunately, the only place he could get a usable phone signal was in a distant corner of the hospital carpark – a roundtrip walk of almost 30 minutes. As Mark was unwilling to repeatedly leave his wife's side at such a time, his communications and updates became understandably sporadic. Had we been able to contact his parents, they wouldn't have known any more than we did. They had just cancelled their holiday and were driving the 100 miles from north Norfolk back to Essex.

For a while, the birth had progressed normally. Things went extremely well, then they didn't. When it became obvious young David was unwilling or unable to make his scheduled appearance, the midwife and doctor remained calm. Readings were taken and drugs were administered. Mark was told there was nothing to worry about. These things happen, they said. It'll be fine. Joanne was uncomfortable, but doing well. During a lull in the proceedings, Mark jogged outside and sent his message telling us nothing had happened.

The medical staff watched and waited. Several other patients had come in, given birth, and left the ward, but Joanne was still no further along. Despite pushing and panting and doing everything she was asked, the baby wouldn't come. She was tearful and felt as if she was at fault. Don't worry, they said, everything is fine – but there's an operating room on standby, just in case. An hour later, the doctor decided the risks of surgery were preferable to prolonging the labour. Unable to enter the operating room, Mark ventured outside and sent another update.

Either the medical staff were being overly optimistic to calm Joanne and Mark, or they were caught off-guard, but on the way to the operating room mother and baby began to deteriorate alarmingly. Suddenly, the calm walk became a gallop, with the trolley pushing people aside and noisily bursting through doors. Within minutes of arriving in the operating room, David was born via an emergency caesarean section. The baby was fine, but Joanne needed further surgery the following day to repair some substantial internal damage. As a family, we could not have been more thankful for the calm professionalism of those doctors, nurses and midwifes.

Not to be left out, Kia, our lovable black collie, decided it was her turn to have some surgery.

A couple of days after David was born, we decided to give the dogs a bath.

"Somebody stinks," I remarked, "and it isn't me."

The dogs eyed us suspiciously, but remained warily calm. However, when I got the shampoo and old towels from where we keep them in the utility room, our pooches all scampered for cover.

"It's like they've got some sixth sense," Lesley laughed.

Using a combination of bribery and threats, we began to corral each of the dogs. Being the smallest, Amber was easy to capture and wash. After the initial excitement passed, Lady and Jack had both fallen asleep. They were easy to catch, but unwilling to go quietly, so I had to carry each dog up the stairs to the bathroom. Once washed and dried, Lady bounded back downstairs and proceeded to scamper around the sitting room, rubbing her face and sides on every available surface.

"I hardly ever do that," I joked. "It must be a dog thing."

With his myopic vision and timid nature, Jack had to be carried up and down the stairs. It was no easy task to transport such a big dog. Fortunately, he had the presence of mind to desist from his squirming escape attempts once we were on the stairs. His fur was like a sponge, retaining water even after a brisk towelling. Accordingly, after the downstairs leg, I was soaked through.

Kia has always had a fear of men. We suspect she had been mistreated by a previous owner, which left her mentally scarred and cowering in fear whenever I tried to pick her up. To avoid any unnecessary anguish, and the inevitable puddle of pee, Lesley took over with the bathing duties. Consequently, it was she who discovered two huge lumps hiding beneath Kia's thick black fur.

"I think they're probably lipomas," our vet said, after an examination. "These subcutaneous masses are common in dogs. They are usually benign and can be left alone, but this one…" she pointed to the grapefruit sized mass on the back of Kia's hind leg, "has got to come off. It's too large and will probably do internal damage, if it hasn't already."

Kia's quick trip to the vet, turned into a week of hospitalisation with intravenous fluids and regular changes to the dressing on her leg. The lump was indeed benign and despite its remarkable size, there was no damage to Kia's leg, other than a two-centimetre gap where there wasn't enough skin to close the wound. With regular cleaning and antibiotics, her leg remained infection free, but it took several weeks for the hole to heal.

Once again, we were grateful for the skill of our local vets.

***

Six weeks after the birth, Lesley flew to the UK to visit her grandson.

"Make sure you spoil him rotten, Grandma," I advised. "I think it's the law, or something."

My joke was met with a valiant attempt at a stern face and a steely look.

"Don't call me Grandma…" she growled.

I laughed. "Get used to your new title. David will be using it sooner than you think."

My wife was quick to counter. "I'm sure you're right – Grandpa."

"Oh…" My face fell. "I'm a grandad. I hadn't thought of that." It was true. I really hadn't.

Lesley had an enjoyable few days in England. She stayed with her mother who, whilst being no better, seemed no worse than before. Perhaps the dementia drugs were working. Muriel was delighted to meet her great grandson for the first time. Although she didn't feel strong enough to hold him, Muriel tickled his chin and whispered sweet baby nonsense in his ear. David smiled a lot and appeared pleased his great grandmother didn't have a chance to drop him on his head – so everyone was happy. As seems to be the fashion for new mothers these days, Joanne had recently had a professional photoshoot done. Although David was a handsome and very photogenic child, the photographer had clearly excelled herself, producing some wonderful pictures of mum and son together. A framed version of the best picture now had pride of place on Muriel's mantlepiece.

Joanne had sent me a link to the photographer's website, so I could view the entire photoshoot. The pictures were poles apart in quality from the grainy snaps we have of my very young wife holding Joanne when she was a baby. Although Lesley had lavished David with cuddles and gifts during her trip, I wanted to get the happy parents a more personal memento in time for my forthcoming visit. The photographs gave me an idea.

A couple of days after Lesley returned, we went to the town of Gort to do some food shopping. Before heading home, we stopped for lunch at a cosy little café, just off the high street. After filling up on good wholesome food, we ordered a second round of beverages and leaned forwards in our seats to have a chat.

"I've ordered a gift for Joanne and Mark," I said. "Hopefully, it will be ready before I fly over."

"What is it?" Lesley asked, her eyes watching me inquisitively over the rim of her coffee cup.

"I was looking on the internet for someone to do the cover artwork for a book I'm planning, when I came across this." I showed her a web page I'd stored on my phone. "This lady is in Indonesia. She does these brilliant caricatures from photographs. She's really talented and not overly expensive, so I've ordered a group shot with Joanne and Mark holding David."

Lesley didn't have her reading glasses, so she squinted at the picture like someone trying to perform telekinesis on a super tanker. After a moment, she gave a nod of approval.

"These caricatures look very good. It's a lovely idea. Mark and Joanne will be delighted. Did you send this lady some pictures?"

"Yes," I replied. "I picked a lovely photograph of Joanne and David from her photoshoot, but for some reason we didn't have any good pictures of Mark. The wedding pictures were too formal. I wanted a casual pose, but the photos we had weren't any good."

Lesley looked to the heavens and gave an amused snort. "I'm not surprised. Mark's such a joker. He's always pulling faces

146

whenever there's a camera around."

"I guess that would explain it. Not to worry though. I found a few nice pictures of him on Joanne's Facebook page, from just before they got married. They weren't quite face-on shots, so I sent two, just to be on the safe side." Proud to have chosen a unique and interesting gift, I grinned. "Once this lady emails her finished work, I can print it on photo paper and put it in one of those nice frames you bought last year."

"I'm sure it'll be lovely. I can't wait to see the finished product."

I stretched back in my seat and laced my fingers behind my head.

Lesley leaned a little closer. "What's this book you're planning?"

"Ah!" I sat forward again, excited to share my idea. "I want to write a thriller. Something with an interesting and exciting plot, but with characters which are…" I hunted for the right word, "believable."

"Believable?" My wife frowned in confusion. "What do you mean?"

"Well, when I read thrillers, even the best sellers, it's always irritated me that the hero is usually some huge ex-military sniper who goes around killing dozens of people without any justification or apparent consequences. Someone as big and obviously capable, wouldn't get picked on in a bar, or walk away from a bunch of bodies. In real life he'd be pursued to the ends of the earth by an emotionally broken and flawed alcoholic policeman."

Lesley laughed at my last comment. "I don't read many thrillers, but I understand what you're getting at."

"I want my hero to be as normal a person as possible," I explained. "He's just an ordinary guy, thrust unwillingly into an extraordinary situation."

"Okay. So far it sounds reasonable."

I loved that my wife wasn't challenging or doubting my ability to write a thriller.

"So…" Lesley put her elbows on the table and rested her chin on her interlocked fingers. Her cool blue eyes held me in a steady gaze. "What's this book about?"

"I'm still fleshing it out, and I've weeks of research to do before I can begin writing, but I was thinking of some recent news stories. Do you remember the strangely convenient death of that inconvenient whistle-blower?"

Lesley nodded.

"Good. So, I thought, what if there was some non-government group, perhaps even a company, which does killings, bribery and the like, but for a fee? No job too small, no task too difficult."

"It's an intriguing idea." Lesley nodded. "And your hero works for this company?"

"Oh no!" I exclaimed. "He's chasing them. Thrillers are all about the chase." I wiggled my eyebrows. "Can he catch them, before they find him?"

"It sounds as if you've got a winner."

Her tone of voice wasn't entirely genuine, but I appreciated the support. Lesley pushed the saucer containing the bill towards me.

"Pay this and we can head home. No time to waste," she declared. "You need to get writing!"

I reached over and patted her hand, grateful for her unwavering support.

The following morning I found my caricature order had been delivered. I opened the email and printed the picture. Once I'd stopped laughing and dried my eyes, I took the picture to show Lesley – making sure I'd brought her glasses. My wife was in the polytunnel.

"Put these on." I handed over her spectacles.

"What is it?" she asked, trying to see what I was hiding behind my back.

"You remember I said that artist was from Indonesia?"

Lesley nodded.

"I think we've had a slight breakdown in communications." I grimaced and showed her the picture and the accompanying email thread. It was a superb and beautifully drawn caricature, but there were four people in the picture.

"Why…?" It took a moment for the coin to drop, then Lesley began laughing too. She pointed from left to right. "That's Mark, Joanne, David and Mark again."

"Remember I sent her a couple of pictures of Mark," I explained, "so she'd have a good profile to work with. In my email I said, here's a picture of my daughter, her son, and two of her husband. But in her reply, she said here is the drawing of your daughter and son, with her two husbands!"

Lesley wiped the tears of laughter from her eyes with her sleeve. "That's definitely a cultural misunderstanding!"

The lady was kind enough to fix the mistake, at no additional cost. I printed and framed the corrected caricature, but before wrapping the gift, I added a copy of the Two Husbands picture.

I knew it would give Joanne a good laugh too.

14 – The Final Straw

It was the middle of October and I was meeting my fellow golf professional, Andrew Rich, at his local club. Although it was mild and sunny when I left Glenmadrie, once I reached the valley, the temperature dropped considerably and the countryside was shrouded in dank fog.

As I climbed from my car, shivering in the sudden cold, I spotted my friend hobbling towards me across the carpark. Puffing a dragon's breath in the chill air, he walked with all the caution of a man who'd recently been kicked in the groin by a mule – an observation ironically close to the truth.

"I fell off me fecking horse!" he explained.

"What happened?"

"I was out with the hunt last week…" Andrew must have seen the involuntary tightening of my expression. He raised a calming hand. "I know you veggie types don't abide hunting, but we never catch a fox. It's all about the chase."

I shrugged a silent acceptance.

"Anyway," he continued, "it's country living, so get used to it."

"It's okay, I'll probably murder a carrot or two later today." I waved a hand, casually dismissing his concerns. "So, what happened?"

"We were on the road, down yonder." Andrew pointed a finger vaguely over my shoulder. "Me horse is a big hunter, 17 hands and as twitchy as a long-tailed cat in a room full of rocking chairs."

I laughed at the image. Andy's accent and terminology became noticeably more Irish when he was agitated.

"Anyways," he continued, "some eejit on a motorbike came haring by and that was that. The big fella stood up like he was tryin' to start a Mexican wave – it was real sudden like – and before I knew what was happening, I was flat on me back seeing blue sky and stars, all at the same time."

"Wow!" I exclaimed. "You were lucky you didn't break anything."

"Aye, that I was." Andrew nodded at the memory. "It ruined me best riding hat though."

"Was the horse okay?"

"He was grand. Just spooked was all."

I was about to get my golf clubs out of my car, but Andrew shook his head. "There's a frost down below. The course is closed until it burns off." He pointed his chin towards the clubhouse. "We'll have a pot of tea while we wait."

He hobbled slowly up the hill. I walked alongside, feeling as if I was taking my mother-in-law shopping.

"Surely you can't play golf like this," I said. "You can barely walk."

"I'll be grand," he grunted, through gritted teeth. "I've reserved a golf buggy."

I groaned inwardly. My bad back did not respond well to such a mode of transport. "After bouncing around on a golf buggy for four hours, I'll probably be as crippled as you."

"Call it a handicap. I need all the help I can get."

"I guess that's true," I teased. "After all, I am four games ahead."

"Anyway, the buggy's for me." He gave an evil grin. "You can run alongside."

Our, so called, friendly golf games were intensely competitive affairs. Playing for nothing but pride and bragging rights, we ground out our scores as if our lives depended on the result. As I tended to have the upper hand, albeit by a narrow margin, Andrew often resorted to verbal baiting. This affable gamesmanship irritated me intensely; something Andrew knew well. But I was incapable of hiding my ire and this only served to encourage him further. In truth, a little psychological irritation was a small price to pay. Back when my dad was still alive, this week in October was always reserved for some autumnal father/son golf. In some way, my matches with Andrew paid homage to those happy days, so I was always grateful for his company.

"How did your trip to England go?" I asked. Andrew had recently attended a one-day training course at the prestigious Belfry golf club, near Birmingham.

"The course was grand…" he rolled his gaze to the sky, "but the day didn't start well."

"Do tell…" I narrowed my eyes and leaned forward.

"Well, to begin with, the flight was late, which put me on the back foot. Then I got lost looking for the hire car place. Turns out it was up in the arse end of beyond."

I tutted and nodded my sympathy.

"To make matters worse," he continued, "while I was wandering around hunting for the office, it started lashing rain. There was nowhere to shelter and in a couple of minutes I was soaked. As I was only there for the day, I didn't have a change of clothes either."

I chewed my lip in an effort to keep a straight face.

Andrew sipped his tea before pressing on with his tale.

"The car hire office was packed, so it took ages to get sorted. They gave me this poxy little Korean motor. I think it was called a hunchback or sommit!"

"You mean hatchback," I laughed.

"Well, whatever it's called, I felt like a hunchback trying to drive it." He shook his head. "And then the fun began. You see, I'd never driven in England before."

My dear friend owned a large Toyota 4x4. Comfortably slouched in his seat and with one hand casually resting on the steering wheel, he drove everywhere at a sedate 40 mph. Doing a quick calculation, I mentally plotted his route from Birmingham airport to the Belfry.

I blanched at the thought of an inexperienced driver trying to cope with the hectic English traffic for the first time.

"So, in an underpowered and unfamiliar car, you came out of the airport and drove straight onto the motorway?"

He nodded sadly. "It was lashing rain and there was huge puddles everywhere. I couldn't see 50 yards, yet everyone was driving like it were a race."

Even though I had many years of British motoring experience, the last time I'd driven around Birmingham had been a scary experience too. Picturing Andrew in his tiny hire car, wide-eyed and white-knuckled, trying to join one of the busiest motorways in England, whilst half of Birmingham bore down on him like angry race car drivers, it was all I could do to maintain a straight face.

"I can imagine it was pretty terrifying," I said.

"Anyways, I got there late and had to sit all day in me wet clothes. My arse was freezing!" Andrew grinned. "On the upside, I didn't die." Suddenly serious, his eyes narrowed. "Do the people in England drive like that all the time?"

153

"Pretty much," I admitted. "They certainly did when I lived there."

"You Brits are certifiable." Andrew shook his head. "Fecking certifiable!"

"Many of them are," I laughed. "And now you know why I live here!"

Our progress around the golf course was sedate. I walked and Andrew rode his buggy as if it were an invalid carriage. Despite his initial optimism, it quickly became obvious Andrew was unable to swing a club in any meaningful fashion, so we discarded our planned competition in favour of enjoying the day and having a good chat. Along the way, he asked me about my recent trip to England.

"It was a bit hectic," I explained. "In five days, I visited my mum, both of my sisters, had lunch with an old work mate, saw Lesley's mum and then spent three days getting to know my grandson."

"Phew!" Andrew rolled his eyes. "Congratulations on becoming a granddad, Granddad!"

"Thank you," I replied.

In my practical mind, I had expected to remain emotionally ambivalent about my grandson, at least until he became old enough to hold a meaningful conversation and learn golf, but I was wrong. From the moment I made that little bundle of nappies and baby drool laugh by bouncing him on my knee, I was smitten. Once I began telling Andrew about my grandson, it was difficult for me to stop.

For half an hour I waxed lyrical about young David, swooning about his beautiful eyes and cheeky grin. Like the good friend he was, Andrew smiled, nodded patiently and even stopped driving for a while, so he could look at the pictures I had stored on my phone.

"Is that your mother-in-law holding him?" he asked, pointing at one of the pictures. "The lady with dementia?"

I nodded.

"You said she's coming over to live with you" Andrew continued. "When's that happening?"

I snorted and patted my fingertips on my lips while I looked for an easy explanation.

"Much like her health, that decision is rather on-again-off-again," I explained. "It's been that way for a couple of years now. Although Muriel isn't entirely against the idea, she's not too keen either. By her own admission, she's hoping for a quick and painless death, just so she won't be a bother to anyone."

"I guess a lot of older people feel that way. They don't want to be a burden."

"That's certainly true." I sighed at the thought. "Anyway, she's definitely coming – eventually. But, as we can't kidnap her, I'm guessing it'll take some dramatic event or crisis to push her into taking that final step."

After nine holes, Andrew was in obvious discomfort, so we scrapped the game and headed back to the clubhouse for an early lunch. While we waited for our food to arrive, I found myself reflecting back on the disappointing lunchtime meeting I'd had with John Pieters, my old friend and work colleague in England.

"John and I worked together for eight years, back before I moved to Ireland," I explained. "We were in the same team and spent a lot of time together on various projects. At first, we didn't hit it off. The company maintained a very competitive environment, so I guess, for a while, we circled each other like feral cats. But, after a few months and a bit of team success, we got on better. Soon we became really good friends and stayed that way until I moved here."

"Did you stay in touch?"

I nodded. "I made a few phone calls, but we conversed more regularly by email. He left the company a month before me, began a new job and moved house, so email was the easiest way to stay connected. As I was passing close to where he lives now, we agreed to meet for lunch. I thought we'd instantly be back laughing together and remembering old times, but it wasn't like that at all."

"How so?"

"Back then, John and I were so similar, it was like we were brothers. Now we're very different people. I was expecting a relaxing lunch, but he was all business. Even before our drinks had arrived, John opened his briefcase and pulled out a thick file. Would you believe he'd brought along some documents and notes from a project he was working on? He wanted to pick my brain. It was the same old work stuff we'd done years before. Of course, I was happy to help, even though my heart wasn't in it.

Afterwards, I tried to chat about Ireland, but he really wasn't interested. In the end, it was quite an uncomfortable meeting. I think we were both glad when it was over and we could go our separate ways.

"Later that day I got to thinking about how much John had changed. He was no longer the carefree and happy guy I remembered. When I tried to describe County Clare to him, or talk about Irish culture and the pace of life here, he became quite disparaging. Even though he's never been to Ireland, John was rather dismissive and insulting, almost to the point of racism. I got rather sad, until I realised John hadn't changed at all. He was exactly like I remembered. It's me that's changed.

"When I lived and worked in England, I was all business; focused on being the top dog, getting wealthy and having nice stuff. Since moving here, I've become more relaxed, more sociable and less interested in status and sparkly tangibles."

Like an old man, nursing a beer in a pub whilst sucking thoughtfully on his pipe, Andrew nodded slowly.

"Aye," he said, "Ireland will do that to yea."

***

A little good news arrived in mid-December. Some observers had described the 2009 financial crash as the worst crisis in Ireland since the potato famine. Left with no other option, the government entered a bailout programme under the Troika, the name frequently given to the combined forces of the European Commission, the European Central Bank and the International Monetary Fund.

During four years of crushing austerity there was a public sector wage and hiring freeze, leaving the health system and many public services in disarray. At the same time, investment stalled, the economy ground to a halt, social security payments were slashed, taxes soared, countless jobs were lost and a generation of doctors, nurses, builders, plumbers, electricians and other essential workers moved abroad in search of new lives with bright horizons.

Now, the country was ready to stand on its own feet again. A few weeks before Christmas, our finance minister shook hands with the Troika officials for the last time and Ireland became the first European country to exit the bailout programme. There would be a long way to go before the country returned to anything resembling the glory days of the Celtic Tiger, but at least we were free once again.

With regard to another problem, Lesley and I were experiencing déjà vu…

Muriel had been taken ill again. An hour after the home help had finished her morning visit, a neighbour found Muriel wandering along the street in a confused state and called an ambulance. The paramedics decided to leave her at home, but called Joanne at work and told her she needed to take her grandmother to the doctor. Despite risking the wrath of her less than understanding employer, our daughter cancelled her meetings and drove the 50 miles from London to Braintree in record time. The doctor diagnosed another bladder infection and prescribed some stronger antibiotics. After several cups of tea and a light meal, Muriel was feeling much better. Nevertheless, Lesley took the next available flight to England. She stayed for a week.

"That home help is flipping useless," Lesley said. I'd just picked her up from the airport and she was updating me on what had happened. Her voice sounded tight and tired.

"I thought you were going to cancel the home helpers while you were there," I said.

"I changed my mind, and it's a good job too," she growled. "It gave me a chance to see them in action."

I nodded. "Good thinking. How did it go?"

"Badly." She spat the word as if it were a sour grape. "They didn't know who I was and I kept well out of the way. Not that it mattered, I didn't see the same girl twice the whole time I was there."

"That can't be good for Muriel. She'd be very uncomfortable with such change."

"Oh she was!" Lesley's lips were tight with repressed anger. "Not that those girls were there for long. By the time they'd come in, said hello and made mum a cup of tea, it was time for them to move on to the next client."

"I thought they were supposed to help her wash and dress," I said. "That's what they're being paid to do."

"Well, that's definitely not happening," she snapped. "When I got there, mum was wearing six layers of clothes. Four vests

157

and two jumpers. I doubt she'd had a shower for a week."

"That's completely unacceptable," I groaned. "Did you talk to the company?"

Lesley ignored my question.

"And there's another thing…" Her voice was becoming louder and more emotionally charged. "She's got new double glazing."

"Yes, I know," I replied, slightly confused by this sudden change of track.

"YOU KNEW?" she shouted.

"Of course I knew." I raised a calming hand. "Don't you remember? It was fitted at the beginning of last year. I had to call the company during my last visit because the lock on the kitchen door was sticking. They sent a guy to fix it." I looked at my wife and continued, cautiously. "I told you about it."

Lesley sighed expressively and rubbed her face with her palms.

"I'm sorry, I didn't make myself clear. Mum's house has new double glazing and doors. It was installed last month."

"WHAT?" I exclaimed. "But the other stuff was only a couple of years old. It had a ten-year guarantee. She didn't need new double glazing, or doors."

"I know that. Unfortunately, some scabby salesman was going door-to-door down the street. He must have seen her as an easy mark. You know how she's always cold, even at the height of summer?"

I nodded, silently focusing on the road ahead.

"Obviously, her feeling cold is because of her age and poor circulation," she continued, "but he convinced her the double glazing was shot and needed replacing."

"How much did it cost?"

When Lesley told me, I growled and called the unknown salesman an unpleasant name.

"So, Muriel's been conned into wasting a large chunk of her hard-earned savings?" I said.

"Oh, it gets worse," she warned. "He got her to take out a high interest loan. I'm guessing it earned him some extra commission."

In anger, I thumped my fist on the steering wheel. "I'll call her bank tomorrow. This is obviously a rip-off. Perhaps they can cancel the loan."

"I already tried." It was Lesley's turn to shake her head. "I met with the manager. He said, because she's under 80 and still has most of her mental faculties, there's nothing they can do. Apparently, scamming thousands of pounds from a vulnerable old lady for unnecessary double glazing might be morally unacceptable, but it isn't a crime."

I sighed and rubbed the back of my neck. "Your mum must have been upset when she realised she'd been duped."

"She was," my wife admitted. "It was very upsetting for her."

I reached over and patted her knee. "I'm so sorry."

She squeezed my hand.

"On the upside, this was the final straw. Mum has accepted she can no longer cope. She's agreed to move to Ireland."

"Really?" I was both surprised and relieved.

Lesley nodded.

"It's time."

15 – A Familiar Spirit

Muriel agreed to move to Ireland as soon as it was practical. As she owned her house and wanted to rent the property, there was a good deal of work to be done first. Lesley was planning to return to England soon after Christmas to manage the arrangements. Joanne had kindly offered to help where she could. As the house would be rented unfurnished, as is often the case in England, Muriel's furniture would need to be sold or gifted to charity. Apart from clothes and a few keepsakes, her remaining personal possessions would be given to friends. Knowing she would be leaving the house which had been her home for 45 years, never to return, it was likely to be a distressing experience for Muriel, Lesley and Joanne. Once her mum was safely settled here in Ireland, Lesley would return to England once more to decorate the house, order new carpets and make final arrangements with the letting agent.

At the same time there would be plenty for me to do here. Although the wing at Glenmadrie had been designed as a separate granny annex, it was far from ready to be used as Muriel's bedroom. At around 250 square feet, it was large enough to feel like an apartment, whilst remaining cosy and welcoming. All on one level, the granny annex was split into three rooms. The bedroom and sitting room were actually one large space, partially divided by a thick stone wall – a feature we had retained from when the original building was a cowshed. There were windows on both sides, with the largest providing a view of the courtyard and bird table. The granny annex also had a separate bathroom with a toilet and shower.

Before Muriel arrived, I needed to decorate, install some grab handles for the toilet and shower, and double the heating capacity of the radiators. We also needed to source some furniture which would be more appropriate for someone of Muriel's age and limited mobility. Later she would need handrails, grab handles, ramps, a wheelchair and a special bed. There was certainly a lot to do. However, our first port of call was to meet with the local social services manager.

I had previously done considerable research to ascertain Muriel's rights to enter the country and reside here whilst accessing the health system, but I wanted to be sure I had my facts straight. Although we were committing our time and resources to ensuring her comfort and wellbeing, it was inevitable she would eventually need outside medical support.

We were expecting to hear about austerity cuts and dwindling resources, but that was not the case.

"I'm really surprised," Lesley said as she looked at the comprehensive list of support Muriel would have available. "This is so much better than she was getting in England."

The social services manager was a gently spoken lady, with jet black hair, dark eyes and a soft County Clare accent. She smiled sweetly and reached out to squeeze Lesley's hand.

"Don't you worry about your mum. Here in Ireland, we value the contribution family members make to supporting their loved ones in later life. You'll do fine. We're here to help."

With our pockets stuffed full of leaflets and contact numbers, we set off for home. We were both feeling considerably less apprehensive about what was to come, but there was one concern still nagging at my mind. As I was driving, I waited until we were out of the town traffic and safely into the countryside, before I began my tale.

"Did I ever tell you about the day I saw a ghost?" I asked.

"Ghost?" she exclaimed. "There's no such thing as ghosts."

"I know that. Of course I do." I nodded and raised a palm. "But bear with me. This is a true story."

Unconvinced, and always cautious of my odd sense of humour, my wife shrugged dismissively and looked out of the window.

"Go on then," she sighed.

"Back when I worked in financial services, I visited a family in Suffolk. I think the father had taken out a pension policy and I was doing a routine compliance visit to check the agent had followed all the correct proceedur–" I stopped and dismissed that train of thought with a flick of my fingers. "Sorry, that bit isn't important.

"Anyway. They were a lovely family. It was my last call of the night. I'd finished the interview and we were having a cup of tea and a chat. I think Tony Blair had just been re-elected and they were quite excited about it.

"We were sitting in their living room. It was one of those Victorian houses, where the wall dividing the sitting and dining rooms had been knocked out to make one long space. I was sitting at the right end of the room, near to the kitchen door, and to my left…" I pointed to each person in turn, "was the husband, wife, daughter and youngest son. Beyond them was the door leading to the hall."

"And where was the ghost sitting?" Lesley quipped.

"Alright, alright!" I gently waved her comment away with my free hand. "I was just coming to that."

"I can hardly wait," she whispered, without any apparent enthusiasm.

Aware Lesley was close to losing interest, or throwing herself from the moving car to escape my seemingly pointless story, I pressed on with some alacrity.

"Right. So…Eric, the husband, was just telling me about his quest to acquire planning permission to turn his small front garden into a parking area, when a woman, wearing one of those old fashioned ankle length white nightshirts came into the room from the kitchen. She was a very elderly lady, almost ancient, with long white hair and skin so pale and translucent, I could clearly see the blue veins in her arms. With her bare feet making no sound on the thick carpet, she silently walked the length of the room. I had chills and it took me a moment to realise why. I was the only person who had seen her."

"Nooo!" Lesley gave me a disparaging sideways glance. "Surely you were imagining it."

I shook my head.

"I swear it's true. Not only did Eric continue with his story without missing a beat as that ghostly apparition passed by, but nobody in that room so much as twitched an eye." I held up a finger to emphasise my point. "And that is nigh-on impossible to do deliberately. There's always an involuntary glance towards something moving through your field of vision – it's what saved us from being eaten by tigers when we first came down from the trees."

"Well it certainly sounds odd," Lesley admitted. "Did you say anything?"

"I didn't need to," I replied. "Rather than walking through a wall or going out of the door into the hall, this spectral mystery turned around and casually strolled back through the room, once again unseen by everyone but me. As she reached my chair, she did a little twirl, gave me a delightful smile and wafted out through the kitchen door. Beyond all reason, I'd just seen a ghost."

"Good grief!" my wife exclaimed.

"For a moment, I sat there open-mouthed in surprise and wonder. Suddenly, I realised Eric had stopped talking and everyone in the room was staring fixedly at the carpet. A moment later, the wife broke the silent tension by whispering venomously, 'That bitch,' then Eric sighed and said, 'I'm sorry'.

"The lady I had seen wasn't a ghost." I paused and sighed at the sad memory. "She was Eric's mother."

Lesley frowned, but remained silent.

"Over another cup of tea, the story came out. Seven years earlier, Eric had brought his mother to live in their family home. She had Alzheimer's disease and (he was quite frank about this) the doctors didn't expect her to live much longer."

"But she did," Lesley suggested.

I nodded.

"She was thin and frail but otherwise quite healthy. However, her memory had gone. It was so sad. This woman was once a loved and valued matriarch, a school teacher respected in her local community. Now she was just a hollow shell, with the mind of a child; a stranger, living in a house full of strangers. What's more, she had become so disruptive as to make their lives a living hell. Eric had tears in his eyes when he told me how they had started out with the best of intentions, but the Alzheimer's gradually turned his mother into someone they didn't recognise and couldn't love. At first, they hated the disease, but soon they began to detest the victim – so much so they had all but blanked her from existence."

My wife brought a hand to cover her mouth. "Oh how awful for them."

I sighed deeply.

"Even after all these years, the memory of that conversation brings a lump to my throat. I felt so desperately sorry for those poor people, and my heart ached for Eric's mother too. Even though her mind had changed beyond all recognition, when I think back to her doing that little twirl and smiling at me, I know, somewhere down deep inside, she was aware of their overwhelming repugnance."

I remained silent, waiting for Lesley to make the connection. It didn't take long.

"And now you're worried this might happen to us?" she asked.

"No," I replied, taking her free hand in mine. "I want us to promise ourselves it won't. We don't know what's going to happen once Muriel gets here, but whatever it is, and however long it takes, we have to make sure we stand strong together and do what's right for her."

Lesley didn't answer, but the nod of her head and the squeeze of my hand spoke volumes.

***

"There's a car stopped in the road at the front of the house," Lesley said, peering out of the window. "It's right on the bend too."

"Tsk. It's probably someone making a mobile phone call," I replied, moving inquisitively to her side.

"Whatever," Lesley shrugged and turned away from the window. She wasn't a morning person.

It was early on a Saturday morning, a couple of days before Christmas. The rising sun was just a pink smudge on the easterly horizon. In the fading darkness, the car's tail lights glowed brightly through the swirling vapour of its exhaust.

Although Glenmadrie is remote and the road at the front of the property only serves to link two other slightly larger roads, it is not entirely unheard of for vehicles to pass our house. However, most of the traffic is likely to be tractors, delivery vans or a familiar clapped out old car belonging to one of the local farmers. In a small community like ours, far away from the nearest police station, any unknown vehicle acting suspiciously is likely to draw attention. For a minute I watched the car with detached interest.

"I guess we should be grateful he had the courtesy to stop. Unlike some I could mention."

"Ack!" she grunted in disgust.

Although it was very much against the law, driving whilst using a mobile phone was still prevalent in County Clare. A few years earlier, Lesley had a nasty car crash when she was run off the road by someone too busy talking on their phone to pay attention to the road.

I went back to eating my breakfast. "Whoever it is, they'll probably move on shortly."

But they didn't. Twenty minutes later, Lesley was back at the window.

"It's still there."

I didn't say anything.

"I said, it's still there," she repeated a little louder.

I sighed. "Do you want me to go out and see what's happening?"

"Yeeess." She had accentuated the word into a frustrated exclamation as only a wife can do.

"Then why didn't you say so?" I hissed.

Without waiting for an answer to my largely rhetorical question, I slipped on my wellington boots and, forgetting to wear a coat, went outside. By strolling along in a casual manner, I hoped to convey the air of a man who wasn't nosey at all, but just happened to have walked down his driveway, through the gate and along 100 yards of tarmac, only to discover a car haphazardly parked in the middle of a dangerous bend.

As I got closer, I could hear the engine running and the radio quietly playing some country music. Moving to the edge of the road, so as to create a wide berth and avoid startling the driver, I approached the car from behind. As I drew level, I could see there was only one occupant. The driver was a man in his forties. Unshaven, with unkempt hair and scruffy clothes, he sat with his head back on the seat and his slack mouth hanging open. Although his hands were still gripping the steering wheel, he was obviously unconscious.

Realising I had found someone in the grips of a medical emergency, I instinctively reached for my mobile phone. Unfortunately, I had left it indoors, along with my coat. I glanced up at the house, but Lesley's interest in our visitor must have waned and she was not in sight, so any hope of miming a request for help was lost. Should I run back up the driveway and call for an ambulance, or attend to this poor fellow first? Obviously the latter was the sensible option.

Moving closer to the car, I called, "Sir? Hello Sir. Can you hear me?" But there was no response.

Standing alongside the driver's door, I put a hand through the open window and shook the man by the shoulder. Still nothing. I could see he was breathing, but unconscious, so I reached in and turned the engine off. As it was certain another vehicle would come speeding around the corner at some point, I would have preferred to move the car to a safer position, but for now my patient came first. He was still unresponsive, probably the result of a heart attack or a seizure. Perhaps feeling suddenly unwell after working a nightshift, he had heroically brought the car to a stop and engaged the handbrake, before passing out.

Recalling my first aid training, I leaned through the window and used my knuckles to rub hard on the centre of his sternum. When this also failed to elicit a response, I rubbed harder and shouted, "Sir? Hello Sir, wake up."

The man grunted and moved his head, but his eyes remained firmly closed. I repeated the process, only longer, harder and louder. Suddenly, he stirred.

"Waah?" His eyes flickered open and I saw confusion as he tried to focus on my smiling phizog. "Weerth the feeck?" he slurred, breathing a veritable wall of alcohol fumes into my face.

It was at this point I finally spotted a dozen discarded beer cans (of the extra strong variety) and an empty quarter bottle of whiskey in the passenger foot well. Apparently, and not for the first time in my life, I had completely misread the situation.

"You're in the middle of the road," I explained to the befuddled driver. "You'd passed out at the wheel. It's a miracle you didn't crash."

"Feck…gerrth...misklip.." he mumbled. His eyes bouncing around in their sockets as he attempted to resolve his confusion.

"Sir? You can't drive in this condition," I said. "It's not safe." As an afterthought, I reached forward to extract the car keys, but my hand was slapped away.

"Gerroff!" he growled.

With impressive dexterity for someone recently comatose by an overindulgence of libation, he started the engine, disengaged the parking brake and sped off. Had I not been so nimble, he would have made my foot his first casualty of the day. I could only hope there wouldn't be another.

"You're welcome!" I yelled after the receding vehicle.

As a final insult, he stuck his hand out of the window and presented his middle finger. Only in Ireland!

***

To any animal lover, every encounter with a new creature, however short, adds some additional flavour to the delicious soup of life. That was certainly the case for us on yet another cold and rain lashed winter night.

It was a few days into the new year. My wife and I were toasting our toes in front of the fire and watching one of a dozen movies we'd recorded over the Christmas holidays. Feeling a little drowsy in the warmth, I yawned expansively and asked Lesley if she wanted a coffee. Not wanting to lose count of her stitches, she bobbed her head in response, but didn't break the soft rhythmical clicking of her knitting needles. I made our drinks and returned to my spot on the couch.

"Have you heard from Joanne," she asked, before sipping cautiously at the hot liquid.

"Not today."

"I thought you were going to phone her this afternoon."

"That was the plan," I replied, "but she texted just before I went shopping to say they were out all day and she would text when she got back."

"But she didn't?"

I nodded.

Lesley snorted softly and smiled. Since David was born, our daughter had become notoriously difficult to track down. To avoid calling when she was snowed under with motherly tasks or missing her altogether, or worse, waking the baby, phone calls now had to be arranged by text beforehand. That was all well and good, but what to do when she didn't answer my text messages?

"I didn't have this problem when Joanne was a baby," Lesley said.

"Perhaps you were more organized," I suggested. "I think she's just having a little trouble getting adjusted to being a mum."

Lesley pointed at me with her chin. "Text her now."

"Okay." I looked around the room before doing a mental inventory of my recent movements. "Blast! I think I've left my phone in the car."

"Well you'd better go and check!" Lesley laughed. "It would

be ironic if Joanne's been phoning all afternoon and it was you who missed the calls."

A harsh wind had been battering the windows with cold sleety rain, ever since I'd arrived back from town. Although the car was parked quite close to the house, I donned my coat, hat and wellies before venturing outside. But as I opened the front door and warily peered into the raging tempest beyond, my trepidation was interrupted by a questioning, "Meow?"

There on the doorstep before me was a tiny tabby kitten, as small as my hand, and as wet as a fish.

I said, "Well, hello!" and crouched low to give the little fellow a gentle fuss.

He had a soft beige coat of long fur, dappled with streaks of dark brown, and highlighted with a white bib that sat below a handsome and intelligent face. While I stroked the side of his chin, he purred contentedly, with a deep rattle like a defective refrigerator. As if this was a new experience, the tiny kitten circled and writhed ecstatically, twisting his head and rubbing against my hand. I tried to lift him up, but as I gently slipped my hand under his belly, the little cat flicked his tail, dived between my legs and made his way indoors. With a gasp of dismay, I spun on my heels and raced after this petite furball because, just around the corner, there were four large dogs gently roasting in front of the fire.

Being unaware of our dogs' reputation as cat haters and feline chasers, the kitten trotted boldly through the kitchen, bounced energetically up the steps and marched confidently into our sitting room exhibiting all the bravado of a Navy Seal and the superciliousness of a celebrity entrepreneur. After pausing momentarily to assess his new domain, the cat meandered casually through the canine obstacle course and hopped nimbly onto Lesley's lap. After kneading her thigh for a moment and finding it to be satisfactorily comfortable, our tiny visitor began cleaning himself and purring like a toy motorbike. Lesley was delighted with this interruption to her knitting, although understandably surprised, but not as comically flabbergasted as the four dogs which now sat staring, open-mouthed in shock, at this brazen interloper.

16 – The Cat in the Hat

As we were unprepared for feline guests, we had to manage as best we could on that first night. Despite arriving at our door soaked through, the little kitten stunk and its fur was matted with what looked like motor oil, so a good wash was in order. He agreed with our assessment and stoically endured the indignity of a warm bath in our kitchen sink and didn't complain at all when we removed several ticks from the back of his neck. After a rubdown with a fluffy towel and a gentle warming blast from a hairdryer, the kitten was purring contentedly in Lesley's arms.

"What shall we call him?" she asked.

"We shouldn't name him," I warned. "You'll get attached and he'll probably be off to his rightful owner tomorrow. Anyway, you said we couldn't have a cat on account of it killing all the wild birds."

Since moving to Glenmadrie, we had spent a small fortune on bird seed, fat balls, worms and peanuts. Consequently, our little corner of County Clare was now a veritable hub of wildlife activity. A cat was likely to cause havoc and get rather fat in the process.

"Yes, but…" Her bottom lip twitched.

"But what?" I asked, rolling my eyes heavenwards.

"But…" She stroked the little kitten's forehead. "Perhaps it'll only kill vermin and leave the birds alone."

I ignored her comment, primarily because it was the same one she had rejected out of hand when I had suggested getting a cat just six months earlier.

"Anyway, we can't have a cat with your mum coming. She's unstable enough as it is, without having a kitten under her feet. Muriel is too frail to risk a fall."

"Perhaps it'll just sit on her lap," Lesley offered. "She'd like that."

"Look, I like cats too and I would normally jump at the chance of having such a pretty fellow in the house, but we need to be practical." I gave him a stroke. His fur really was very soft. "I'll check with the vet and the pound tomorrow to see if anyone has reported him missing."

"He's dreadfully thin and undernourished," Lesley pointed out. "I think he's a stray."

"How on earth did he get all the way up here?" I asked.

"It was cold today when you were in town. Perhaps he climbed up under the bonnet and inadvertently took a ride."

She had a point. During cold weather, it's not uncommon for cats to curl up in a dry and dark corner of a warm engine bay, but not all of them survive the subsequent journey to their new homes as well as this kitten had. I suspected he was in a deep sleep, or just too terrified to move.

"You could be right," I admitted. "Why don't you take him to the vet tomorrow? They can check him over and test to see if he's got a microchip. If he hasn't, I guess he can stay for a while, if he wants to."

Lesley grinned and nodded, delighted with the prospect of proving her theory and thereby claiming ownership.

We didn't have any cat food to hand and we figured offering dog food would be insensitive as well as being unsuitable for his tiny tummy, so Lesley sacrificed a tin of her favourite wild pacific pink salmon.

"I think he's got hollow legs," Lesley remarked, listening to the kitten's strident demands for third helpings.

"Or worms," I suggested.

"I can't believe he's still hungry."

"Please, Sir, I want some more." I joked, using my best Oliver Twist little boy voice.

Lesley's eyes met mine and she smiled as if she'd just caught me with my hand in the cookie jar.

"That's it! We'll call him Oliver."

My shoulders slumped and I groaned internally, for I knew, as we'd bathed, fed and now named this gorgeous kitten, he was here to stay.

And so it came to pass, a tiny underweight stray kitten, matted in engine oil and covered in ticks, acquired the name Oliver and came to live at Glenmadrie.

***

While Lesley was in England working round the clock helping Muriel sort her belongings and preparing her house for the rental market, back in Ireland, I was keeping busy – or trying to.

As it had been underused for several years, the granny annex had become something of a storage area, so my first task in making it into a safe and comfortable apartment for Muriel, was to empty the rooms and give everything a good clean. That part went well, as did the decorating and installing a television and an aerial, but trying to source the many new items we'd need proved to be rather a frustrating exercise. Living on a budget, our shopping lists lean towards being repetitive and predictable. It was ages since I'd bought plumbing supplies and I'd never shopped for mobility equipment. Where to begin?

After several years of tough trading conditions, I'd expected Ireland's embattled retailers to have become lean, mean fighting machines, with slick comprehensive websites, competitive pricing, easy ordering and first class customer service. A quick internet search proved I was mistaken. Although in a perverse way it was reassuring to discover many traders had survived the recession by relying on 60 years of intergenerational local trade and without wasting money on extravagances like advertising and websites, it made it maddingly difficult to identify what I needed and even harder to buy. In the end, I resorted to doing my research and pricing on English websites and trying to buy the items in Ireland, but it was not to be.

"I don't suppose you could fit a Kudox 1200mm type 22 double-panel convector radiator in your suitcase?" I asked Lesley during our regular morning phone call.

"I don't think it will fit," she laughed. "Are you having problems?"

"I'll say," I groaned. "It's for Muriel's new bedroom. I need a specific type. Basically it'll be the same radiator as the one that's in there, but twice as deep. Otherwise I'll have to knock holes in the plasterboard to change the plumbing and I've just finished decorating."

"Oh dear. I'm guessing you can't get one in Ireland. I know you were hoping to shop locally."

"I've tried," I explained. "The shops I contacted either don't stock that model, or they say they'll call me back, but they never do. I found a place down in Cork, but they wouldn't deliver to Clare. It's a similar story with the grab handles and rails. Most of the companies only supply the local authorities and they won't order anything for us until an inspector has done a site visit and that's something they wouldn't consider arranging until after Muriel has moved to Ireland."

Lesley growled in frustration. "But that would take months! Mum's quite unsteady on her feet already. Those handles and rails must be installed before she arrives." The last couple of sentences were whispered, so I guessed Muriel was nearby.

"I know," I sighed. "That's why I've ordered most of what we need from the UK. We'll just have to take a hit with the delivery charges."

The cost wasn't an issue, but I was genuinely disappointed I couldn't buy what we needed in Ireland. Fortunately, there was some better news to share. My quest to find some suitable furniture for the granny annex had been heading similarly downhill. Because she can't stand up easily from a sitting position, Muriel wanted a tall armchair, just like the one she had in England. But most of the furniture shops I visited only stocked modern low level chairs. Fortunately, one kindly gent pointed me in the right direction. A local charity had a large warehouse hidden at the back of an industrial park, where they sold a wide variety of donated items, including furniture.

"It's a huge place, packed to the gunnels with the sort of old fashioned stuff she wants," I told Lesley, "and most of the furniture is brand new, or very good quality second-hand."

"I think these days second-hand is called previously loved," Lesley joked. "Did they have what we need?"

"Yep!" I couldn't help grinning. "I've put a deposit on a nice drop-leaf table with a couple of dining chairs, a tall armchair and a bed. You can see them when you get back."

"A bed?" Lesley exclaimed. "I thought we'd agreed to source one of those adjustable beds."

"That we did," I agreed. "So I wasn't looking for beds. But…when I told the manageress why I was buying the furniture, she asked if we needed an adjustable bed. It turns out they had two. They're brand new, with electric controls and orthopaedic mattresses. They were just sitting under plastic sheets at the back of the warehouse. Apparently, they'd been gifted the previous week direct from the manufacturer. As they are not a popular item, she was delighted to sell one."

"Oh, how wonderful!" my wife said. "I'm sure Mum will like it."

The day after Lesley returned, we visited the furniture

warehouse to pay the outstanding balance and arrange for delivery. My wife approved my selection without any fuss but added one further item. A three piece leather suite.

"It's a recliner," she said, pointing to the couch. "Mum can put her feet up and relax while she watches television."

"But it's huge!" I exclaimed. "Wherever will we put it?"

"In our sitting room of course!" She smiled sweetly and gently shook her head at the misunderstanding. "We'll gift our old suite to the charity. It's in excellent condition."

I did a quick mental calculation of what we'd spent. "It's not really any cheaper here, but they've got what we want and the money is going to a good cause."

"It's a shame they don't sell radiators and grab handles too!" she joked.

I smiled and pointed towards the checkout. "I'll go and pay."

The following afternoon an ancient delivery van arrived at Glenmadrie, laden with our new furniture. The driver and his two assistants were volunteers at the charity. They were all in their late 60s and proud owners of beer bellies, bad backs and heart conditions. Being the youngest and fittest by far, it fell to me to do most of the lifting and carrying. The final item to be moved was the three seater couch. With its substantial steel frame and thick leather covering, it was astonishingly heavy. Transporting such an unwieldy lump and keeping it undamaged on a meandering route across the lawn, along the side passage, through two narrow gates, down some steps, under the coverway and in through the French doors, would be a tough task for a group of professional furniture movers, so for three old men and an author with a sprained wrist, it proved to be hard work. Nevertheless, after 20 minutes of groaning, swearing and puffing, several skinned knuckles, a strained back and an enforced break when the van driver went down on one knee and clutched his chest, the deed was done. I gave the crew a hefty tip, sent them on their way and returned indoors to help Lesley unwrap our purchases.

Everything was fine, but later, whilst trying to wrestle the unwieldy settee into place, one of the seatbacks came away in my hands.

"At first, I thought it was broken," I explained to Lesley, "but then I realised the couch was designed to split into eight lightweight sections for easy transportation."

Eyes wide, recalling the trouble we'd had moving the couch, my wife covered a laugh with her hand.

"On the upside," I continued. "We've got the furniture we needed, your mum will be comfortable, the charity is substantially better off and we didn't kill any of their delivery drivers!"

***

Even though Oliver clearly considered himself to be a dog with some unique climbing skills, as a prudent precaution, we let him sleep in the laundry room overnight. He seemed happy with this arrangement, but rejected the fluffy towel we'd offered as a bed, in favour of snuggling into an old upturned trilby hat. There he was safe from the dogs, but still free to climb out of the open window to do his business or to engage in some nocturnal hunting.

After a little jockeying for position in the hierarchy, Oliver settled in nicely, becoming a loyal playmate for our terrier Amber, albeit one lethally armed with razor sharp claws and lightning fast reflexes. Although he was woefully underweight, and riddled with ticks and worms, Oliver was otherwise in good health. With the aid of two hearty meals a day and supplemented by the dog food he stole, he quickly began to gain weight and muscle. It was a credit to the forbearance of our four pooches at mealtimes, that they tolerated this little kitten's head shoving its way between their noses and food bowls, in search of a few tasty treats. Oliver was certainly living up to the appetite and recalcitrant attitude of his namesake.

As Lesley had predicted, the little kitten found the prospect of trying to catch birds too tempting to resist. Despite our shouted chastisements, he spent much of those first few days quietly hanging around the bird table in anticipation of a feathery meal. For a while, we were concerned he would totally decimate our flock of avian friends, or at best send them all away to a safer feeding ground. However, despite many hours of slyly tracking the birds at ground level, and hiding behind bushes, he had no success. Next, presumably working on the basis he must eventually get lucky, Oliver took to quietly sitting in the centre of the bird table like a furry alligator, whilst waiting for a suicidal finch to fly into his open mouth. When this cunning plan failed, he began hanging upside-down in a tree and playfully swatting at his prey as it flew by. Even though his antics were thoroughly entertaining to watch, they delivered no results. Without one bird kill to his name, Oliver quietly switched to hunting rodents.

Although we saw little evidence of Oliver's nocturnal hunting success, he must have been working away diligently, because the local rodent population slumped noticeably. To justify his exorbitant wages, or perhaps to show us what a clever boy he was, sometimes Oliver would arrive home with a half-dead mouse or a tiny vole. He would then spend a happy hour showing me how he had caught the pesky vermin. Like a ruddy faced golfer propping up the bar at the 19th hole whilst recounting the majesty of his best-ever round, Oliver's mimed replaying of his hunting feats would become ever more dramatic and longwinded. Frequently, the poor mouse would get bored with all this waiting around to die and quietly sidle off into the undergrowth in search of something more interesting to do.

A few days after our new friend arrived, I was taking the dogs for their early morning walk when I noticed we had some company. Oliver was 20 yards behind and slightly off to one side, cautiously following along, curious to know where we were going. After a hundred yards, he stopped, but for the next hour I could hear his wretched cries of abandonment and discontent. On our return, Oliver greeted us with typical feline enthusiasm, feigning disinterest until we were within yards. Only then did he acknowledge our presence, as if to say, "Oh, there you are. I was so busy looking at this interesting leaf, I didn't even notice you had been away for the last hour and 12 minutes!"

Despite his apparent indifference, the next day, Oliver shadowed our mile-long trek from a discreet distance, all the way around the forest walk and back to the house. Two days later, he was jogging along at the back of the pack. Within a week, he had claimed his place alongside the lead dog. From then onwards, every time I took the dogs for a walk, Oliver would be there, either trotting along at the front with his tail held high, or a few yards ahead, hiding in the long grass preparing to pounce on his unsuspecting victim. For their part, the dogs took his presence in their stride. They accepted Oliver as one of the pack, expecting him to chase after the ball, or assist in the hunt for the cunning fox.

***

From the day he arrived, the little kitten had a dry cough and was often prone to bouts of violent sneezing, particularly at mealtimes. When he went to have his gonads removed, our vet had again checked him over carefully but still found nothing amiss. As a precaution, she prescribed more worming tablets and antibiotics, along with a homeopathic treatment to cure the coughing, but the symptoms stubbornly remained. A few days later, things came to a head. It was breakfast time for the animals and Oliver was in the laundry room, perched on the chest freezer where he could supervise as I filled the bowls. Suddenly, he had another violent bout of sneezing. As this prolonged and involuntary sternutation subsided, I noticed what looked like a small length of grass hanging out of Oliver's left nostril.

"Lesley?" I shouted. "I think I've found why Oliver's been sneezing!"

With my wife's help we wrapped the little cat in a thick towel – as much for our protection as for his – and with a pair of tweezers, I gave the offending item a gentle tug. Like a master magician performing a slight-of-hand trick, I slowly removed a 14-inch parasitic worm which had been living in the poor kitten's sinus. I skipped breakfast that day and we didn't eat spaghetti for the next month, but Oliver was instantly a much happier cat, and I never heard him sneeze again.

***

With outbuildings, cover-ways and a single-storey wing, our home has a considerable amount of roofing which is accessible to a determined and imaginative feline – and Oliver was both those things. The warm moonlit nights were perfect conditions for a young lad to practise his hunting skills, confident he would be able to return at dawn and sleep all day.

Late each evening he would slip out of the laundry room window and disappear into the darkness. In the morning, at around half-past sparrow fart, like a drunk returning home from a late night binge, our little cat would noisily clump his way along the roof, stop below my bedroom window and meow incessantly until I let him in.

178

"The laundry room window is still open!" I testily pointed out. "You climbed out of it not five hours ago."

Perhaps wondering why I wasn't serving his needs as swiftly as he would expect, he stared at me innocently and blinked.

"You certainly have no problems getting in through that window whenever I rattle the cat food tins!" I snapped.

Oliver purred loudly while he performed a seductive Argentinian tango around my legs.

"Maybe you learned it from Lady," I suggested. "She does the same thing with doors."

Even though most normal people would still be in the arms of Morpheus for another three hours, once I was up, Oliver would expect to be fed and played with. Unlike human teenagers (those adroit hibernators), once one of our pets is awake, they will all rise and noisily demand to be fed, walked, and fussed. Furthermore, they will ensure every human in the house is also roused, before settling down for a good day of sleeping. These early morning disturbances became so unbearably frustrating and annoying, even the dogs began to show their displeasure. My simple solution was to shut the laundry room window, forcing Oliver to remain indoors overnight, with only a few spiders and a cat litter tray for company. This brilliant and infallible strategy delivered peaceful sleep for precisely two nights.

At 4am on the third night, our slumber was rudely interrupted by an enormous crash and the frenzied barking of the dogs. Tousled haired and sleepy-eyed, I sprinted down the stairs to investigate the source of the disturbance, painfully stubbing my toe along the way. Bursting into the laundry room, with nothing more than a lavatory brush for protection, I found the tumble dryer had been forced from its shelf and fallen to the floor. Feigning innocence, Oliver was lying on his bed and blinking at the unwelcome intrusion. His guiltless little face said, "That tumble dryer just jumped off the shelf all on its own."

I didn't believe a word!

After a similar disturbance the following night, I bought some earplugs and reverted to leaving the window open. Sometimes I envy Lesley's ability to sleep through Armageddon.

A couple of days later, I went into the laundry room to load the washing machine. In passing I gave Oliver a kindly stroke and immediately sensed something was troublingly different. Although he was in his usual place, curled inside my old hat beside the dented tumble dryer, and happy to accept my outstretched hand for a fuss, he seemed to have changed colour. Our previously beige tabby cat was now a deep black, with a white nose stripe, and intense green eyes. I suspected an impostor and my suspicions were confirmed when I spotted Oliver peering warily through the window. It seemed we had a new cat!

17 – Skunk and Disorderly

The new cat drowsily luxuriated in the unexpected attention he was receiving, but only for the few seconds it took for him to become fully awake. Like a tussled-haired teenager rising early on the first morning back after a long school holiday, he stretched, yawned and slowly blinked his big green eyes at his unfamiliar surroundings. I watched with growing curiosity as he looked in turn at his bed, my stroking hand and then Oliver, who was cautiously peering around the open window. The sight of another male cat caused this interloper to deliver a sudden double-take so funny, it could have won a television comedy award.

Suddenly fully aware of his surroundings, the cat bellowed with rage and exploded into a flurry of fangs and claws. Like someone who had inadvertently touched a hot stove, I attempted to pull my hand away, only to discover the cat had sunk his teeth into my thumb. Yelping in pain, I shook my hand as if it were on fire and attempted to push him away. The stray took considerable umbrage at the introduction of another hand into what he now perceived as an unwarranted attack. In response, he employed his full arsenal of offensive weapons, grinding his teeth into the bone of my thumb, slashing my left hand with his claws and peeing down my leg – although the last bit could have been me. As I flailed my arms helplessly, trying to dislodge this vicious furry bundle of fangs and talons, without doing further damage to him or me, it was Oliver who came to my rescue. Without a thought for his own safety, he climbed through the window, stepped nimbly across the utility room sink and, with a single bound, reclaimed his now empty bed. My hero!

Fortunately, the presence of a second cat in such a confined space, was enough to convince the interloper it was time to leave. In a flash of black and white fur, he sprung from my arms and dashed through the window. With my aching hands clutched protectively under my armpits, I turned to admonish Oliver for his inactivity, but he was already deep into an innocent sleep.

"He must be another stray," I said, wincing as Lesley applied some antiseptic to my wounded thumb.

"That's hardly likely up here." Her brow furrowed as she considered the alternatives for his sudden appearance. "He's probably a feral cat."

"That would explain why he was so vicious," I hissed through gritted teeth.

"The poor thing was probably terrified."

"Well Oliver was a fat lot of good," I complained, rolling my eyes for dramatic effect. "He's supposed to be protecting his territory, not inviting stragglers in to share his bed."

"What shall we call it?" Lesley asked.

"I doubt we'll see it again," I replied, sniggering at the memory of the cat's dramatic exit. "Especially if it is feral."

"We could still give it a name," Lesley said, hopefully. "Felix would be good."

I wasn't too keen on the idea of naming a strange cat, especially since my recently chewed thumb ached and my trousers were rather damp. Nevertheless, I could see my wife wanted my input.

"How about this?" I proposed. "Today we said, a cat came in. If we see it again, we'll call it that cat, if it comes twice more we'll say the cat. If it's still here next week, we can call it our cat, and if we're feeding it after ten days, we'll name him Mike."

Lesley laughed at my suggestion. It always made me feel good to see my wife smiling.

"Why Mike?" she asked.

"Mike cat," I explained.

She frowned, oblivious to my joke.

"It's where he was sleeping…Mike cat…In MY HAT!"

She groaned and stopped smiling.

"Or we could name him Felix," I conceded.

***

There was some good news on the publishing front as well.

"Look!" I said, excitedly jabbing the computer monitor with my finger.

"What?" Half blind without her glasses, Lesley squinted at the screen.

My Irish manuscript had been selling well and receiving some great reviews – along with a few stinkers too, but today was a landmark moment.

"It's a number one bestseller!" I exclaimed.

"Really?" Lesley's face was a delightful picture of joy and

surprise. "Where?"

"There." I tapped the screen again.

She closed her eyes and tutted as if she were trying to explain her vehicular transgression innocence to an officious parking warden. "Which country?"

"Canofulorous," I mumbled into my chest.

"Where?"

I sighed, keen to protect this fleeting moment of glory for as long as I could.

"Canada," I conceded, reluctantly. "It's the number one memoir in Canada."

"Oh…" Perhaps sensing the fast melting of my ego under the sun of truth, she added quickly, "But that's good…isn't it?"

"I suppose so. It's probably only sold a thousand or so copies…" my voice trailed off.

"A thousand?" she replied, patting me on the shoulder. Her voice cracked with genuine excitement. "But that's great. You must write another."

"Another memoir?"

"Or finish that thriller," she suggested

"Or that," I agreed. "I should probably do that."

***

Somehow, my name had finally reached the top of another list. This one was medical. After what felt like years, I had an appointment for an endoscopic examination.

I recall travelling to the hospital, filling out dozens of forms and meeting with the gastroenterologist. It wasn't the same man I'd met before, but he was very polite, professional and knowledgeable. I remember him explaining the procedure and telling me not to worry.

"We'd usually just sedate you," he explained, "but as we're also doing a colonoscopy, we'll knock you out."

"Oh. Is that necessary?" I asked.

"It'll be best." He gave me a reassuring smile and a nod, then added a twirl of his index finger, as if he were asking the waiter for the bill. "I'll probably do a little maintenance while I'm up there…"

I didn't know what maintenance he had in mind and I didn't ask.

"Do you have someone to drive you home?" he said, tapping his pen on the form.

I nodded. "My wife."

He made a note of Lesley's phone number and finished by reading through a long list of medical disclaimers.

I couldn't help adding a few warnings from my days in financial services. "Stocks can go up and down. Your home is at risk if you do not keep up repayments on a mortgage or other loan secured on it. This quotation is only provided as a guide."

He half-smiled at the joke and handed me his pen. "Sign here please."

I vaguely remember being asked to wear a plastic shower cap and a paper gown which was draughty and refused to close at the back. My recollection of the operating room is of stark lighting and strangers with kind eyes wearing gowns, gloves and masks. As I climbed on the table, I made a nervous joke about hoping everyone had washed their hands. It fell rather flat.

"Tough crowd," I said.

The anaesthetist was suddenly at my side. He waved a huge syringe which appeared to be full of milk.

"Don't worry about a thing. This is the good stuff." His voice was soft and the wrinkles around his eyes told me he was smiling. "Just count backwards from a hundred."

"100, 99…"

"Good afternoon," Lesley said.

And just like that, I was standing in our kitchen. The clock showed 2pm. I was dimly aware of mental cobwebs and a furry tongue. My brain wasn't functioning properly. "Wha…?"

My wife filled the kettle. "How are you feeling?"

"Err. Okay, I guess." My thoughts wobbled around in my head like a drunk trudging slowly through a syrupy fog of confusion. "The hospital? Is that today?"

Lesley laughed and shook her head. "No dear, that was yesterday."

"Oh." I frowned and rubbed my face with my palms. There were two plastic hospital bracelets on my left wrist, one red and the other white. "I don't remember anything," I mumbled. "How did I get home?"

My wife laughed again and with good reason. Apparently, the 'good stuff' the anaesthetist administered had left me as happy as Larry and as drunk as a skunk. Despite being fully conscious, but almost unable to walk, I had insisted I was capable of driving home with such confident exuberance, Lesley had resorted to strapping me into the back seat. Had I managed to undo the seatbelt, she would surely have needed to tie me down for my own safety. Fortunately, my drug addled brain was far beyond coordinating my eyes and fingers in a manner sufficient to facilitate the pressing of the seatbelt button. After a while I gave up and entertained myself by giving my wife driving tips. When these back-seat observations failed to elicit the expected appreciation, I kept myself occupied by singing loudly all the way home. To this day, I have no recollection of those 24 hours, which is probably a good thing as I have an inkling my dear wife may have been rude to me at some point.

***

Perhaps encouraged by the award of an official moniker, Felix soon began gracing us with regular visits. Particularly on cold nights when Oliver was out hunting, Felix would slip in through the utility window and curl up in the warmth of my old hat. Although Oliver was a considerably smaller cat, and without a feral bone in his body, Felix was quick to vacate the bed the instant the rightful occupant returned. After a few tense exchanges and one extraordinarily loud bout of feline fisticuffs, the two cats reached an amicable level of tolerance. When they demonstrated a desire to dovetail their hunting and sleeping schedules, we had to provide a second bed in the utility room, albeit at a discrete distance from Oliver's.

Despite the softening in the feline relationships, Felix remained as feral as ever towards humans, firmly resisting any of our attempts to make physical contact. The dogs took a dim view of this bad mannered interloper and, despite our strident admonishments, chased him off whenever the opportunity presented.

"That cat can certainly climb trees," Lesley observed.

"It's a good job the dogs can't," I replied.

My wife laughed and pointed to Amber, who was scrabbling at the base of a huge pine tree. "It's not for the want of trying!"

Although he wasn't above stealing any unattended cat food, Felix refused to eat alongside Oliver. At meal times, we fed the

185

new cat on an old patio table positioned outside, just below the utility window. There he could munch happily on his kibble and take the occasional break to check if Oliver had left anything in his bowl.

Felix was obviously older and more experienced than Oliver, perhaps by as much as a year and two testicles. Not wanting to risk castrating someone else's pet, we elected to wait for a few months before taking him to the vet. In any event, Oliver and Felix were the only cats we'd ever seen at Glenmadrie, so the risk of an unwanted litter was small – at least for now.

 Relinquishing his responsibility as senior feline, Felix seemed happy to follow Oliver's lead on most matters. The older cat may have been lazy when it came to taking the initiative, but I prefer to think he was just being a polite companion. Naturally, Oliver did his best to lead Felix astray. When the tumble dryer mysteriously fell off its shelf one night, I found Felix staring at it in guilty horror, whereas Oliver was cuddled up in his hat and pretending to be asleep. Whenever they played chase up a tree, it was always the older cat who was encouraged to climb the highest and most dangerous branches.

Perhaps my assessment of these events is just the product of my overactive imagination, but I have no doubt it was Oliver who taught Felix which bedroom window was mine. I was less than happy to be woken in the early hours by plaintive meowing, only to discover the older cat's steady green eyes peering cautiously through the glass. As soon as he was satisfied I was awake and out of bed, Felix turned tail, trotted happily across the roof, nimbly hopped to the ground and disappeared into the forest until it was time for his breakfast.

***

My expectations of spending some quality time with my daughter and grandson during a relaxing trip to the UK were trashed when Mark and Joanne announced they were moving house. They'd been hunting for a suitable property since before she'd fallen pregnant, but when they'd finally found their dream home, a long chain of linked house purchases had delayed completion of the sale for several frustrating months.

It was an old and very rundown three bedroom house, sitting on a corner plot in a quiet Essex village just a few miles from where our daughter grew up. This was their first home as a family. As the house needed some extensive repairs and alterations, they'd wisely decided to remain in their rented house for a few more months until the lease expired and the worst of the building work was finished. Unfortunately, things didn't go to plan. As is often the case with a project involving plumbers, electricians, builders and plasterers, all trying to occupy the same space, the renovations got substantially behind schedule. Strewn with rubble, draped with wires and without any heating, Mark and Joanne's new home was almost uninhabitable. But, short of renewing their rental agreement for another six months, they had no choice but to move in at the end of the month. The race was on to get the house to a liveable state.

"I'm so glad you're coming," my daughter said when I phoned. "You'll be able to help us clear up."

"Me?" I exclaimed. Clearing rubble wasn't the holiday I'd visualised.

"Yes. I know you love getting your hands dirty.

"I do?"

"Of course you do," she laughed. "It'll be great fun."

"Fun?" I stammered.

Although I'm inclined to look for the joke in even the darkest shadows, I never considered our seven year long renovation project as being fun. It was a necessity, born out of poverty and an inability to find an available builder. Although it may have turned out to be a satisfying and memorable achievement, it certainly wasn't fun. Playing golf was my idea of fun, as was walking across the moor, going to concerts, or bouncing my grandson on my knee.

Perhaps sensing my reticence, Joanne's voice changed as she pleaded for sympathy. It brought to mind an image of her former self, seven years old and standing alongside the sweet counter.

"Pleeese?"

How could I resist?

In the end, my trip hadn't been the disaster I'd anticipated, but it hadn't been much fun either. Mark was heavily engaged in a new project at work and too busy to lend much help at the new house. Young David was as delightful as ever, even though he was going through one of those baby phases where he had a head cold, a hacking cough and displayed some magnificent snot

187

bubbles. The poor boy felt dreadful and found his world to be constantly irritating. Seemingly unable to sleep, eat, or stay awake, he was a relentless drain on his mother's time, energy and good humour.

Although most of the structural changes at the house were complete, the new heating system had yet to be commissioned and some of the upgraded electrical wiring was unfinished. The plumber and electrician were due to return after my trip, so the house would soon have heat and light. The big problem was rubble and rubbish.

Mark's idea had been to save money on long-term skip hire, by storing all the debris created during the renovations on site and clearing everything at the end. It had seemed a good plan, but in practice the growing piles of bricks, plaster, copper pipe, off-cut wood and old wires became dangerous obstacles. Furthermore, without access to a skip, the builders began dumping their rubbish in the nearest convenient clearing. By the time I arrived at the house, most of the ground floor and half of the garden looked like a three dimensional map of a mountain range. Until we moved some of the rubble, there wasn't even a clear space for a skip. Joanne and I spent every day at the new house together. With David demanding almost constant attention from his mum, I'd done much of the humping and sweeping myself. Although it was lovely to see Joanne, Mark and David, particularly in the evenings when the day's work was done, by the end of the week, I was more pleased than usual to head home.

As I'd flown out in the early morning and would be returning late at night, to avoid dragging Lesley out of bed, I'd left my car at the short-term parking. She was still awake when I got back, but only just.

"How was David?" Lesley asked.

"Tired and irritable," I replied.

"And Joanne?"

I gave an ironic laugh. "Tired and irritable."

"I guess she's having a tough time."

"She is." I nodded. "And this house move isn't helping."

"Did you get the rubble cleared?"

"Yes. A replacement skip arrived, so I finished the last of it yesterday." I puffed my cheeks and rolled my eyes at the memory. "That was some day. Joanne had an appointment at the mother and baby clinic and couldn't drive me to the house, so she popped me in a taxi. The weather was horrid, cold lashing rain all day and the traffic was so awful that 20 mile trip took 90 minutes!"

"Good grief," she exclaimed. "However much did that cost?"

"Don't ask... Anyway, as I only took a carryon suitcase on the flight, I didn't have a lot of clothes with me and I'd already run out – except for clean underwear. Knowing I was moving rubble outside all day, I wore my dirtiest jeans and a sweatshirt."

"You should have taken your overalls," Lesley suggested.

"I thought so too, but it wouldn't have made any difference. It was raining so hard, I made up a protective suit from a roll of dustbin bags. Even then, I was soaked through within an hour and my shoes were wrecked. That evening, Joanne had to take me to the shops so I could buy some new clothes."

Lesley nodded knowingly towards my unusually fashionable attire. "Ah, that would explain it."

I smiled. My wife knew I favoured function over fashion with most of my shopping, particularly clothes. Living in a rural community where wellies and overalls were acceptable attire for most social gatherings, I was unlikely to get much use out of the patent leather shoes she'd just noticed I was wearing.

"It's Joanne's fault," I said, with mock severity. "I wanted to go to a cheap clothes store, but the nearest one was miles away, so our daughter insisted on taking me into this high-end retail park we were passing." I groaned at the memory. "It was reeeally expensive."

Lesley grimaced and pointed at my new and ridiculously pointy footwear.

"Italian loafers aren't really your thing are they?"

"I feel like I'm wearing clown shoes," I sniggered. "One misstep and I'm likely to stab myself in the calf."

"Did you get any time with David?"

"Oh yes," I replied. "As we'd finished at the house, today we had the whole day together. It was proper grandad time. I cuddled him when he was asleep, fed him when he was hungry, and inbetween, bounced him on my knee. It was the highlight of my week."

Lesley smiled like a doting grandma. "That's nice. Did

Joanne take you to the airport?"

I shook my head.

"As the house they're renting is so close to the bus park, it was easier for me to get the airport coach." I frowned at the memory. "Something odd happened though. An old lady sat next to me on the bus. Just after she sat down, I noticed she stank of stale urine. It was so horrid, I had to breathe through my mouth the whole way."

Lesley didn't look very sympathetic. She knew I had an unusually strong sense of smell and was particularly sensitive to such things.

"Anyway…" I pressed on with the story. "Sitting so close on a hot bus made the smell seem even worse. It was so bad it seemed to hang in my nose long after we got off the bus. To make matters worse, on the plane, I found myself sitting next to this big old farmer, and guess what?"

My wife's eyes narrowed. "He stunk of stale urine too?"

My eyebrows involuntarily rose in surprise.

"Yes. However did you guess?"

Lesley used her index finger to beckon me closer. She sniffed experimentally and immediately wrinkled her nose in disgust.

"Phew!" she groaned. "You smell like a skunk!"

And she was right. At some point during the day, my grandson had christened my new trousers. Unnoticed, the wet patch had dried and begun to fester. In the heat and humidity of the bus, the smell became overpowering.

I laughed and grimaced in embarrassment.

"There was I thinking I'd had the misfortune to meet a succession of incontinent geriatrics, when all along, it's me that stinks!"

18 – Chainsaws in the Mist

In the decade and more since we moved to Ireland, we have experienced around 40 Atlantic storms. From our perspective, many of these tempests were no more noteworthy than the average foul-weathered Irish holiday weekend. But this year had been particularly bad. A succession of violent storms had already battered the west coast, damaging houses, blocking roads and ripping down power lines across the country. Although heavy rain and flooding is becoming more common in Ireland, it's the winds that can quickly cause serious damage, injury, or even worse. As Glenmadrie sits high on a hill, we have no real fear of flooding and our mature trees seem impervious to wind, but I do worry about the risk of structural damage to the house and outbuildings.

With another storm pounding the west coast overnight, we lay awake listening to the rain lashing against the windows and the roof creaking as the cold wind whistled under the eaves in search of a way in. In the morning, I went outside to check the house and land for damage. All I could find was some dead foliage and a few loose twigs. The violent overnight winds had been replaced by slack humid air. In the eerie quietness, I could pick out the distant sound of chainsaws echoing through the mist. With my tour complete, I headed back indoors.

"So far so good," I reported.

"No damage at all?" Lesley sounded sceptical. "Listening to that wind last night, I was sure we'd have lost a few tiles or something."

"I guess we were lucky again." I shrugged and smiled with relief. "There must be some trees down somewhere though. I can hear several chainsaws."

Lesley pointed at the television which was showing the morning news.

"There's power lines down all over the west coast. I guess we got lucky there too."

"Since they replaced the wires up here and upgraded the network, we haven't had a single outage," I observed. "Those electrical engineers don't get enough credit. Some people might have been sitting indoors without any telly last night, but they were out in the worst weather, cutting back trees and replacing power lines. I wouldn't fancy doing it."

"Me neither." Lesley nodded towards the television which was showing a map of Ireland overlaid with tightly packed isobars. The forecast looked grim. "There's more bad weather on the way."

Despite the dire warnings, the next weather event was almost an anti-climax, producing nothing more startling than a steady gale. For 20 hours, the storm blew a consistent stream of moist air across the country from the southwest, like a wind tunnel on full power. Just after dark, I cautiously ventured outside, to check for damage and to ensure the dogs didn't blow away whilst doing their business before bedtime. The air was full of flying debris and the ghostly sound of the wind groaning through the trees. It was certainly a wild evening but compared to our usual storms, all pretty mild stuff. I staggered indoors with my hands full and struggled to shut the door against the force of the wind.

"What's it like out there," Lesley asked.

"Perfect weather for kite flying," I replied. "Provided you've got forearms like a weightlifter."

"What's that?" She pointed to the tangle of metal I was holding. It was about the size of a beachball.

"Right now, it's scrap metal. A minute ago, it was the spinner on our chimney. It blew off and just missed hitting me on the head."

"Oh…" Lesley sighed. "That's a shame."

"A shame it fell off, or because it missed hitting me on the head?" I joked.

She tapped her lip with an index finger and looked at the ceiling. "Tough question…"

Despite the steady wind and the occasional rumble of thunder, the night was reasonably quiet and we both slept well. In the morning, I was pleased to note the electricity was still on and our water pump continued to work – all good evidence there hadn't been a lightning strike nearby.

"It seems another storm has passed without incident," I said.

"Lucky us," Lesley replied.

It was getting light outside, so I opened the curtains. For a moment, I stood boggle eyed in shock.

"What's wrong with this picture," I asked, pointing out of the window.

Lesley gasped. Our view of the moor was completely blocked by branches. We went outside to investigate.

Four big trees had fallen along the length of our front garden. The tallest, which was now the longest, was a pine tree easily 120 feet from the base to the tip. Alongside it were two slightly smaller pine trees and an enormous beech tree. During the night, this group of trees had been uprooted, silently falling across the lawn as they narrowly missed the front of the house.

I had never before had the opportunity to inspect recently fallen trees at close quarters. My first impression was one of absolute chaos. There was such a confused shamble of branches it was impossible to get anywhere near the trees, except by approaching via the trunks, two of which were more than four feet thick. As this group of trees had quietly tipped over, they had also lifted a huge slab of earth and roots, which now stood upright to a height of 20 feet. Many of the branches were twisted and crushed into a confusing tangle beneath the trunks of the three largest trees, and those that were not – some over a foot thick – now stood upright, 30 feet high and waving gently in the fading wind. Closer inspection revealed that a fifth tree, a 30-foot willow, was lying crushed under the labyrinth of broken and twisted wood.

Although these trees had fallen without making a sound, their last moments had clearly been one of considerable violence. Peering through the mess of wood and foliage, I could see that many of the larger branches had been snapped by the sheer weight of wood and that several had been driven deep into the earth. Furthermore, the trees had fallen down the hill, so the tops were now some 20-feet below the roots. Even though the trees were down, they had clearly not finished falling. Every few minutes a loud crack would ring out as another branch snapped and the trees would settle a few inches lower.

"You'd better keep back," I warned.

"I can't believe we didn't hear this lot falling," Lesley exclaimed.

"I'm pleased they missed the house," I replied.

The row of trees at the southern end of our garden now had a 20-foot gap, like a missing tooth in a goofy smile. Lesley grimaced when she noticed one of her flower beds had also been squashed.

"What a shame," she sighed.

"On the up-side, we won't need to order firewood for a while."

My wife slapped her forehead. "My mum is coming in a couple of weeks. You'll have to get this lot cleared before she gets here!"

I looked forlornly at the complicated jumble of wood.

"Oh, good..." My answer lacked any real enthusiasm.

Whereas I was delighted with the prospect of so much firewood making itself available, it was obvious the task of clearing these trees was going to be difficult and potentially dangerous. All I had at my disposal was a bad back and a tiny chainsaw. I was going to need something a lot bigger. I called Cormac at our local tool hire shop, hoping to rent a chainsaw with a long enough blade to cut through the thick tree trunks. I knew Cormac from when he used to play golf. His son had attended my junior golf academy.

"No can do. Sorry, mate," he said. "We're not allowed to rent chainsaws."

"Why ever not?" I asked.

"Feck knows!" he growled. "We used to, but now we can't. It's probably because the health and safety Nazis have finally taken over at the Ministry of Common Sense!"

Lesley was unsympathetic to my problem.

"Why don't you just buy a bigger chainsaw?" she asked.

"I considered that, but I'd need one with at least a 48 inch blade," I replied. "It's not the sort of thing they stock at the local hardware shop. These professional chainsaws are prohibitively expensive. Buying one makes no financial sense, unless I'm planning to go into the logging business full time."

"I guess we'll have to call someone in," she suggested.

"I tried that too. The tree surgeons I spoke to all wanted to keep the firewood as part of the deal. Otherwise, their charges would have been so high as to make it more economical to leave the trees where they were, and burn our money instead!"

Fortunately, while I was searching through the local advertisements for ideas, I came across one advert that piqued my interest. Apparently, a local artist was looking for large slabs of wood to make rustic furniture. He was an experienced woodsman and had his own equipment. After a quick phone call and a bit of negotiating, the deal was done. In exchange for a few offcuts, he would assist in clearing my trees without further payment.

**

Nigel was a polite and energetic English lad, probably around 28 years old. He spoke like a lumberjack, but had the physique of a ballet dancer. Over the phone, he had explained his passion for making tables and other pieces of rustic furniture from those parts of trees that were normally too large or knotty for domestic use. Carefully following my directions, he got hopelessly lost and didn't arrive at our house until late the following afternoon. We shook hands and exchanged some pleasantries, as Englishmen abroad are genetically inclined to do, but all the time his eyes were looking over my shoulder at the trees. I was as keen to get the work underway, as he appeared to be, so I led the way across our lawn. Seconds later, Nigel was climbing around on the trunks and between the broken branches. His eyes gleamed with excitement, like an inquisitive child getting a behind-the-scenes look at Disney World.

"I was going to try cutting them up myself," I explained, "but my chainsaw isn't big enough."

"Good job you didn't." He pointed at the massive beech tree. "That lot's under tremendous tension, one wrong cut and it may all let loose."

As if to back-up this observation, there was an ominous cracking sound as one of the trees settled.

"So it's not very safe then?" I asked.

"Definitely not, people have died doing this."

"Good to know," I whispered, suddenly feeling rather less manly. "So what's the plan?"

"I'll make some cuts to release the tension, here and here," he waved his hand vaguely towards the trees. "Then we can clear some of the branches together."

"Ok," I said, a little cautiously.

"Don't worry, it'll be safe," he said, perhaps noticing my concern. "Once it's clear for me to work, I'll come back in a few days and remove the sections I want. After that I'll cut up the rest. Ok?"

195

"Sure," I nodded enthusiastically. "Shall I get my chainsaw?"

He gave me a pat on the shoulder. "Yep, let's get started."

A few moments later, I stood by the trees, mannishly bedecked in my safety gear of purple overalls, leather gloves, boots, and goggles. Lesley had come out to watch the fun. She frowned as I held my yellow chainsaw at the ready, like a 14-inch phallic symbol. A moment later, Nigel emerged from behind his van, brandishing his 60-inch long monster. My proud tool slowly drooped in wretched embarrassment. Lesley covered a giggle with her hand and turned away.

"Well, that'll do the job," I said, trying not to sound impressed.

"You betcha," he replied with a roguish smile.

Despite my desire to have the trees turned into usable firewood, I was mildly gratified with a small but childish victory on the phallic symbolism front, when Nigel's massive Stihl Magnum chainsaw refused to start. I was even happier when my little yellow job worked flawlessly and his kept cutting out at the critical moment. Apparently, it's not what you've got, it's how you use it that matters.

After a little adjustment to the engine and some colourful verbal encouragement, Nigel soon got his massive machine running and he set to work. With his experienced eye identifying the best places to cut, he soon released the tension and allowed the trees to settle to the ground. Once he'd cut a path through the tangle of branches, Nigel was able to reach the trunks.

"Right, you'd better stand well back. This next bit is likely to be a bit tricky," he said. "I have to cut through the trunks and allow that slab of soil to fall back into place. Once it's down, it should be safe enough for you to start cutting the branches away."

From a safe distance, I watched bravely as Nigel began to cut through the trunks. He stood with his left shoulder against the enormous upright slab of soil and cut as closely as he could to the base of the trees. With its powerful motor, his chainsaw sliced through the thick trunk like a hot knife through butter. Other than the cut end of the trunk rising by a couple of inches as it was freed from the tree, nothing much happened. The second tree was problematic to cut. Each time it moved, the chainsaw blade became trapped. But by using a car jack to add a little upward pressure and a pry bar to keep the cut open, things progressed nicely.

By now, Nigel was halfway through cutting the four trees and yet there was no sign of the huge slab of soil falling back into place. I removed the car jack and pry bar and moved again to a safe distance. Nigel stood with his back to the trunk of the smallest pine tree, and then began to cut through trunk number three, the large beech tree. His mighty chainsaw sliced through the tough wood with ease and just 30 seconds later he was through. In the next three seconds, two things happened almost simultaneously. The enormous beech tree, finally released from its stump and the mud slab, settled down the hill, snapping and cracking the branches underneath its massive weight. At the same time, in the blink of an eye, the massive slab of earth fell back into its hole with a ground-shaking thud. The fourth pine tree, which was just an inch behind Nigel's back, became erect with the speed and violence of a counterweight trebuchet. I swear I saw several pinecones efficiently dispatched towards America along with what looked like a very surprised squirrel. I definitely saw Nigel flinch as the tree whipped by the back of his head.

"Feck, that was close!" he squealed, not quite remaining true to his lumberjack persona.

"You were lucky," I laughed. "If a branch had caught your belt, you'd be well on your way to America with that squirrel."

We walked together to look at the small pine tree. It now stood 30 feet tall, so upright and solid, it was hard to imagine a moment ago it was resting recumbent across my lawn. Furthermore, the slab of soil had fallen so perfectly back into its hole, we couldn't even see the join. Nigel looked at me and shrugged casually, trying to mask his surprise.

"That was a good shot," I said, "I guess we'll leave that tree where it is."

And we did.

***

Nigel never returned to cut the wood for his rustic tables. He was due to come back the following week, once Lesley and I had cleared away all the remaining branches, but the weather intervened. A couple of days after his visit, a massive storm slammed into the country with devastating force. Across Ireland, thousands of trees were torn down and tens of thousands of houses were left without power. Locally, several golf courses had so many trees uprooted, they were closed and unplayable for weeks. On the phone, Nigel was apologetic but adamant, he had enough paying work to keep him busy for six months and would probably not have the time to return to my house. Fortunately, he had already cut the thickest and most difficult pieces. Anyway, with my new TimberPro 20-inch chainsaw (bought online for €99 with free shipping) I was confident I could manage the rest.

Although the work cutting and splitting the trees for firewood progressed at a decent pace, I must admit to being surprised by just how many branches there were. Even though our land has a hundred or so trees and we live alongside a forest, until several of these giants were adorning my front lawn, I had never really appreciated just how many branches each tree had. During the following week, Lesley and I got miserably wet and tired, working every daylight hour cutting the branches away. We saved some of the larger sections for firewood and dragged the remainder up a muddy hill, to where they could be safely burned – should it ever stop raining. Once all the branches were cleared, we were finally able to see the tree trunks.

"Wow," Lesley exclaimed. "Were going to have a lot of wood."

I did a quick mental calculation.

"Together, these three trunks measure around 240 feet. Cut into 20-inch sections, then split and dried, that's about 1,500 logs."

"Like I said, lots of wood."

And there was more to come.

A couple of days later, after what could only be described as a typically blustery Irish weekend, I discovered the lumber fairies had visited again. The farm track at the rear of the house was completely blocked by a neat line of four horizontal trees. They had originally lined the fence on the left of the farm track but now lay directly across the lane, with their tops reaching well into the forest on the right. With the track now impassable, even for walkers, clearing the trees became a priority. I took my trusty chainsaw and got to work.

Yet again, there were hundreds of branches to be removed

before I could get anywhere near to the trunks. I had to cut very cautiously, as the falling trees had raised another huge slab of soil along with their roots. The trees were very unstable. Suspended by a mass of broken branches, they spanned two fences, three deep ditches, and a small stream. Without the aid of a lumberjack's knowledge to guide me, I had to find a satisfactory way to work in reasonable safety. After some careful experimentation, I developed a technique of cutting through a section of tree and then running away as fast as I could. Once I was reasonably confident nothing was going to trap my leg, or fall on my head, I could cautiously return to cut through another section. It was good exercise, but rather time consuming. Anyway, as it turned out, it wasn't my head I needed to worry about.

The only way to clear the lane was to cut a 20-foot section from the centre of each of the trees. Once this wood had been cleared away, I could safely leave the top third of the trees where they had fallen, over the fence in the forest. These treetops were securely out of the way, ready to be turned into firewood the following year. Although the path was now clear enough for dog walkers, the gap wasn't yet sufficiently wide for a tractor to pass. On the left, the thick trunks were still attached to the large slab of earth and partially blocking the lane. Confident in my new lumberjacking skills, I began slicing wheelbarrow-sized chunks from the stumps until the path was clear.

When the trees had fallen, they had also flattened the barbed wire fences which lined the sides of the lane. The largest tree stump needed one last cut, but to reach, I had to straddle the rusty remains of the barbed wire fence. After years of karate training, I have very flexible legs, but even for me, it was quite a stretch. Given I had already cut the trunks without incident, I assumed these stumps were going to remain permanently in their horizontal arrangement. However, as I began to make the final cut, I saw the stump move upwards by a couple of inches. Disturbed by the vibrations of the chainsaw, the large mud slab was about to flip back into place. Looking down, I saw the barbed wire of the fence vibrating ominously just an inch below my crotch. Feeling like a man straddling a nuclear bomb, I turned off my chainsaw and cautiously cocked my right leg clear of the wire. The instant my booted foot reached hip height, the tree stump, along with its huge slab of earth, tipped back into its hole with a thwack, like someone hitting an elephant on the bum with a cricket bat. At the same time, the rusty barbed wire fence whipped upright, taut and erect, some six feet from where it once lay. Had I moved a moment later, I am sure my gentleman's dangly bits would have been left hanging on the fence like a ghoulish Christmas decoration. Lucky me.

19 – A Row of Ducks

I love my lists. Planning ahead, having all my ducks neatly lined up and trotting confidently forward towards a predictable outcome gives me great comfort. Unfortunately, not everything in life can be planned and predicted in such an orderly fashion. Caring for a loved relative suffering from dementia is definitely one of those unpredictable things.

Sure, we prepared. Even before Muriel had a diagnosis, back when we were seeing the early signs and started pleading with her doctor for help, Lesley and I began planning what we would do if Muriel's health deteriorated. At first, our conversations were no more than vague discussions about care homes in England, or the prospect of moving her to Ireland, but as it became obvious Muriel's gradual mental decline couldn't be entirely dismissed as a symptom of old age, we began planning in earnest. But here's the problem. You don't know what you don't know. In preparation for what was to come, we had read and researched as best we could, but there were holes in our knowledge. There were things we didn't know and things we couldn't have known. We planned carefully for things that didn't happen and were caught out by events we never could have predicted. But whatever the outcome, we did our best and tried to put Muriel's needs above our own.

Through discussions with the doctors and our own research, we knew vascular dementia is a general term describing problems with reasoning, planning, judgment, memory and other thought processes caused by damage from impaired blood flow to the brain. There are two main types of vascular dementia. Multi-infarct dementia is caused by a stroke and subcortical dementia results from a disease of the small blood vessels in the brain.

Based on her symptoms and medical history, Muriel was believed to be suffering from multi-infarct dementia. In her case it was probably caused by a series of small strokes. These strokes can be so tiny no-one notices them happening, but the person may suddenly get worse then stabilise until the next stroke happens. Consequently, this type of dementia often happens in downward steps, rather than the steady gradual changes seen in Alzheimer's disease. Although the progress of the disease can vary greatly, the typical life expectancy of someone suffering from vascular dementia is no more than five years. While she was still able to make such an important decision, Muriel had made it abundantly clear to both Lesley and her doctor, that when the time came, she did not want her death delayed by the use of heroic medical measures, machines, or feeding tubes. It was a brave decision and one we accepted and respected.

Muriel's dementia had been worsening for a couple of years. Now she was exhibiting signs of slower mental processes, trouble with her speech, having difficulty remembering recent events, problems with planning, concentrating, making decisions and organising, as well as short periods of sudden confusion. As a result, Muriel would have difficulty preparing the simplest of meals, or forget to eat at all. Along with balance issues, she also had problems with depth perception and spatial awareness. These would cause her to become disoriented and frightened when presented with unfamiliar surroundings, like a change to the layout of her local shop.

Although on first impressions she still appeared to be alert and responsive, because of her inability to think on her feet, Muriel was becoming more vulnerable and open to manipulation. Consequently, she was inclined to comply with suggestions, even when wrong, rather than question their veracity. If asked, "You've had breakfast, haven't you?" she'd almost certainly say yes, even if she hadn't. This may go some way towards excusing the person who sold her the double glazing she didn't need, but not much.

People with vascular dementia can also suffer from delusions, strongly believing things which are not true. In Muriel's case, she was convinced one of her neighbours was stealing from her. Given their long relationship and close friendship, the accusation seemed unlikely and, given Muriel's state of mind, we had to give that person the benefit of the doubt. Sadly, it was only later we discovered Muriel's suspicions had been correct.

Because of how dementia attacks the brain, the disease eradicates the personality and destroys the person long before it kills the body. In many cases, the patient no longer recognises their own children and they in turn are left caring for a human shell who looks like someone they once loved. Such a commitment is a tough ask.

We knew all these things and more, but there was much we didn't.

In retrospect, I wish we'd been trained how to talk with a dementia patient without every conversation becoming a frustrating argument. There is a knack to keeping the discussion in the present moment, only talking about one thing at a time, focusing on the immediate environment and using specific commands with simple language. These are skills we learned through trial and error, without ever becoming proficient.

Because the disease is unique to each person, we didn't know how quickly her symptoms would develop and worsen, how long Muriel would survive, or what the end would look like. Nobody told us Muriel could suffer pain, become depressed, agitated, angry, aggressive, incontinent or develop a blank expression. We didn't know she might have difficulty eating, lose her sense of taste or find the texture of certain foods to be suddenly unbearable. We weren't told to expect socially inappropriate actions. Most of these things we discovered as they happened, but others were only revealed in hindsight.

Although nobody really warned us how hard the road ahead could be, we had some sense of what was coming. Lesley and I committed to doing our best for Muriel and, no matter what stage of dementia she was in, to try and enjoy our time together.

***

Muriel may not have been a rich or famous person, but she was good and kind. A child of the Second World War, she was brought up in Birmingham, England, where her life revolved around the simplicities of factory work, chatting to friends over the garden fence and drinking at the local pub. A down to earth woman, without pretension or hubris, Muriel was content to live a modest life. Although she was by no means perfect, she was an affectionate and caring grandmother, generous with her time and happy to offer some extra pocket money or a shoulder for Joanne to cry on. She enjoyed knitting, gardening, card games, quizzes, jigsaws, television game shows, reading, talking and laughing.

It was March when Muriel moved to live with us in Ireland. By that time, the chatty, funny and slightly irreverent lady we once knew was gone. The blue twinkle in her eyes had been replaced by a flat grey stare of confusion and her once lyrical voice could only produce a few slurred words or a groan of exasperation.

Lesley drove to England and stayed a couple of days to load the car with the remainder of Muriel's possessions, before setting off towards Ireland. The return journey took two days, with an overnight stay at a hotel in Wales so they were ready for the early morning ferry to Dublin. I was waiting in the driveway with a friendly wave and a welcoming smile as they arrived at Glenmadrie. With ironic timing, as we helped Muriel take the dozen or so faltering steps across the gravel from the car to the front door of her new home, a cold, hard rain began to fall.

"Aggh!" Muriel exclaimed. "Wrainink."

"Don't worry, Mum," Lesley said. "You'll soon be indoors. Then we'll have a nice cup of tea."

"Gaghh!" Like a puppy refusing to walk on a lead, Muriel shook her head and dug her heels in. "Whant goow home."

"This is home," Lesley replied gently.

"Whant myhh home!" she shouted angrily and stamped her foot.

The look of pain in my wife's eyes made my heart ache. I gave her a stiff sympathetic smile and nodded towards the door.

"Come on, Mum," I whispered gently, whilst encouragingly tightening my grip on her elbow. "We're all getting wet here."

Muriel grunted angrily once more, but after a few seconds, with the rain falling harder and the last vestige of her reluctance fading, she moved forward again.

After a tour of her new apartment and some lunch, Muriel went to bed for a midday nap.

"It's been a tough couple of days for her," Lesley said. "What with the early ferry and such a long drive, she must be exhausted."

"I'm sure she is," I sighed sympathetically. "That's probably why she was a bit grumpy earlier."

"Getting pounced on by four excitable dogs was probably a bit overwhelming too," Lesley snorted a laugh. "She seems to be settling in now."

"After seeing so many pictures of Jack, Mum was delighted to meet him in person." I nodded towards the sitting room, where our rough collie was sprawled on the floor. "He was very polite, especially for a dog who is so wary of strangers."

"Mum's not so keen on cats though," Lesley warned. "Oliver's keeping his distance for now."

I rolled my eyes skywards and made a praying gesture. "So far so good."

"She seems to be coping alright getting around though." Lesley pointed to the doorway. "Those handholds you installed are really helping."

Muriel wasn't as mobile as I'd anticipated. As our house was considerably more spacious than hers, without furniture within easy reach, her balance issues were obvious to see. I suspected she felt less confident too.

"We'll probably need to get a wheelchair soon," I said, almost to myself.

Lesley nodded. "And some ramps."

I frowned. "Ramps?"

"For the sitting room and kitchen steps," Lesley explained.

"But it's only a couple of steps. Surely we can just bump the wheelchair down?"

"You may be strong enough, but I certainly am not. Anyway, Mum won't appreciate being bounced up and down the steps."

"Okay." I nodded. "I'll see what I can do."

Lesley pursed her lips in thought.

"Wait until she's seen the doctor," she said. "I think he'll be able to point us in the right direction."

Unlike England, where Muriel had to wait a fortnight for an appointment and seldom saw the same doctor twice, here she saw our family doctor the following morning. We didn't even need to book.

"You were a long time," I said, when Lesley and Muriel returned. "How did it go?"

"It was fine." My wife smiled. She was obviously very happy and bursting to share some news. "Doctor Mark was really nice and helpful. He did a full examination and a cognitive dementia test too."

"Wow!" I exclaimed. "She had to wait a year for that test in England."

"It was two years," Lesley corrected. "Doctor Mark took charge of the medical records I'd brought over. Though he seemed rather shocked it was all on paper."

"I'm not surprised," I laughed. "That stack of records was about four inches thick. It's going to take ages to type it all into his computer."

Lesley glanced cautiously over her shoulder. Muriel was on her recliner chair watching a gameshow on television. Satisfied her mother's attention was elsewhere, my wife leaned closer and spoke *sotto voce*. "He concurred with her dementia diagnosis and referred us to the district nurse. She's in the same building, so we saw her right away. Pat's a lovely lady. She's coming up this afternoon to check out the facilities here and see what we need."

"Oh that's wonderful." I was truly delighted. "I'm so impressed with the efficiency here. It bodes well for the future."

Lesley crossed her fingers and smiled hopefully.

The district nurse's arrival shattered the quiet calm of our post lunch afternoon like a bursting balloon in a library reading room.

I heard a car pull into the driveway and quickly shut the dogs in the kitchen, before sprinting to the door. In typical Irish fashion, the district nurse had knocked once and let herself in. I found her standing in the porch, looking around expectantly and trying to decide which door to try next.

"Hello. You must be Pat," I said, offering a welcoming handshake. "I'm Nick. Muriel is through here." I led the way into the annex.

Pat wore a blue nurse's outfit with a hat, and carried a medical bag. Disproportionately thin for her height, she had jet black hair, dark eyes, a strong Limerick accent and the manic intensity of someone on a mission and far too busy for idle chitchat. When she spoke, her words came in a blinding rush, like tsunami waves flooding over a breakwater. To keep up with the conversation, I had to listen very carefully and replay almost every sentence in my head. My tactic of feigning deafness came in handy, but I worried how Muriel would respond, particularly as she struggled with most conversations and had yet to become acclimatised to the Irish accent. Such a brisk demeanour would easily have been mistaken for indifference had Pat not been so obviously sweet and caring.

Muriel was laying on her bed watching television when we

came into her room. This was her private space, so I always knocked before entering. She smiled at the intrusion and nodded politely at Pat, although I was sure she didn't recognise her as the same person she'd met that morning.

"Hello, my love." Pat spoke slowly and clearly as she leaned over Muriel and patted her hand reassuringly. "How are ye feeling?"

As often was the case when she was tired or had just awoken, Muriel's response was slow and faltering. From my side of the room, I couldn't make out the words.

"Ah that's grand, Muriel." Pat turned to me and nodded towards the door. "I need to examine her. Would you mind...?"

I nodded and pointed a thumb over my shoulder. "I'll wait in the kitchen with Lesley. Give me a shout when you're done."

Half an hour later, Pat came through. As she opened the kitchen door, the dogs exploded from their beds and rushed forward to perform either a joyful welcoming or a menacing canine haka, depending on who they met.

"Mind your head!" Lesley and I shouted in unison.

With the low stone lintel above our kitchen door, this had become our traditional greeting. Pat ducked, but a moment too late. I winced at the impending collision, but fortunately the only damage was to unseat her nurse's hat.

"Hello, doggies," she laughed, crouching down to share some love and desterilise her hands at the same time. Pat stood and nodded towards the wing. "Muriel's having a sleep. It's a good thing you're doing for her."

"Thank you," Lesley said. "We've been trying to get her to come for a long time, but she wanted to maintain her independence for as long as she could."

"That's a very common attitude with older folk and perfectly understandable." Pat nodded knowingly and shrugged. "You can only do your best. Anyway, that's a grand setup ye have out there. It's as good as a private room in a hospital. I'm sure your mum's going to be just fine here."

"Oh that's good news," Lesley replied. "We tried to make it as homely and practical as possible."

"You'll have to do something with the shower though," Pat added. "That corner cubical won't be suitable for long."

"I was planning to change it to a low level walk-in shower," I explained. "Would that be okay?"

"Yes, that should be fine. As long as there's enough room for a bath chair and someone to help her wash."

I nodded. "No problem. I'll get it done as soon as I can."

Despite her busy schedule, Pat joined us at the kitchen table and, over a cup of tea, carefully explained what she would do in her role as the coordinator for Muriel's healthcare. I could see the delight and surprise in Lesley's eyes as she listened.

In the few hours since the morning, Pat had already arranged for daily visits from a care assistant to help Muriel get showered and dressed. She had also booked a site visit from the local health service representative to assess Muriel's need for mobility support. This would focus on things like further handholds, measuring Muriel for a wheelchair and a correctly fitted walking frame, arranging for ramps, an electric hoist to lift her in and out of bed and a special bed with an air powered mattress designed to prevent bedsores for when she became bedridden. Pat had also arranged for a disabled parking badge and put us on the list to receive deliveries of adult nappies and some special high energy foods, specifically made for people who have trouble eating.

"It looks like baby food," she explained, "but it will help a lot when she begins to lose her ability to swallow."

"Thank you." Lesley sighed a smile. "It's been so hard to get anything for Mum in England. I can't believe you've done all this in a morning. It's incredible."

"Tsk!" Pat waved away the compliment with a shy smile. "Think nothing of it. Ye guys are going to do most of the work. Over here, we appreciate the contribution families make to support their loved ones."

"Thank you anyway," I added. "We're most grateful for all you've done."

Pat smiled sheepishly. "The care assistant has your number, so she'll call to arrange her first visit shortly. I've put ye on the list to have respite. I know Muriel has only just arrived, but she obviously can't be left alone. That's going to be a terrific burden on ye both. In a few months, you'll be glad of a break. When the time comes and you need a few days off, there'll be a bed waiting for her at a nursing home."

"That's most kind," I replied.

"And most generous," Lesley added.

"In the meantime," Pat continued, "I've arranged for someone to relieve you for three hours once a week. There's a nice local girl called Linda. She'll come and read to Muriel, or play cards, just so you've got the chance to get out of the house for a bit. Three hours isn't long, but it's enough time for you to visit the shops or have lunch together." Pat took a leaflet out of her bag and slid it across the table. "There's a dementia day care centre in Ennis. It would be good for Muriel if she could attend once a week. They have lunch, do exercises, speech therapy, play cards, sing songs, watch television and read stories. Muriel might even make some new friends."

By that time we'd run out of superlatives to express our gratitude, so all I could do was say thank you again and offer Pat another biscuit. She stroked her silver crucifix neckless before grinning guiltily and selecting a couple of chocolate hobnobs. I smiled back.

"One final thing before I go," Pat said, her face suddenly serious. "Ye all have a tough road ahead, but you're not alone. We're here to help, so call me anytime if there's something you need." She leaned in to take Lesley's hand. "Nobody wants your mum to suffer," she whispered, "and there's no reason why she should. If you think she's in distress or pain, you must tell me."

Just an hour after Pat left, my phone rang. It was the care assistant calling for directions to the house. Her name was Dezera and her accent definitely wasn't Irish. As she was nearby, I explained how to find the house and arranged to meet her at the gate.

Ten minutes later, a brand new, top of the range sporty Lexus swept into the driveway, missed my toes by a couple of inches, and skidded to a halt in a dusty shower of gravel. As I jogged back towards the house, Dezera bounded energetically from her car and waved at me as if I were a much missed close friend, arriving at the airport. Of medium height and build, Dezera had skin the colour of milk chocolate. Her long straight black hair was pulled tight by a high ponytail, adding a misleadingly hawkish quality to her thin angular face, high cheekbones and full lips. She wore a loose grey cotton t-shirt above tightfitting elasticated sports leggings and brown leather flipflops. Despite her casual clothing, her carefully applied makeup and red nail polish spoke of someone who took great care of her appearance.

"'Ello, Nick!" she shouted. Her accent was noticeably east London.

"Hello," I replied. "It's nice to meet you, Dezera."

"Call me Dizzy. Everyone does." She giggled. "Dizzy by name and dizzy by nature!"

Her sudden burst of laughter came from deep within her ample chest. She was genuine and unrestrained. I liked her immediately.

"Dizzy, I'm delighted to meet you." I gave a respectful half-bow. "Nice car, by the way."

"Ta." She smiled, her teeth gleaming white in contrast to her bloodred lipstick. "Wiv da miles I do, it pays to 'ave a decent motor. I gets a new one every year."

"I've heard they're very reliable, so that makes sense." I nodded appreciably at her car. "It looks a bit low slung and sporty for rural roads though."

"I know I should be driving one of them four wheel drive SUVs, but where's the fun in that?" As if it were her favourite dog, Dizzy lovingly stroked the car's black paintwork. "Anyways, it helps that I'm a bit of a petrol head."

I laughed and gestured towards the front door. "Shall we go in?"

Dizzy followed me into the house. In the kitchen, she fell to her knees and bestowed each dog with equal measures of hugs and kisses. After chatting with Lesley, she made a quick tour of the apartment, introduced herself to Muriel and helped her out of bed and through to the kitchen where her supper was waiting. Leaving Muriel to eat, we stepped into the sitting room to discuss Dizzy's homecare visits.

"I have a busy schedule," she explained, "but as luck would 'ave it, I pass the house every morning. Starting tomorrow, I'll be here at nine for an hour. That should be enough time to get Muriel out of bed, washed and dressed."

"Oh, that's wonderful!" Lesley exclaimed. "I'd be happy to assist."

"Thank you. I'd appreciate some help. I expect it'll be easier for your mum if you're there as well." Dizzy looked at me and grinned. "You look like a strong lad. We'll be okay for a bit, but as Muriel gets weaker, I'll need help lifting her."

I nodded. "No problem. Lesley has a bad back, but I'll be

ready whenever you need me."

Dizzy smiled and looked around. "Cor, blimey!" she exclaimed, as if noticing our home for the first time. "Dis ain't 'arf a nice place!"

I grinned. "Thank you. It's certainly nicer now than when we bought it."

"Did you 'ave it done up?"

"Sort of," I replied. "We did all the work ourselves."

"Did you, by golly?" Dizzy rolled her eyes skywards. "Lord, luv a duck!"

I smiled, secure in the knowledge we were going to get along just fine. It seemed our ducks were lining up rather well.

20 – A Matter of Routine

From that point onwards, our freewheeling and relaxed lives were willingly surrendered to the necessary routine of being fulltime carers. No longer could we leave our beds when we wished, enter the day without a plan, or go for a day trip on a whim. Now we became clock watchers, plotting our time and location like busy parents juggling triplets through a variety of after school classes. Muriel's needs and the regular visits of the various care assistants, nurses, doctors and health service inspectors blocked timeslots in our calendar and left little space for our own activities.

However, even though Muriel came first and could not be left alone, life had to go on. At some point one of us would need to visit Joanne in the UK, leaving the other to look after Muriel. I was still teaching golf – albeit sporadically – and needed to show my face at the club whenever I could. My work and practice days were now limited to a few hours combined with a quick dash around the shops before heading back home. Lesley needed her space too, probably more than me, so I made myself available to do the housesitting whenever she wanted to visit a garden centre or meet some friends for lunch. All too soon the gardening became a problem.

"I thought Mum would help me, or sit and chat while I worked," Lesley whispered, just after I arrived home from a shopping trip. "But we were only outside for 20 minutes before she wanted to come back indoors. She didn't want to watch the television and I couldn't leave her alone, so I had to sit and play cards."

"Oh dear," I replied, pulling my wife into a hug. "I'm here all day tomorrow. You can garden then."

She pulled a grim smile. "I've so much to do out there, but it's forecast to rain all day tomorrow. That's why I was trying to get it done today."

So the gardening was added to the list of activities that needed preplanning, along with DIY, shopping, housework and my efforts to write another book. Our lives had become a matter of routine.

***

I awoke two minutes before my alarm clock was due to sound. In the darkness, the red display glowed brightly. I reached over and flicked the switch. It was 05.58 on a Tuesday morning, three months since Muriel came to Ireland.

Silently slipping out of bed, I dressed in yesterday's clothes and tiptoed downstairs. I didn't need to wake Lesley yet, I'd let her have a bit more rest. Goodness knows she needed it. Our dogs slept in the conservatory, a wide corridor, connecting our courtyard with the kitchen and Muriel's apartment. When I opened the door they were still deep in slumber. Although they were excited to see me, somehow I managed to muster the unruly mutts outside without any unnecessary barking. Some mornings, Oliver would slip out of the utility room window and join us in the courtyard, but not today. Perhaps he was tired too.

Leaving the dogs to have a sniff and a pee in privacy, I filled a plastic jug with seed and restocked our bird table, ready for the early birds who can't be bothered to catch worms. It was almost light, so I refilled the jug and made my way up the hill past our polytunnel to the chicken run. Our hens were already awake and tapping impatiently at the door of their coop. They were happy to see me, more so because I had brought food. Now a regular part of my morning ritual, one brown hen stopped at my feet and squatted low in a display of subservience. She probably thought I was a very large cockerel. Not willing to disappoint, I reached down and ran my fingers along her back several times, gently stroking the silky feathers from head to tail. After a moment, the chicken gave an ecstatic shiver and flapped its wings, before moving away in a coy shuffle, her head hung low as if in embarrassment.

"Tart!" I laughed. With a smile on my face, I headed back to the house.

Lady, Kia, Amber and Jack were waiting patiently in the courtyard. To avoid making unnecessary noise in the conservatory, I led them back into the house via the French doors. By the time I had made my tea and toast, they were all fast asleep in the living room, scattered around like so many discarded toys. There was a chill in the morning air, so I flicked the central heating on. I normally wouldn't bother, but the house needed to be warm for Muriel.

To avoid waking anyone, I ate my breakfast watching the

television with the sound turned down low. The Greek debt crisis dominated the news once again. There was talk of another bailout. After rinsing off the dishes, it was time to take the dogs for a walk.

As a rule, I preferred looped walks to those which go out and back along the same path. Jack had the opposite view. If I took the dogs up the forest logging road, he'd stop at the entrance gates and wait, secure in the knowledge we'd eventually come back. The same thing happened when we walked on the moor. When he first came to us, this beautiful rough collie was undernourished and showing signs of juvenile rickets. Since then, with the benefit of good food and some dietary supplements, he'd put on a fair bit of weight and become much healthier, but he still needed regular exercise to strengthen his weak hip joints. Fortunately, my work on cutting paths through the forest had gone well, creating a delightful meandering looped walk.

Our route took us down the hill towards the river, before branching off to cut through a small wooded area. Climbing a steep embankment, we squeezed under an old barbed wire fence and entered a meadow. Walking through the waist-high grass, I saw dozens of purple and white orchids along with yellow buttercups, ragwort and hundreds of other wild flowers. The air was rich with the delicate scent of gorse and the sweet smell of honeysuckle. The tall grass swarmed with butterflies and bees, hungry for nectar. Fortunately, the biting midges were absent on this beautiful morning. At the top of the hill, I paused for a moment to take a snap of Kia. Like a supermodel, she waited patiently while I framed the picture. Sitting on some short meadow grass and backlit by the rainbow rays of the rising sun, it became one of my favourite photographs of our soppy black collie.

After passing through two fields, we turned right at the waterfall, climbed an embankment and entered the treeline. Following the banks of the stream, we climbed 200 feet up a steep hill, before turning right again. This was a commercial forest. Although there were some areas of native woodland around, these were rare. The forest around Glenmadrie was planted in huge squares of either European larch or Sitka spruce. Under the thinly spaced larch trees, the forest floor was green with moss, ferns and swathes of white flowering shamrock. There were frequent signs of deer, badgers and the ever present hares. My path followed a ridge alongside a natural drainage ditch. It was 20 feet wide, deep enough to swallow a car and impassable to all but the most athletic animals. Even so, there were a few points where the deer crossed. The trampled grass, occasional footprint and wisps of dark hair on the barbed wire were as obvious to me now as signposts on a London street. On the other side of the ditch, there was a wall of thick bushes and bramble. Beyond that, the hill rose steeply towards the distant skyline. There lay the oldest part of the forest, its huge pine trees and spooky grottos beautiful and intimidating at the same time. It was an area I have only explored via the logging road above. That hike was tough and dangerous, the sort of adventure I shouldn't have taken on my own. Even so, I hope to do it again one day.

A hundred yards ahead, the path cut through a large area of Sitka spruce. Here the canopy of dense branches blocked all but the brightest sunlight, making this part of the forest seem dark and foreboding. Below my feet, the ground was soft with a thick carpet of pine needles, silencing my footsteps like coffee-coloured snow. Although my route followed a ridgeline of firm ground, I knew from experience there were swampy areas nearby, where the pine needles hid several muddy bog holes. These seemingly bottomless pits were filled with stinky liquid goop, the consistency of custard and the colour of crude oil. They had been known to swallow cattle and hapless hikers too, so I stuck to the safety of my path.

While this part of the forest was incredibly dark and the floor below the huge spruce trees seemed lifeless, that was not the case. The warm and permanently moist peat was an excellent growing medium for fungi, of which Ireland has around 3,500 species. In the autumn, this area would be rich with fascinating toadstools and beautiful wild mushrooms, but for now the ground was dominated by colourful lichens. They covered the tree stumps and devoured any fallen branches. Just below the surface, the soil was crisscrossed with microscopic hair-like fibres, signs the forest was actually part of a huge organism constantly sharing and processing nutrients.

Although this was commercial forest, focused on turning a

profit, there were exceptions to the regimented lines of trees. Alongside inaccessible hedges, on rocky terrain and between the planted areas were small gaps where the sunlight could reach the ground. These clearings, some the size of a tennis court and others no more than a few paces across, quickly became an oasis of exuberant growth and extraordinary colour. Like islands of sanctuary in an ocean of high trees, these leafy dells were a haven for wildlife. Many had their own microclimates. Where the weather on the forest floor remains quite consistent, the open spaces may be covered in snow during the winter and bathed in sunshine during the summer. I find it incredible that just two paces from the dark brown peaty forest floor, there was an ecosystem diverse enough to make a botanist drool.

For me, these forest glades were a liquid well of suspended time, a peaceful place where I could sit on a mossy rock and let my woes melt away while I listened to the birds. Each of these clearings had its own unique character, driven by the soil conditions and available light. My favourite forest oasis was on a small plateau near the top of a hill and only existed because a couple of car-sized rocks prevented trees being planted there. Squeezed into such a narrow gap and surrounded by towering pine trees, the moss and ferns received very little direct sunlight. Consequently, the green coloured chlorophyll in the plants was unusually concentrated and dark. In the weak light of dawn, like a phosphorescent shipwreck tableau in a darkened aquarium, this eerie but beautiful glade glowed as if it were hiding a treasure chest of iridescent turquoise jewels.

These days, my time for sitting around and staring into space was limited. Lesley and I had to get Muriel up and fed before Dizzy arrived. With a sigh, I whistled for the dogs and set off for home. Pausing only momentarily to take a picture of Jack posing on the top of an embankment, the remainder of my forest walk took 20 minutes.

Lesley was sitting at the kitchen table drinking her coffee when I returned.

"Oh, you're back," she said, her eyes flicking involuntarily to the wall clock. She isn't really a morning person.

I checked my watch.

"There's plenty of time." I leaned down and gave my wife a kiss. "While you finish your coffee, I'll have a quick shower and get dressed. Ten minutes? Then we can wake Mum. Okay?"

Lesley nodded.

At 8am we woke Muriel, helped her out of bed and slowly walked her through to the bathroom. Whilst Lesley did the unpleasant stuff like changing her mum's adult nappy and cleaning up, I went to the kitchen to prepare her breakfast. Not long after Muriel came to Ireland, we realised she couldn't concentrate for long enough to eat a meal alone, so someone always had to be on hand to help her. Within a couple of months, her coordination had deteriorated to the point where she needed to be spoon fed all the time, with the exception of sandwiches and cake – those she could manage on her own. Perhaps because she felt embarrassed to show such weakness in front of her daughter, Muriel preferred it when I fed her. One painfully slow spoonful at a time, it took her almost an hour to consume a small bowl of porridge and some mashed banana.

Like all good trusting Irish country folk, we leave the front door unlocked when we're expecting visitors. Without knocking, at exactly 9am Dizzy breezed in on a whirlwind of energy, perfume and laughter.

"Watcha, Muriel!" Her greeting was always warm and accompanied by a genuine smile. "'Ave ya ha yer breakfast yet?"

"Yhess." Muriel smiled and nodded slowly.

"We had porridge today," I added. "Mum ate it all up. I think she was hungry."

"Oh, well done!"

Mum smiled again.

Dizzy crouched and gave each of the dogs an obligatory head pat. Standing up, she turned her attention to Muriel once again. "Come on then, my love, let's be having ya."

Muriel took my arm and we began the slow walk back to her room.

"I see Social Services brought you a present," Dizzy said, pointing to the wheelchair in the corridor.

"Not exactly…" I grimaced and sucked my teeth. "I had to take Mum to the hospital yesterday. She was being assessed for respite. As you know, she struggles with that walking frame. I think it's difficult for her to get the coordination right. Because she was taking so long to walk to the assessment ward, the hospital lent us a wheelchair. Afterwards, a nurse put it in the boot of my car. She gave me a wink and said to bring it back if Social Services ever delivered the proper one."

"That was nice." Dizzy smiled conspiratorially. "Where did you get the ramps from?"

"Those I bought," I admitted. "I doubted we'd ever get the proper ones from the health service, so I found these online."

I was very proud of that purchase. After a day of fruitless phone calls, I'd spent an evening hunting the interweb before finding a specialist UK supplier. We now had two lightweight aluminium wheelchair ramps.

"They're different lengths," I explained, "so they'll be perfect for our steps and they fold away for easy storage. There's even a carrying handle."

"Well, I tink they look great." As we helped Muriel into the bathroom, Dizzy nodded towards the new shower tray I'd just installed. "Them ramps are almost as good as dis walk-in shower. You've done a proper nice job dare. Very professional."

"Thanks." I think I blushed a bit. "We're just trying to make Mum as comfortable as we can."

"You're both doing great." Dizzy patted me on the shoulder.

Once Muriel was safely seated on the shower chair, I stepped away and went back to the kitchen. Lesley's back pain had worsened recently so, whenever possible, I was the one lifting Muriel out of bed, onto the toilet and into the shower. Such situations were unavoidably up close and personal, but for Muriel's sake, I did my best to look away and pretend she wasn't undressed. Once Dizzy had finished with the washing and dressing, she called me through to help manoeuvre Mum into her wheelchair.

"Fanks very much for yer 'elp," she said, giving me a wave. "I'll see ya dis evening."

"Thank you," I replied gratefully.

Dizzy's help made a big difference to our daily routine. Having a professional carer washing and dressing Muriel was better for both Lesley and her mum. Dizzy was definitely someone we could easily have made friends with, but she never had the time to stop and chat – and she never would. As delightful as she was, Dizzy was all business. All of her clients were terminally ill or terminally old. She knew each of her clients were going to pass on in the near future. It was an unavoidable truth. For her own emotional protection, she had to maintain a professional distance.

Every Tuesday and Thursday Muriel went to the Ennis Dementia club from 10 until 3 pm, so as soon as Dizzy left, I took Mum out to the car. On a good day, the trip to Ennis takes 40 minutes. I had no golf lessons booked and we didn't need any shopping, so once I'd helped Muriel into the building and chatted with the nurses, I headed home.

"Much traffic?" Lesley asked, when I arrived back at Glenmadrie. She was in the front garden, attacking the weeds on one of her flowerbeds with a hoe. With Ireland's temperate climate and fertile soil, weeding at Glenmadrie was a never-ending task.

"Not too bad." I nodded stoically. "Except for one impatient lady driver wanting to get past when I was trying to get Mum into her wheelchair."

Lesley clicked her tongue and shook her head sadly. Although most people we encountered were understanding when their passage was slightly delayed by an elderly lady being helped out of a car, there had been a few who had displayed obvious impatience or even outright anger.

"What are you going to do now?" she asked, nodding towards the house.

I checked my watch and my eyes widened in surprise. It was already after 11 am.

"I think I'll hoover up and clean the bathrooms. After lunch, I might squeeze in an hour's writing before I have to head back to collect Mum."

"Okay." Lesley smiled. "I've already cleaned Mum's room and I changed her sheets too."

"Thank you. That's a big help." I gave Lesley a hug and kissed her head. Her hair smelled of shampoo and insect repellent. "Those ladies at the dementia club are a scream," I added. "I think some of them know socially inappropriate behaviour is an expected symptom of the illness and they use it as an excuse to push the boundaries."

My wife raised a suspicious eyebrow.

"Did that lady grope your bum again?" she teased.

"I feel so violated," I joked.

"Don't worry, dear, you'll get used to it." My wife patted me on the arm in mock sympathy. "Given time, you may even grow to like it!"

With a dozen patients being collected from the dementia club at the same time, it took longer than usual to get Muriel into the car. On the return journey, we caught some traffic, got stuck behind a tractor and didn't arrive home until just before 5pm. By the time Lesley had made Muriel's supper and I had fed her, there was just enough time for Lesley and I to eat our meal before Dizzy arrived.

Putting Mum to bed was the reverse of the morning process, but with a flannel wash in place of a shower. Again, I stepped out of the room while Dizzy did her thing. After Dizzy had left, Lesley and I tucked Muriel in for the night, pulled up the cot sides to prevent her from falling out of bed, switched on her nightlight, locked the doors and went back to the main house.

With the dishes washed and put away, we slumped gratefully onto the couch. At last we had some time alone.

"Do you want to watch some television?" I asked, sleepily.

Lesley squinted at the clock and shook her head.

"No. It's after nine. I think I'll go to bed."

I nodded stoically. This was our life now.

"You know we're lucky, don't you?" I mumbled.

Lesley frowned. "What do you mean?"

"I know caring for Mum is hard work and disruptive to our…" I added a heavy hint of irony to my voice, "previously perfect lives–"

Lesley snorted a laugh then sleepily waved a hand, beckoning me to continue.

"But at least Mum sleeps through the night. Dizzy said about half of her clients need to be checked on every half hour, otherwise they'd wander off or do something dangerous."

My wife nodded again.

"I agree. Things could be a lot worse."

Lesley yawned and stretched like a geriatric cat.

"We don't get woken a dozen times every night…" she leaned over and patted my knee. "and you get your bum groped twice a week. That seems like a fair trade."

She had a point.

221

21 – Lost and Confused

Although we were committed to caring for Muriel and putting her needs ahead of ours, life still had to go on, albeit in a substantially truncated fashion. Even though Dizzy came by twice a day, and a different care assistant, the lovely Judy, was available one afternoon a week to housesit, in planning our activities we were always mindful of Muriel's current state of health.

We had been primed by the doctors to expect Mum's mental and physical capacity to degenerate in a series of downward steps, triggered by microscopic brain bleeds, and that certainly happened. In between these events, there might be periods of days or weeks when Muriel's health stabilised or even noticeably improved. These upturns were like distant ship-smoke on the horizon for a desert island castaway, a cruel illusion of a non-existent brighter future. Even so, like pools of sunshine in the darkness of a forest, these temporary improvements in Muriel's health had their memorable moments.

A few months after she arrived, Muriel developed yet another bladder infection. Despite being treated with antibiotics, she quickly became confused and listless. Unable or unwilling to eat or drink, she was soon bedridden and appeared to be slipping into terminal unconsciousness. During the lunchtime break at his surgery, Doctor Mark kindly drove up the hill to Glenmadrie to check on his patient. After his examination, he pulled Lesley and I to one side and shared his verdict in a hushed voice.

"Not long now, I'm afraid," he whispered, his lips white in a tight smile of sympathy.

I pulled my wife into a hug.

The doctor continued, "Without fluids, there isn't any hope…"

Lesley nodded her understanding. "Mum was insistent. She doesn't want a drip or feeding tube."

"I understand," Doctor Mark replied, patting Lesley's arm. "It's all in her notes. We must respect her wishes."

Two days later, Doctor Mark stood open mouthed in surprise when he saw Muriel sitting at the kitchen table, eating her lunch unaided and reading the newspaper.

"Goodness, what a turnaround!" he exclaimed. "If I hadn't

seen it with my own eyes, I wouldn't have believed it possible."
While he was obviously delighted with Muriel's improvement,
as were we, I suspect he felt a little embarrassed too.

Muriel smiled gleefully, gave Doctor Mark a small wave and
mumbled something. With a half-masticated sandwich
interfering with her already slurred speech, it was hard to
decipher what she said, but it may have been "I'm not dead yet!"

***

During one of her remission phases, Muriel was accepted
into a local care home for two weeks' respite. Not wanting to
squander this short period of guaranteed freedom, Lesley
disappeared into the garden and I took the next flight to England.
Any hopes I'd held of spending a week playing golf and visiting
friends were but a dream, Joanne and Mark had moved into their
new home and they wanted me to fit their kitchen.

It was lovely to see my grandson and marvel at how quickly
he was growing, but my kitchen fitting assistant was noticeably
absent.

"Where's Mark?" I asked.

"Ah…" Joanne grimaced. "He's in bed with the 'flu."

"Real 'flu," I frowned suspiciously, "or 'man 'flu'?"

"Oh, it's definitely real." Joanne looked grim. "The poor
baby's been in bed for 36 hours and before that, he spent an
entire afternoon in the toilet."

"Eek!" It was my turn to grimace. "I guess I'll be fitting the
kitchen on my own…"

She patted my arm. "Don't worry. I'm sure he'll be up and
about soon."

"Let's hope so," I said, rolling my eyes skywards. "While
we're waiting for Lazarus to rise, perhaps you can help me to
assemble some of these units?"

"I'd love to!" Joanne nodded enthusiastically. "I can't wait to
see what they look like. It's been months since we've had a
proper kitchen."

Their builder had done a fine job changing the layout of the
ground floor to something more appropriate for a young family.
The old dining room had been sacrificed – knocked through to
provide space for a downstairs toilet, a much bigger kitchen and
a family room opening into a large conservatory. Although the

builder had finished his work, there was still a lot of decorating to be done and flooring to lay before the renovation could be declared a success. And that was just the inside. Mark and Joanne hadn't even begun work on their garden, which, despite my efforts to clean up during my last visit, looked more like a building site than ever. It had even acquired another skip.

Unlike the clutter and jumble in other parts of the house, the kitchen was just a large empty space smelling of plasterboard and fresh paint.

"It looks like we've got square corners and perpendicular walls to work with," I observed happily. "Perfect for fitting kitchens!"

Joanne frowned in confusion, so I explained.

"If the walls are out of true, or the corners aren't square, it's a bugger to get the units to line up properly – or at all."

She nodded. "Good to know. I guess you learned a lot doing your kitchen."

I grimaced and rubbed my ear doubtfully. "We'll see…"

Joanne laughed.

The flatpacks containing all 28 kitchen units were piled behind the couch in the sitting room and mixed in with dozens of almost identical boxes containing doors, draws and various other kitchen unit accessories. Our first task, which would take a couple of days, was to identify and assemble all of the carcases, then stack them in the centre of the kitchen ready for fitting. Assuming Mark recovered in time (or at all), he and I would spend the next three days installing and levelling the units, before adding the doors, draws, handles, pelmets, worktops and kickboards.

While Joanne and I worked, she quizzed me about Muriel and how Lesley and I were coping with being fulltime carers.

"I won't lie to you, sometimes it's been tough. Apart from the obvious disruption to our lives and the loss of freedom, it's–" I paused while searching for the right word, "it's unpleasant, watching someone gradually degenerate, both physically and mentally."

"I imagine it would be," Joanne said, her voice tinged with sadness.

I nodded. "More so for your mum. She'd appreciate a visit from you."

My daughter's mouth tightened. For a moment she chewed pensively on her lip.

"Video chatting and phone calls are great, but not the same as face-to-face," I added. "I know it would be difficult for you to come over while all this building work is going on, especially now you've got a baby."

"And expensive," Joanne added. "It'd be better if Mum could pop over here for a couple of days."

She had a point, but there was something else on my mind.

"Perhaps you could fly over on your own," I suggested. "Just for the weekend."

"Would Muriel even recognise me now?" Joanne asked, her voice no louder than a whisper.

"Probably not," I conceded. "I don't think she knows who we are any more. Muriel spends most of her days asleep, or sitting on her chair in the sitting room glaring at anyone who walks past. Even the dogs are getting uncomfortable around her, especially Jack. I guess he's the most sensitive of the dogs, perhaps he senses her confusion."

When Joanne didn't reply, I tried a different tack.

"It would be a chance to see Muriel one last time."

For a couple of minutes, my daughter worked quietly screwing a kitchen unit together. The tip of her tongue poked between her lips as she concentrated. When she finally spoke, her eyes were wet with tears and her voice trembled with emotion.

"I've already said goodbye and seen her for the last time." She nodded slowly, as if confirming a thought to herself. "I want to remember her how she was. That smile. Her kindness. The hugs."

I reached out and Joanne fell into my arms. We stood in silence as she sobbed into my collar. My daughter was very close to her grandmother. I understood the conflict she was experiencing and her wish to protect and preserve her happy memories of someone she loved. She was in pain and didn't want to make it unnecessarily worse. It was her decision to make, not mine. I understood and supported her choice and told her so.

As she dried her eyes on my handkerchief, I added an afterthought. "In your place, I'd probably do the same thing. It

226

was hard to see my father when he could no longer talk and didn't recognise me. That's a memory I wish I didn't have."

Joanne squeezed my arm and gave me a tight smile. "Thank you."

I nodded. "And I will try to get your mum over for a few days. Goodness knows, she could do with a break."

That evening, although still rather pale and clammy, Mark felt well enough to join us for supper. By the morning he was like a new man, raring to crack on with fitting the units.

With the aid of an impressive 3D rendition of the finished kitchen he'd made on his laptop, we worked out where everything belonged and began attaching the still bare carcases to the walls and each other. There was a good bit of adjusting, jigging and poking to get everything straight and level, but gradually the kitchen came together. While we worked, Mark asked me how my book was coming along.

"Which one?" I asked.

"There's more than one?"

"You have to keep up, Mark!" I quipped. "I've almost finished writing my third book. That's why I brought my laptop with me. I wanted to do some editing in the evenings and at the airport while I'm waiting for my flight."

"Good plan." He pointed at my face. "Are the new glasses because of old age, or eyestrain from all that squinting at a computer screen?"

"A bit of both!" I laughed.

"Is the new book about Ireland too?"

"No." I shook my head and grinned excitedly. "This one's a thriller!"

"A thriller?" Mark's eyebrows shot up, indicating his genuine interest. "I like reading thrillers. What's it about?"

"Well, I haven't finished polishing the marketing spiel yet…" I frowned and rubbed my nose with the palm of my hand. "It's tough to summarise a story without giving away the plot."

"I can keep a secret." Mark gave me a beckoning wave and a conspiratorial wink. "Have a go!"

"Okay. It's about a regular sort of guy called Eric Stone, who discovers his friend's apparent suicide was engineered by the British government, using a secret fixer organisation called the Wrecking Crew. Stone joins forces with a former police officer and together they try to track the bad guys down and bring them to justice. Somewhere along the way, the Wrecking Crew find out they are being investigated and the hunters become the hunted. From there on, it's a hectic chase to a climatic finish. It's taken ages to write because of all the research I've had to do. There's loads of computer stuff and hacking in it. I even took a course on lockpicking so I'd have my facts straight for one particular scene."

"Sounds intriguing," Mark said. His face showed genuine interest. "I'd love to read it."

I smiled and nodded my gratitude. "I'll make sure you get one of the first copies."

"That'd be great. How's your golf?"

"Ha!" I snorted an ironic laugh. "Since Muriel came, my golf teaching business has dwindled to almost nothing and I haven't really had the chance to play myself. Of course it's not her fault, but the time restraints and responsibilities of being a carer means it's very hard to make myself available. Obviously, the economic crash in Ireland hasn't helped much. Paying the mortgage and feeding the kids ranks way above golf lessons for most people. Anyway, I've had very few enquiries for lessons and when someone did call, most of the time, I wasn't able to fit them in. I don't like things being up in the air like that so, for now, I've cancelled all the advertising and closed my website."

"Will you go back to teaching…" Mark paused as he struggled to find the appropriate word. "After?"

I chewed my lip and sighed doubtfully. "We'll see. For now, I'll just play for fun and relaxation, when and as I can."

"And how's that working out?"

"Not well," I admitted stoically. "I love golf but, although it's important to me, it's hardly a priority just now. Muriel and Lesley's needs come first. Anyway…" I smiled triumphantly. "I now have my own practice ground at home, so there's hardly any need for me to go out!"

"A practice ground?" Mark's eyes widened. "Have you cut all the grass on your land?"

"Yep." I nodded proudly. "Except for some areas we've deliberately left wild, I've cleared around four acres, A few months ago, I sold that huge unwieldy lawnmower and bought a proper ride-on lawn tractor. It's an American model. Small enough to fit in my shed, but big enough to make short work of cutting large areas of grass. On a good day, I can cut all four meadows in around two hours."

"That must be fun," Mark said, grinning with boyish glee.

"Oh, it is," I replied. "For about five minutes! Going endlessly around and around is quite cathartic, but rather boring. On the other hand, this model doesn't have any brakes, so going down the hills can be quite exciting."

"No brakes?" Mark frowned. "That doesn't sound right."

"That's what I said, but the guy at the shop told me it's quite common on these American models. I guess they're designed with flatter ground in mind. Second-hand, it cost as much as Lesley's car, so it's a good model. It was fully serviced and guaranteed."

"I guess that makes it okay." Mark shrugged, still unconvinced. "How do you stop without brakes?"

"Ah!" I held up a finger. "Think ahead, engage a low gear and pray!"

He laughed.

"On the upside," I continued. "I've had some of my best writing ideas whilst cutting the grass and now I've got enough space to hit golf balls whenever the mood takes me."

Throughout the week the kitchen fitting progressed pretty much according to the plan Mark and I had worked out. Although I was confident the job would be finished by the end of my visit, Joanne thought otherwise. With a new baby to look after whilst she was trying to start her own wedding makeup and hair business, the prospect of being left with an incomplete kitchen was too much to bear. There was some shouting, a few tears and the slamming of several doors, before she disappeared into the sitting room. I waited for five minutes then cautiously peered around the door. Joanne was sitting on the couch, staring blankly at the television, her arms tightly folded as if trying to hold in her anger.

"I've made you a cup of tea," I said, softly.

She took my offering without comment. I waited while she sipped the calming brew. It's difficult to remain angry once the caffeine hits the brain.

"I'm sorry," she whispered. "I shouldn't have got so cross. You've come especially to help and all I've done is shout at you.

It was ungrateful of me."

"It's okay. I'm used to it. You're just like your mother."

She snorted at my ironic joke.

I smiled gently. "I know the kitchen looks rather messy just now, but we're making good progress. It'll be finished long before I leave."

"I know..." She nodded, as if to herself. "David can be rather a handful... What with the house being such a mess..."

For a minute she stared into her cup, seemingly lost in thought. I waited.

"I guess I'm upset about Muriel's illness too. Probably more than anything."

I sat on the arm of the couch and put my arm around her shoulder. Unable to think of anything else to say, I pulled my daughter into a fatherly hug. It seemed to do the trick.

***

Back at Glenmadrie, Lesley got on with the gardening and I cracked on with my to-do list of chores. No rest for the wicked, or so they say.

My first task was to visit the local tip. We don't have access to a rubbish collection service, so every couple of months one of us has to load the car and head to the recycling centre in Scariff. Once the car was empty, I decided to make a social call.

Although there were still nine days left before Muriel was due to end her respite, the care home was just around the corner, so I thought it would be nice to pop in and say hello.

The secretary at the reception desk greeted me with a warm smile.

"Goodness, that was quick," she exclaimed. "I've only just phoned."

"Excuse me?" I asked in obvious confusion.

"You're Muriel's son-in-law aren't you?" she replied. "I presume you've come to take her home."

As if to confirm her point, just then a nurse wheeled mum along the corridor in her wheelchair. Muriel was wearing her coat and clutching her small suitcase to her chest.

"But, but she's not due home for another nine days," I said.

The secretary leaned forward and whispered. "I'm afraid Muriel is refusing to eat. We've had a dreadful time with her."

She lowered her voice further. "You see, this is a care facility, not a hospital. If she won't eat, she can't stay here. I was just explaining to your wife on the phone, that's why I thought you'd come to pick her up."

"I only came to say hello," I explained.

"Well, you're here now…"

"So much for our respite," I thought.

Of course they were right. If Muriel was refusing to eat, it would be wrong to leave her at the care home. Half an hour after we returned to Glenmadrie, I watched her hungrily tucking into her lunch. It was a sight both reassuring and frustrating.

"I guess Mum was uncomfortable eating in unfamiliar surroundings," I suggested, once Muriel had gone for her afternoon nap.

"It's nice she thinks of this as her home now," Lesley replied.

"I'm sorry the respite ended so abruptly."

Lesley shrugged stoically. "Can't be helped."

After five days away, and with the sun shining, my next task was to cut the grass. As I droned around in ever decreasing circles, I had a chance to enjoy the scenery and let my mind wonder. Like the butterflies, flitting on the gentle breeze over the wildflowers, my thoughts drifted aimlessly.

On my final day in England, with the kitchen finished, Joanne treated me to lunch at a local pub. As it was a warm and sunny day, we joined a group of her friends sitting on the grass in the beer garden. Protected from the busy road and the pub's septic tank by a stout fence, the children could run and play, whilst we ate our sandwiches and chatted amicably. Largely excluded from the conversation by virtue of age, gender and not being able to hear over the roar of the traffic, I was content to eat my meal and watch the cars crash into each other. Because of a new road layout on what was already a dangerous roundabout, there were three accidents in the space of an hour. In the aftermath, the road rage and shouting quickly lead to colourful language and threats of violence. In one case, the police had to intervene. It was all terribly exciting.

Looking back, I realised I knew most of the mums from when they were Joanne's friends at school. Now they were all grown up, with children of their own and sitting alongside was my daughter, well into her 30s and with a child of her own. In one of those ah-ha moments, it suddenly occurred to me that Joanne was no longer the little girl I pictured whenever I heard her name, but a mother in her own right. That revelation both warmed and chilled me in equal measure, but in a good way. She was older and wiser. I too was older, but not necessarily wiser.

And so my butterfly brain flitted on, seeking another thought to examine.

Why didn't my mower have brakes? Admittedly the machine didn't have a brake pedal, but short of throwing out an anchor on a chain, there was no way to stop in an emergency. Americans are reputed to be very litigious people, so it seems odd a garden vehicle would be manufactured there without giving thought to stopping should the need present itself. Perhaps later, I'd ask Google.

And another thing. That morning I'd taken the dogs along one of my favourite looped walks and become surprisingly lost and confused. The paths I'd cut now went deep into the forest, providing about a dozen interlocking routes of various lengths and difficulty, depending on how energetic I was feeling. Regardless of which path I was taking, I habitually entered the forest at the northern extremity and exited in the south. On this particular morning, with the field to the north occupied with a dozen cattle and their new-born calves, I decided to enter and exit the forest from the south. Cattle with calves can be wary and aggressive, particularly when confronted by dogs, even if they are on a lead. Better to be safe than sorry.

My plan was to walk my usual route, but in reverse, make a circle using three intersecting shorter paths at the north end of the forest and return home the way we came in. However, even though I had walked this particular path hundreds of times, I quickly became disoriented and several times lost track of the path completely. By travelling in the opposite direction, the visual indicators previously so recognisable to my eye, were now jumbled, out of place, or invisible. After just a dozen paces in the wrong direction, I became lost and unable to reacquire the path. The dogs had disappeared and suddenly my friendly and familiar forest had become a confusing wall of seemingly identical trees. I began to feel stressed and a little apprehensive. Then it hit me. Is this what dementia feels like? When Muriel had a breakdown in her shop after they'd moved some of the products, was this what she was feeling? At the time Lesley was confused as to why someone swapping the bread aisle with the breakfast cereals would cause her mother such distress, but now I understood. Just like me in the forest, with those subliminal signposts removed, Muriel couldn't find the correct path. She too was lost and confused.

"Our lawnmower now has brakes!" I declared, wiping my dirty hands on the legs of my purple overalls.

"That's nice," Lesley mumbled, somewhat unconvincingly.

My wife was sitting at the kitchen table shelling peas into a Pyrex bowl. Kia and Lady were sitting alongside the table, expectantly waiting in the hope of being fed a deliciously fresh pea. Amber is a less patient dog. She had already pinched an empty pea pod from the green waste bin beside Lesley's chair and was happily transforming it into a blob of fibrous green pulp.

"Where's Jack?" I asked.

"Sunning himself in the courtyard," she replied.

I peered into the sitting room. Muriel's chair was empty.

"Is your mum in bed?"

Lesley nodded. I dipped into the bowl to grab a few peas, but quickly whipped my hand away to avoid a slap.

"Hey!"

"Wash your hands!" Lesley chided, in a singsong voice.

I went to the kitchen sink and ran some water.

"So you've fixed the brakes?" she asked.

"Yes," I replied, proudly.

"But I thought the guy at the shop said that model didn't have brakes?"

"He lied," I chuckled. "Looked me in the eye and lied."

"Why would he do that?"

"I don't think there was any ill will intended," I observed. "It's not like when we bought that car. I'd already paid for the mower. It was only after it was delivered and he was showing me how it worked that I asked about the brakes. He probably didn't know the answer and was too embarrassed to admit it."

"But you've fixed it now?"

"Yep!" I grinned and thrust out my chest.

Lesley silently continued shelling peas. Perhaps she knew I was fishing for compliments, or maybe Craftsman lawnmower brakes were genuinely beyond her sphere of interest. Undaunted, I pressed on.

"You see, normally brakes are positioned on the wheel hubs, but this mower has a brake inboard, on the rear axle. The mechanism is tiny and it was totally covered with dirt and rust, which is why I didn't notice it before – and why it wasn't working. Once I'd stripped and cleaned all the parts, it worked fine. It made such a difference cutting those slopes, now I can stop."

Lesley nodded to herself. Clearly my fishing attempts were to remain unrewarded.

"By the way," I continued. "The top meadow looks like a bomb site, or it did, before I repaired it."

This got her attention.

"What do you mean?"

"The top meadow was full of holes," I replied. "It looked like a polo field on a wet day. I had to refill the holes and replace the upturned turf.

She snorted dismissively. "That'll be Amber, digging for chafers."

Our little dog had a particular liking for the juicy grubs of the chafer beetles. Amber would frequently disappear for hours, happily rooting in the grass for these tasty treats. Oblivious to our calls, she would dig dozens of holes in the lawn and only return when her belly was full or her nose became sore from being repeatedly thrust into the ground. But Amber's trademark lawn holes were quite small and directly proportionate to the size of her snout. The damage I had seen was on an entirely different scale.

"I don't think so," I replied. "These holes were bigger than Amber. I think it was badgers."

"Badgers?" Lesley exclaimed, excitedly. "Oh how wonderful. I love badgers."

"Me too. I've seen them wandering along the road at night, but never on our land." I rubbed my hands together in glee. "There must be a set nearby. I'll try to find it."

"Well, we'd better keep quiet if you do," she said, her face suddenly serious.

"Why?"

"A lot of farmers believe badgers cause tuberculosis in cattle. If they hear there's a badger set, they may kill them."

"Oh…" I touched a finger to my lips. "We'll keep it our secret then."

That was a good day.

***

"Has Pat gone?" I asked. The district nurse had popped in earlier to check on Muriel.

"Just now," Lesley replied. "I asked if she wanted to come into the kitchen for a coffee, but she's got a lot of work on and had to rush off."

I gestured my chin towards Muriel's room. "How did it go?"

"As well as can be expected." Lesley shrugged noncommittally. "Pat wants Mum to go over to Limerick hospital A&E. She's given me a letter."

"Is it because of this persistent bladder infection?" I guessed. My wife nodded.

I sighed. "What time have I got to have her there?"

"For once, you're off the hook," Lesley smiled. "She's arranged for an ambulance. Because it isn't an emergency, they probably won't be here until this afternoon. I'll follow in the car so she can get back a bit quicker, assuming they don't keep her in."

"You sure you don't want me to go?"

"It's fine." My wife dismissed my offer with a casual wave. "You can get on with whatever it is you're doing with your book."

"No need," I grinned proudly. "It's all done. Wrecking Crew has officially been on sale since yesterday. I checked earlier and we've already sold 100 copies."

"Oh great! Now we'll be able to afford a meal out to celebrate your birthday."

"Ha! Fat chance." I'd laughed, because I suspected Lesley was only joking. Our busy schedule left little time for such frivolity, even if I was about to turn 56.

"O ye of little faith!" Lesley smirked and wagged her finger. "I've asked Judy to do an extra day. She's coming at 11am and she can stay until 4pm. So we'll have plenty of time for a nice meal. Perhaps we can even stop off at a garden centre on the way back."

"Ah…" I gave my wife a stiff smile. "Visiting a garden centre for my birthday treat. How exciting!"

"Carry on like that," she teased, "and you'll be the one in the ambulance."

As luck would have it, the ambulance driver called a short while later. Unsurprisingly, they were unable to find the house and had phoned me for directions from, of all places, the local graveyard. Fortunately, they followed my instructions to the letter and arrived at Glenmadrie ten minutes later.

"Blimey!" I exclaimed, as the driver climbed down from his cab. He was hefting a huge green bag of medical supplies. "I was expecting one of those hospital minibuses, not a proper ambulance."

"We were in the area, so it made sense for us to take the call." The driver was a ruggedly handsome Irish lad. Probably aged around 30 and well over six feet tall, he had thick black hair, dark eyes and the healthy complexion of an athlete. I correctly guessed he was a keen participant of Ireland's national sport of hurling. Short, tubby and with bright ginger hair, his workmate was the opposite in almost every way.

"I'm Patrick and this is Liam," the paramedic said, pointing a thumb over his shoulder at the smaller man.

"Thanks for coming," I replied.

"We're here for your mother?" Liam asked.

"Mother-in-law," I corrected. "She's got a bladder infection, so the district nurse wants her to be seen at Limerick A&E."

Liam nodded towards the house. "Okay. Let's be having her."

"She's in the kitchen, with my wife." I led the way through the porch and conservatory. As always, whenever we had guests, as I ducked through the low doorway into the kitchen, I called over my shoulder, "Mind your head."

Liam was close on my heels and being shorter than me, he didn't need to duck. But Patrick was much taller...

There was a sickening thud, like a wet hand slapping a cow on the bum. This was followed by a groaned expletive and the sound of someone very tall and muscular falling flat onto his back.

"Oh no!" Lesley squealed, her hand covering her mouth.

Liam and I exchanged a wide-eyed grimace. Slowly I turned to look for Patrick, but all we could see was the soles of his size 12 boots.

"Oh crap!" I exclaimed, rushing forward to offer assistance.

Whereas most people who have misjudged the now infamous

low doorway into our kitchen, would graze their heads, being tall and inattentive, Patrick had walked face first into the lintel. Weighed down by his green bag, the poor lad was squirming on the tiled floor like an upended turtle, whilst trying to nurse his split chin and bloody nose. I was about to attempt some first aid, when I recalled there was another qualified paramedic on hand. However, when I looked to Liam for help, I was shocked to find him kneeling on the kitchen floor and twitching uncontrollably. For a moment, I thought he was having some sort of a seizure, but I soon realised he was actually doubled over with laughter.

"Oow, feck that's funny!" he exclaimed, wiping the tears from his eyes.

"Eck off ye ginger twat!" Patrick groaned. "I'b boken me dose."

At this, Liam gripped his aching sides and howled with laughter. Clearly, we were honoured to be witnessing some ambulance humour.

Eventually, Liam recovered enough composure to offer his mate some assistance. With the blood flow staunched, Patrick was able to proceed with the job at hand. In an efficient five minutes, the two lads took Muriel's temperature, blood pressure, checked her heart, blood sugar and made a cognitive assessment. As Liam was putting their kit away, Patrick gestured for me to follow him into the conservatory. I noticed he ducked so low as he passed through the kitchen door, he almost hit his chin on his knees.

"Here's the thing," Patrick whispered as he leaned closer. "We've just been to Limerick A&E. It's absolutely packed and there were 30 people waiting on trollies for admission. Muriel isn't very well. She's certainly far too frail to be hanging about in a corridor for a day or so. That's no way to treat an old lady."

"Oh dear," I replied. "What would you suggest?"

Patrick chewed his lip and sighed.

"It's not for me to say, but there's a medical assessment unit at Ennis hospital..." He left the thought hanging.

"Can you take her there?"

Patrick shook his head. "We're Limerick only, but you could take her."

"Is that allowed?" I asked.

He did that so-so hand gesture.

"Although you have a letter from the district nurse, it doesn't specifically mention Limerick." He winked conspiratorially. "If anyone asks, just look blank and confused."

"Oh, I'm really good at blank and confused," I laughed. "It's my natural expression!"

So we waved the kindly paramedics on their way and I took Muriel to the medical assessment unit at Ennis hospital. We had to wait almost 15 minutes before seeing a doctor, which was a considerable improvement on the likely two day wait had Muriel gone to Limerick. He was quick, efficient and polite, despite looking exhausted and overworked. Clearly the Irish health system was creaking at the seams under the strain of the budget cuts it had suffered during the financial crash.

After a comprehensive examination, which Muriel didn't enjoy or understand, she was diagnosed with a persistent urinary infection, given some stronger antibiotics and sent home. Before we left, the doctor pulled me to one side for a chat. In a quiet and kindly voice, he told me what was ahead for Muriel and checked we were getting all of the available support. Although he didn't tell me anything about her condition and prognosis I didn't already know or suspect, I was immensely grateful he'd taken the time from his franticly busy day to have that little chat. Yet again, I was in awe of the professionalism and quiet determination of the Irish healthcare staff. All in all, it was a good day.

***

The following Monday was another good day.

It was a gloriously sunny and warm morning, so I took the dogs across the moor for a good hike. Today we followed one of my favourite routes. Departing the road a few hundred yards below the house, we climbed over a dry stone wall and set out across a wide grassy plane, heading for the distant cliffs. Thousands of years ago, this area was covered in a thick layer of ice. As the glaciers gradually retreated, they left behind bare limestone dotted with huge boulders, scattered like discarded toys on a child's bedroom floor. Over time thick moss formed on the rock. When it died, new growth formed, compressing the old moss into rich peat. This process continued year on year until the peat was several feet deep. This flat plane may once have been a lake, but now the water was hidden under a floating mattress of grass and moss. As I walked, the unstable surface shifted beneath my feet. Fair warning that, for all its desolate beauty, the moor was a harsh and dangerous place which demanded respect and care.

To make any progress across the deep moss and long grass, I had to high-step each foot, as if I was a soldier on parade, comically trudging through thick snow. Soon my thighs were burning and cool rivulets of sweat were running down my back. After 30 minutes of hard walking, we reached the cliffs. This series of six 100-foot tall sheer limestone rock faces were interspaced with steeply sloped grass embankments. Here I paused for a moment to slow my breathing, rest my legs and wait for the dogs to catch up.

With his bad hips playing up, Jack had wisely stayed behind, but Lady and Kia were happily bounding around, sniffing for hare and disturbing the many moorland birds. Being much shorter in stature and the oldest dog by a couple of years, little Amber was bringing up the rear. I watched her progress and shouted encouragement, whenever she looked up. Wise beyond her years, or perhaps too small to make progress in any other way, Amber was following the path I'd just created by flattening the long grass with my size ten wellington boots.

Once I'd rounded up my unruly pack of pooches, I led them up the hill to the top of the cliff. On the steeply sloping grass bank, their natural four-wheel drive gave the dogs a distinct advantage and I felt no shame in copying their technique. On my hands and knees, I dug my toes into the soft soil and clutched handfuls of grass as I pulled myself up. From experience, I knew the view was spectacular, but not one to be enjoyed until I was standing safely on flat ground.

As was sometimes the case, as we reached the top, a herd of feral goats appeared from behind the only line of bushes on this section of the moor. There was a large buck with magnificent horns, perhaps ten does and six tiny kids. Despite my frantic shouts, the dogs immediately gave chase, but I need not have worried. This dance was old and well-practised. With the handsome buck in the lead, the goats casually trotted to what they considered a place of safety, perching precariously on the seemingly sheer rockface. Such dexterity, particularly in an animal which seems visually unsuited for rock climbing, always made me smile.

"Perhaps next," I thought, "pigs really will fly!"

The dogs expended a little excess energy by woofing and peering quizzically over the cliff edge, but they soon lost interest and reluctantly followed me as I headed home. Our route back was considerably easier walking, as we had linked up with what was once a busy hiking trail. Since the recession, funding cuts had closed the path to visitors, but even without maintenance, it was still less effort than hiking through the thick grass. Once we reached the bottom of the hill, where the land flattened out, Amber bounded ahead, disappearing behind some bushes around a bend in the path. I had no fear she would race into the road as the little dog knew the routine well. Up ahead was a rock the size of an ancient throne and sitting in the scalloped centre was Amber, looking rather regal – even with her muddy paws – as she waited for me to attach her lead.

After lunch, I took Muriel for a drive. Although she would only look out of the window and occasionally nod or smile, such trips had become a frequent part of our routine. On this day I drove high into the Slieve Aughty mountains and out towards Lough Atorick. At the highpoint of the road, I stopped the car and backed into a layby. This was one of my favourite spots, where we had a magnificent view down the forested valley floor and all the way to the distant windfarm behind the town of Gort.

"Isn't this beautiful?" I said, gesturing towards the windscreen and the wonderful vista below.

Muriel mumbled something unintelligible and nodded, even though she was looking through the side window and could only see the trees a few yards away. Although she wasn't really taking it all in, at least Mum was still able to come out for these little trips. I subliminally shrugged my acceptance and hoped she was enjoying herself in some way. Surely it must be better than sitting indoors and staring blankly at the television.

"You were a long time," Lesley said as she helped her mother through the door. "I thought you'd got lost."

Muriel snorted a laugh, or perhaps it was a cough.

"Actually, we did," I smiled and added an embarrassed grimace for good measure.

"Not another of your shortcuts?"

I rolled my eyes. "That was one time and it was years ago!"

"So how did you get lost this time?" she asked, once Muriel was seated at the kitchen table and happily munching her sandwich.

"After we left Lough Atorick, I decided to take a trip to Lough Derg before heading home. There was this little side road with a sign pointing in approximately the right direction, so I took it."

"And you got lost?" My wife delivered the line with a 'told you so' sing-song quality.

"We weren't lost," I replied defensively, before adding my worst/best Irish accent, "I was just fierce confused for a while!"

Lesley laughed and I saw Muriel smirk.

"Well, at least you got home safely."

"It was touch and go for a while," I admitted. "Especially when we ran out of road at one point. This lane I was following just ended. There was nowhere to turn around, so I had to reverse for about a kilometre. It was all very exciting. Eventually, like a cork from a bottle, we popped out onto the main road somewhere between Loughrea and Gort."

"Good grief!" my wife exclaimed. "That's miles away!"

I shrugged again. Lesley leaned close and whispered.

"Did Mum enjoy herself?"

I smiled.

"She slept well."

Although Muriel's speech had become no more than unintelligible mumbles and we suspected she had little comprehension of events surrounding her, occasionally we saw flashes of the bright, affectionate and funny person she once was. One particularly memorable event occurred later that evening.

Dizzy and I were helping Muriel to her toilet before her bed time. We were both old hands at this routine and, perhaps to disassociate everyone from the unpleasantness of the situation, frequently talked of other things than the task at hand. I was facing Muriel in a gentle hug to keep her upright, whilst Dizzy was around the back wiping and cleaning. I forget what we were discussing, but Dizzy finished her story with one of her raucously lewd laughs. Suddenly Muriel, who was never known to be a mimic, interjected with a perfect impersonation of the same laugh. There was a moment of genuinely stunned silence whilst Dizzy and I shared a wide-eyed look, then we both burst out laughing.

"Well done, Mum," I exclaimed. "Well done!"

That was another good day.

***

On the morning of my 56th birthday, I rose early, fed the chickens and woke Lesley. Although we'd long since skipped birthday cards and gifts on such occasions, Lesley had promised we'd go out for a meal together, so time was tight to get everything organised before Judy arrived. As soon as I'd finished eating my breakfast, Lesley nodded to the kitchen clock.

"We'd better get moving," she said. "If you can take the dogs for a walk, I'll get Mum up and fed while you're out."

"Okay," I replied. "We'll head down to the river. I'll try to tire them out, so they won't hassle Judy too much."

"Fat chance!" Lesley snorted a laugh. "They always get excited when she's here."

With a little encouragement, I managed to get Jack to join our walk. Although Oliver had a feline dislike of traffic, whenever our hikes began at the rear of the house, safely away from the road, our little cat liked to join in. Today he was leading the way, trotting along with his tail held high like a flagbearer guiding a marching band. It was another lovely day. Pleasantly warm with clear blue skies.

"Perfect golfing weather," I mumbled to myself with heavy irony. I hadn't played for months and was unlikely to do so for a while yet.

We'd covered no more than a kilometre when my mobile phone began playing a merry tune. The caller display told me it was Lesley. I frowned and tapped the answer button.

"Do you miss me already?" I joked.

"Come back immediately." Her voice was breathless and serious.

"What's the matter?"

"Mum's collapsed. She's unconscious."

That was a bad day.

It probably took me 20 minutes to corral the dogs and jog back to the house. I found Lesley in Muriel's room. She was sitting on the bedroom floor, cradling her mother's head in her lap.

"What happened?" I asked, breathlessly.

"I was helping her out of bed," Lesley replied, her voice cracking with emotion. "She just collapsed."

I gently took Mum's hand and checked her pulse. I'm no expert, but to me it felt fast and irregular. Her skin was tinged blue and deathly cold to the touch.

"I think she's coming around," I said, hopefully. "Perhaps she just fainted."

Lesley bit her lip and shook her head. She was right to doubt my forced positivity. Although her mother opened her eyes, her uncomprehending expression and slightly lopsided mouth squashed any hope this was just a fainting event.

"This floor is cold," Lesley noted. "We'll have to move her."

"Okay. I'll lift her onto the bed, then I think we'd better call an ambulance."

Over the months, I'd had a lot of experience lifting Muriel on and off her bed, but moving a semiconscious person from the floor was a different matter. Even with Lesley's help, my eyes bulged with the effort and a couple of the stiffer joints in my back popped loudly to indicate their displeasure. With Muriel comfortably positioned on the bed and covered in a warming blanket, we took a moment to check her over. There were no obvious signs of injury, but her level of consciousness hadn't improved. At best, she was only able to grunt and groan.

"She went down quite softly," Lesley commented. "I just couldn't hold her."

"You did your best and you probably saved her from breaking a hip or something," I replied. "Can you stay with her while I call for an ambulance?"

My wife nodded, her face grim with concern.

This time the ambulance found the house without the need for directions. Nobody hit their chin on the low lintel above the kitchen door and we didn't have a laugh. After a thorough examination, Muriel was strapped onto a trolley and carefully taken out to the ambulance. This time they went directly to

Limerick University Hospital Accident and Emergency department. Lesley packed a bag for her mum and set off in her car 20 minutes later. I offered to come along, but she thought otherwise.

"Stay here," she pleaded. "At least I'll know the dogs are being looked after."

"Okay." I pulled my wife into a quick hug. "Take care."

It was late in the evening when Lesley arrived home. As Muriel had been admitted and taken up to the stroke ward, there was nothing more my wife could do – at least for now. Once I'd made Lesley a cup of coffee and popped her supper in the microwave to reheat, she slumped exhausted onto the couch.

"Did you remember to call Dizzy?" she asked, idly stroking Oliver who was purring and turning circles on her lap.

"Yep," I nodded. "I telephoned Judy too."

"Judy!" Lesley slapped her forehead with such force, the little cat took fright and jumped down. "I forgot, it's your birthday. Oh, I'm sorry."

"Tsk!" I waved her worries away. "Don't fuss about my birthday. Muriel comes first. How is she?"

"Not good." Lesley closed her eyes and pinched the bridge of her nose. "The doctor thinks she's had a stroke, or one of those TIAs. He said it's another step down in her condition. Perhaps the last." Eyes wet with tears, she chewed her lip. "Mum woke a little, but she can't speak and she certainly didn't recognise me."

"Did they do a scan or anything?"

"Not that I'm aware of," my wife said, shaking her head. "I don't think they will. There's nothing they can do really, beyond keeping her comfortable. They took some blood and did the usual pulse, heart tracing and so on, but nothing else. Anyway, putting her through a bunch of X-rays and MRI scans is only going to upset her."

"So they're keeping her in for a while?"

"For now." Lesley nodded. "Once she's stabilised, I think the plan is to move her to the Geriatric ward at Ennis."

"The district nurse phoned," I said. "She'd heard what had happened."

"Crikey, she's on the ball!!. What did she say?"

"It seems nothing gets past Pat." I smiled. "She sent her best wishes and told me to tell you there's a space waiting for Muriel at the respite home, as soon as she's out of hospital."

My wife smiled at the good news and Pat's kindness. It was a bright moment in an otherwise dark day.

"That's so nice of her," she sighed.

***

Lesley visited her mother every day, sometimes twice, which was both upsetting and tiring. The hospital was on the far side of Limerick, necessitating a 40 minute drive through quiet and picturesque countryside, followed by half an hour of hectically busy city traffic and a desperate search for parking. At that time the hospital appeared to be overcrowded, underfunded and operating on the ragged edge. It seemed the austerity cuts to the health service were taking a heavy toll, particularly at the larger hospitals. On the fourth day, my wife came home visibly upset by what she'd seen.

"I'm sure the staff are doing their best, but this can't go on," she growled, throwing her handbag and car keys onto the kitchen table.

"What do you mean?" I asked, holding out a calming cup of coffee. I'd put the kettle on as soon as the dogs had informed me her car was approaching the gate.

"That place is overwhelmed. They obviously haven't got enough staff. Mum's nappy had leaked and her sheets were wet and soiled. I suspect they'd been like that all day." She sipped her drink and sighed. Her anger barely contained. "Before I arrived, the catering staff had left her lunch on the bedside tray but, because there was nobody to feed her, it was still sitting there, cold and congealed. Best as I could tell, she hadn't even had a drink. I had to change her sheets myself and then buy some sandwiches from the shop opposite the hospital. I even fed the old lady in the bed opposite."

"Oh, how awful," I replied. "Perhaps we should just go and get her?"

Lesley shook her head. "I almost brought her home with me, but she needs the medical attention. They've got her on a drip and intravenous antibiotics for a bladder infection."

I leaned in and patted her hand. "Whatever you think is best."

"It's not the fault of the staff," she continued, "I'm sure

245

they're doing their utmost. I talked with one of the nurses. She said, because of these budget cuts, there's been a complete ban on recruitment. On paper it might seem like a workable solution to cut costs but, in practice it's been a disaster. Although most of the managers and admin staff have stayed, a fair number of doctors and nurses have left without being replaced. The poor girl I spoke with was visibly exhausted. She was busily updating a huge pile of charts, whilst trying to eat her lunch."

"It sounds dreadful. Almost like a third world country."

"Sadly, it felt that way too."

"Did Muriel eat much?" I asked, conscious she had previously been reluctant to eat when anyone but me was feeding her.

"I made sure she drank plenty. Her mouth was really dry. After that she was more comfortable and happy to eat most of the sandwich and the yogurt I bought," she said. "Tomorrow, I'll take food and water with me."

"Good idea. Did Mum talk much?"

"She didn't talk at all." Lesley shook her head, her mouth tight with distress. "I think she thought I was one of the nurses."

"Oh dear…I'm so sorry." I puffed my cheeks in a long sigh. "Any idea how long she'll be in?"

Lesley could only shake her head.

Muriel was kept at Limerick hospital while the doctors waited for her condition to stabilise. On the sixth day, she was transferred to Ennis. Although this was a much smaller hospital, it was considerably less crowded and much closer than Limerick, with the added benefit of ample free parking. The geriatric ward was housed in a newly built section of the hospital, which was airy and scrupulously clean. Muriel even had her own room.

The geriatric ward seemed to have ample staff. Perhaps because of this, all the doctors and nurses we saw were relaxed, attentive and happy to take a few moments to discuss Muriel's condition. After my third visit, where I spent an hour helping her eat, I popped over to the nurses' station before heading home.

"How did it go?" the senior nurse asked.

"She ate all of her baby food," I joked.

"Good for her," she grinned. "Personally, I wouldn't touch the stuff."

To help keep Muriel's strength up, the hospital had prescribed a special high energy food. In my humble opinion, it looked like puréed mud and smelled like feet.

"I think it was invented by a well-meaning scientist, who has no sense of taste."

"You could be right!" The nurse laughed, then her face became more serious. "Do you think Muriel recognised you?"

I shook my head. She patted my hand sympathetically.

"It's only to be expected," she added. "This was a big stepdown in her condition." She grimaced and continued in a gentle whisper. "It may be her last."

"I know," I nodded, sadly. "Do you think she'll be here for much longer?"

"Only for a couple of days. The district nurse has just been in touch. Muriel's being transferred to the respite care home on Thursday."

"Oh, that's great!" I exclaimed. "Pat's obviously delivered on her promise. Will I need to pick Mum up?"

"No need." She waved away my offer with a wave of her hand. "There's an ambulance all arranged. Leave it to us."

"Thank you so much. Will we be able to visit her?"

The nurse tutted. "You and your wife should take a break and put your feet up. It could be your last chance for a while. If you must visit Muriel, you can go any time after the weekend, once she's settled in."

***

With a short period of guaranteed freedom in the pipeline, Lesley and I decided to get out of the house and meet some of our friends. At least that was the plan.

Pat had kindly arranged for us to receive regular shipments of adult nappies for Muriel. Previously, we'd been buying them from a UK supplier and had almost run out a couple of times – which would have been something of a disaster. Now we would have a regular supply of good quality, better fitting nappies. The following morning, the health service delivery driver carefully reversed his huge lorry up our gently curved driveway and backed straight into Lesley's Skoda Estate.

"I'm sorry, mate," he exclaimed, scratching his head. "I didn't see it."

Exposed to sunshine, lashed with rain, frozen by frost and beaten by roadside briers, over the years our once shiny red estate's paintwork had faded to a dull pink, streaked with moss and scarred by scratches. Nonetheless, she was a loyal and trusty steed, almost irreplaceable for transporting builder's rubble, bags of garden compost, shopping, or wet dogs – sometimes all at once. So it was with some considerable sadness I reviewed the damage. The rear bumper was bent and split, the offside wheel arch was pressing against the tyre and bulged sideways, and the tailgate was dented.

"Crikey. You've done a proper job on it," I sighed.

Obviously well experienced in such matters, he shrugged and gave the rear bumper a gentle poke with the toe of his work boot. In response, the tail light fell off with a clatter.

"Not to worry, mate. These things happen all the time. The insurance companies will sort it out. You should give yours a call." He waved dismissively at our car. "With an old banger like this, they'll probably write it off and send you a cheque."

I balked at the very idea. Our Skoda's book value was negligible, but to us the car was almost irreplaceable. From experience, I knew the chances of finding a suitable replacement would be both time consuming and costly. Better the devil you know and all that. Perhaps there was an alternative. With a little negotiating and a phone call to his boss, we agreed to settle in cash, so I could arrange for the repairs myself.

Consequently, on the day Muriel was being transferred to the respite care home, Lesley's car was in the garage and I was visiting my friend Andrew Rich.

"You're home early," Lesley remarked as I walked into the kitchen. "How was the golf? Did you have a nice time?"

"It was great," I replied, my voice tinged with heavy irony, "for about half an hour!"

My wife's quizzical expression demanded more information.

"Just after Andrew and I teed off, my phone rang," I continued. "It was Ennis hospital, asking why I hadn't collected Muriel."

"What?" she exclaimed. "But Pat arranged an ambulance transfer."

"I guess there was some kind of a SNAFU." I shrugged. "So I apologised to Andrew, loaded my kit back into my car and hightailed it cross country to Ennis."

"That must be 60 miles!" Lesley groaned.

"70," I corrected, "and another 50 from Ennis to the respite home."

"Oh, Nick, I'm sorry. If my car wasn't at the garage…"

"Don't worry about it." I casually waved away her concern. "Anyway, Mum's all settled in and I'm home early. I think I'll cut the grass."

Predictably, Muriel's two week respite lasted less than a day. The following morning, we got the call, Muriel was refusing to eat, could we please come and get her?

Back at Glenmadrie, we quickly returned to our well-worn routine. For the first time since her collapse and fall we had the opportunity to assess how Mum was doing. It wasn't good. She was no longer able to communicate, she couldn't stand or walk and although she could still pick up food from a plate, even small pieces of her favourite cake were more likely to end up on the floor than in her mouth.

"She's doing it deliberately," Lesley whispered, pointing at her mother.

We were in the sitting room watching from behind as she ate. Muriel was selecting morsels of food from her plate and casually tossing them onto the floor.

"Perhaps she doesn't like it," I suggested.

Lesley shook her head and mouthed, "It's her favourite."

"Well they're enjoying it!" I laughed, pointing to the circle of animals, four dogs and one cat, expectantly waiting for the next tasty morsel to fall.

Although it was frustrating to see her deliberately throwing food onto the floor, all we could do was bite our lips and continue trying to maintain her dwindling calorie count. Most parents will have experienced the frustration of trying to feed a hungry child who, despite demanding food, will quickly spit it out rather than swallowing. I'm no expert, but my instinct told me, whereas the infant's sense of taste and feel are developing, Muriel's were diminishing fast. Because Mum had chosen not to receive any medical intervention, including a feeding tube, we knew she would gradually waste away from lack of food. Fortunately, Muriel never showed any sign of hunger, so I guess the misfiring nerves in her mouth were matching those in her stomach. It was only much later I discovered dementia patients can suffer a sensory incongruity where the flavour and texture of any food can become so unpalatable as to make eating impossible. In retrospect, I wish I'd known sooner.

A couple of days later, I was sitting face-to-face with Muriel, spoon feeding her the gloopy special high energy food she'd been prescribed. For a while, she was doing quite well. We were halfway through her second pot of this adult version of baby food, when Muriel stopped chewing and pursed her lips as if in thought. I'd just leaned fractionally closer, with another spoonful prepared, when she spat the entire contents of her mouth into my face.

My instinct outran my brain and before I could gather my thoughts, I'd already reached out and tapped her hand.

"Don't do that!" I snapped.

It had been no more than a firm pat, the sort of touch you would use to attract someone's attention in a noisy room, but my intent was one of admonishment and Muriel knew it. For a fleeting instant I saw a flicker of recognition in her eyes, a momentary flash of confusion and emotional pain before her blank expression returned once more. I drew myself together and professionally and compassionately got on with the business of cleaning away the mess and getting Mum safely into bed.

Later, as I shared the experience with Lesley, the shame overwhelmed me and the tears began to flow. My wife was kind and supportive, pointing out I had only tapped Mum's hand to attract her attention. It was okay, she added. Later, Dizzy said my reaction was understandable and, given the circumstances, somewhat restrained. Although I was grateful for their kind words, the guilt of that event festered on within me. Even now, the memory of that moment of anger, feels like a knife to the gut. I hope, somehow, Muriel understood and forgave me.

Towards the end of September, Pat visited to discuss Muriel's ongoing care. The number and frequency of nursing visits were increased and specialist equipment began to arrive. We finally received a properly fitted wheelchair, so I was able to return the loaner I'd stolen from the hospital (albeit with the aid of a kindly nurse). Next we had a visit from a nice man who checked and approved my installation of rails, grab handles and ramps. He declared there was nothing he would add or change, which was a good thing as he didn't have any spare equipment anyway.

Despite the budget cuts within the health service, the help and support we received for Muriel was first class. I cannot say enough good things about Pat, Dizzy, Judy, Doctor Mark and his team. We are eternally grateful.

Although Mum remained unresponsive, we usually brought her into the sitting room when we were watching television. We also continued to include her in our conversations and shared any news we had. Joanne had sent a lovely picture of David wearing the Ireland rugby shirt I'd sent him for his birthday (along with several toys), this took pride of place by her bedside.

***

On a hot and humid day in mid-October, a huge squall hit the house. As the hail and rain smashed down, Lesley and I cowered under the coverway and peered cautiously out of the gate. Sensing this was more significant than the usual storms, I pulled out my mobile phone and began filming. Perhaps 30-seconds later, a small tornado passed close to the house. While we were battered with a flying soup of mud, leaves, twigs and hail, we clung to the door frame and prayed for the tempest to pass. When the wind reached a crescendo, the gate slammed shut, unceremoniously depositing Lesley and I onto our bums. As quickly as it arrived, the squall passed. Somehow we'd escaped any serious damage. Five minutes later, we stood in the front garden and stared in wonder as the purple cloud gave way to blue sky in a perfectly straight line, like a blanket being pulled away. Suddenly, Lesley slapped a hand over her mouth.

"Mum's in the conservatory!" she exclaimed, her eyes wide in horror. "The noise in there must have been terrifying."

We hotfooted our way back to the house, but we need not have worried. Muriel was fast asleep in her wheelchair, blissfully unaware of what had just passed.

As her condition worsened, the focus of Muriel's medical support gradually transitioned from managing her health to end of life care. In November we took delivery of a special air bed. Rather than a traditional mattress, this clever contraption had dozens of computer-controlled air-filled tubes, which were individually inflated and deflated in a cycle designed to reduce the occurrence of bed sores. It didn't completely prevent these painful wounds from developing, but I was confident the bed would help to reduce their number and size. These beds are expensive to buy and hard to source, so we were extremely grateful our local health service was able to loan one to Muriel.

Perhaps sensing Muriel's decline, or because of the general air of impending doom at Glenmadrie, coupled with an increase in the number of visitors we were receiving, the animals became unsettled. Although Lady, Kia and Amber were usually leading an excitable welcome party whenever we had guests, they had become noticeably standoffish. Felix had always been ambivalent towards human contact, but now he had become positively feral. During the month of November, his visits to Glenmadrie became ever more sporadic and by early December, he'd vanished completely. While we missed his pretty black and white face peering quizzically through the window at meal times, Oliver seemed rather pleased to have his territory once more unchallenged. Whilst continuing to give Muriel a wide berth, in response to his restored freedom, our little cat became noticeably more playful and relaxed. Jack was by far the most sensitive dog in our unruly pack. Already a neurotic and timid animal, he was obviously unsettled if Muriel was in the room and jumped in fright whenever we used the noisy wheelchair ramps. We did our best to keep him calm and even tried using a pheromone spray the vet suggested, but to no avail. Soon Jack was spending most of his days in the courtyard and only reluctantly coming indoors at bedtime.

Watching Jack pacing anxiously around the garden, Lesley summed up our fears.

"He's so timid, I'm afraid he's just one thunderstorm away from doing a runner."

Throughout that winter, as one dark and dreary day rolled into the next, Lesley and I kept up our routine and did our best to maintain some sense of normality in our lives. From December onwards, even when Judy was sitting with Muriel, one of us remained at Glenmadrie at all times – just in case. Aside from grocery shopping trips to Ennis, individually, we only went out a handful of times. Because of her declining food intake, Muriel had lost a considerable amount of weight. Nevertheless, lifting her on and off her bed some 400 times, had taken a toll on my already unstable back. As a special treat, I booked an appointment with my osteopath. I hobbled in looking like a village amateur dramatics version of Richard III and left standing tall and straight. Although I promised to do the back strengthening exercises the osteopath advised, I was unable to comply with his "No heavy lifting" request.

Lesley had two trips out. Her visit to the dentist was a necessity, but the appointment I'd arranged with a hairdresser was a well-earned treat. Even though my dear wife spends most of her waking hours in the garden, which usually leaves her hair tangled with stray twigs and glistening with bug repellent, having her hair cut and styled really lifted her spirits at a much needed time.

Lesley's other trip out was to visit the local undertaker. Ghoulish as it may seem to some, Muriel's passing was an impending inevitability and, as she'd made her funeral wishes clear, arrangements had to be made.

Christmas came and went almost unnoticed. For a while we were snowed in and none of the care or medical staff could come. Fortunately, Muriel was stable and didn't require any medical intervention. Dizzy's husband kindly offered to bring her up in his four wheeled drive jeep but, as Lesley and I felt we could manage ourselves for a few days, we told her to have a break. It was Christmas after all.

Throughout January, our routine continued almost unchanged, except for an increase in the frequency of visits from district nurse Pat and Doctor Mark. Perhaps because we were inexperienced in such matters, Lesley and I expected every day to be her last and every day we were wrong. All the doctors and nurses could tell us was "Soon. Someday soon."

Mum turned 80 at the end of January. It was a benchmark she had always wanted to see. Lesley sat and held her hand for most of the day, even though her mother was no longer aware of her surroundings. That afternoon, I managed to feed her half a carton of her favourite chocolate mousse. Although Muriel continued to receive fluids through a drip, that was the last time she ate.

A few days later, Pat formally handed Muriel over to the palliative care team. To ensure she remained as comfortable as possible, Mum was fitted with a pump which automatically delivered her pain medication. From that point forwards, someone was with Muriel all the time. For the most part, we read, watched television, chatted and frequently wet her mouth with a small sponge on a stick.

I was talking with one of the palliative care nurses a few days later, when Muriel suddenly stopped breathing.

"Oh, she's gone," I whispered.

The nurse placed a kindly hand on my shoulder and squeezed gently, before stepping forward to examine her patient. Perhaps 30 seconds later, Mum coughed and took a deep breath. Knowing Muriel's irreverent sense of humour, I involuntarily gave a wry smile, which I quickly covered with my hand.

"It's called Cheyne-Stokes breathing," the nurse explained. "It's quite common in end stage patients."

"Is it like sleep apnoea?" I asked.

She nodded. "It'll happen a lot now. The non-breathing periods will get longer and the gaps between these events shorter. Then one day…"

"Thank you." Although she'd left the final sentence unfinished, the inference was clear and I was grateful for the information.

Four long days later, I happened to be the one sitting with Mum when she stopped breathing again. Holding her hand, I waited for a full minute, but this time she remained still. Muriel had passed away.

24 – All Good Things…

Lesley was still sitting with her mother and holding her hand when I heard a car pull up outside the house.

"There's someone here," I whispered, gently squeezing my wife's shoulder. She nodded her silent affirmation for me to leave.

Just as I reached the porch, the front door opened and Pat bustled in.

"Oh, hello, Nick," she smiled. Her voice was the usual sing-song rapid fire jumble of words. "I was just passing and I thought I'd pop in and check on Muriel."

"She's just…" I fought for the appropriate words, then gave up, "died."

"I am sorry." Pat sighed and pulled me into a quick hug.

"Thank you." I nodded stiffly.

Lesley was less restrained. She fell into Pat's arms and sobbed. I discretely headed to the kitchen and made a pot of tea.

My father passed away in the privacy of a hospital side room, with my mother and two sisters at his bedside. I was at work 90 miles away and arrived two hours later. Once we'd paid our respects, we stepped into the corridor, pulled the door shut and left him in the care of the nurses. At Glenmadrie, things were very different.

As professional as always, Pat quickly stepped into action. After checking for a pulse and confirming Mum had indeed passed away, she disconnected the drip, called for a doctor, spoke to the undertaker and told Dizzy that Muriel would no longer need her help.

An hour later, a tired and shabbily dressed locum doctor arrived. With the casual indifference born out of repetition, he did a brief examination, declared time of death, signed some forms and left. The entire process took just four minutes.

Pat gave us both a parting hug and set off to attend to her next client. While we waited for the undertaker, my wife brushed her mother's hair, straightened her bedding and tidied the room. The arrival of a sleek black hearse was too much for Lesley. With a distressed groan, she kissed her mum's forehead one last time and tearfully headed back into the main house.

Eamon, the undertaker, and his young assistant were

professional and respectful. We knew Eamon well because, in typical Irish fashion, he also ran the local garage and the village shop. With quiet proficiency, they positioned the simple pine coffin on a collapsible stand next to the bed and prepared to remove the bedsheets. Watching this well-practised routine, I felt the need to be involved in Muriel's care one last time. After carrying her so many times in the previous few months, it seemed appropriate that I should be the one to lift Mum into the casket as she began this final journey. Eamon was unsurprised by my request and consented with a nod. He and his young assistant took a step back to give me room, but remained close enough to render assistance should the need arise. With the deed done, Eamon gently squeezed my shoulder before closing the lid. And just like that, Muriel was gone.

First thing the following morning, a familiar lorry pulled into the driveway. Chatting and joking while they worked, it took just half an hour for the two health service employees to dismantle and remove the air bed. They also took the commode, wheelchair and walking frame, the unused adult nappies and a dozen other items they had supplied to help with Muriel's care. To some people, it may have seemed a little insensitive for the health service to reclaim their belongings so quickly but, air beds and wheelchairs were in short supply, so we didn't mind one bit.

Less than 24 hours since she had died, my wife and I stood together in Mum's apartment. With all of the health service equipment removed and her remaining belongings boxed up for the charity shop, the room was empty. There was no trace of Muriel. Except for our memories, it was as if she had never been there.

Sensing the moment, I gently squeezed Lesley's hand.

"Well…" she whispered to herself. "That's that then."

***

They say 'All good things come to an end' and that was certainly the case with our neurotic rough collie.

Uninvited, but welcome, Jack had arrived at Glenmadrie on a bitterly cold winter night. Despite our best efforts to return him to Brenden, his rightful owner, the lovable pooch had stubbornly refused to comply. Over the course of several weeks, I had repeatedly lifted Jack into my car and driven him the five miles or so back to his original home. There he would stoically climb out of the car, lick my hand and settle down on their driveway for a little late afternoon sunbathing. But, without fail, within a couple of days he would reappear at our French door, peering through the glass and whining to be let in. This to-and-fro dance continued almost to the point of comedy until, on the 23rd occasion, Brenden and I came to an understanding: Jack would be free to live where he chose. For the next four years, he chose to live as part of our family at Glenmadrie. Despite his bad hips, poor eyesight and terrible fear of thunderstorms, Jack was an outwardly happy dog. He was always keen to accompany the other pooches for walks – provided we didn't go too far – and he loved playing with Oliver. Jack enjoyed chasing the chickens and, even when being admonished for some infraction he didn't understand, he would melt our hearts with his one floppy ear and soppy grin. All was well in Jack's world, until Muriel arrived.

Although Mum doted on Jack much more than the other dogs, he was at best ambivalent towards our new houseguest. We speculated her gradually diminishing health heightened his neurosis to the point of distrust. Although it wasn't in his nature to be aggressive, Jack was noticeably standoffish with Muriel and became positively distant as her condition worsened. He made no secret of his distrust for her walking frame, his dislike for the wheelchair was obvious for all to see, and he was positively terrified of the noise whenever we took the chair up the aluminium ramps. Jack's fear of strange and noisy implements was understandable, but his reaction to Muriel's mental decline was surprising. Many dogs are instinctively drawn towards people in pain or distress. That empathy is one of the reasons we so love and appreciate our pooches, but Jack was made in a different mould.

"Jack's gone," Lesley said.

It was a couple of days since the health service had visited to recover their equipment. I had just arrived home with some groceries from the local shop.

"What do you mean, gone?" I demanded. "He was in the garden earlier."

"I saw him walking down the lane," my wife explained. "But when I called him back, he looked over his shoulder and trotted off down the hill. He was so fast, I would never have caught him."

I frowned and rubbed my chin.

"I wonder if he's gone back to his old home?"

"Why ever would he do that?" Lesley asked. "He's been here for years."

"Who knows what goes on in his head?" I shrugged and gave an ironic smile.

"I know he's been a bit off since Mum's been here, but all the same…"

I sighed and gave my wife a calming hug.

"Don't worry. I'll drive down and ask Brenden if he's seen him."

"Thank you." Lesley sniffed into my chest. "I'd be so upset if he went too."

There was no car at the house and I didn't see Brenden, but Jack was there. He was happily sunning himself in the driveway as if he'd never been away. When I climbed out of my car, he trotted over and looked at me with his head slightly tipped to one side, as if to say, "Oh, hello. I remember you!"

With a little coaxing, I managed to get him into the car. For some strange reason, I felt like a dog thief. Back home, the other dogs greeted Jack as if he'd been away for months. He seemed happy to be back home, but his euphoria didn't last. Two days later, he'd gone again.

Once more, I drove down and recovered Jack from Brenden's driveway and brought him back to a welcome befitting a sailor returning from a long stint at sea. He seemed happy to be home, but just after breakfast the following morning, he slipped through the fence and headed off down the hill. The back and forward game continued for a week.

"I don't know what to do," Lesley groaned. "We can't lock him in and I won't chain him up."

"He's never shown any inclination to wander off – except for when he came here in the first place. Frankly, I'm stumped," I admitted. "On the upside, he's unlikely to come to any harm walking across the fields. Also, Brenden doesn't mind, but he was certainly surprised to find Jack sleeping in his shed yesterday."

"Silly old dog!" Lesley laughed. "I guess he's developed a wanderlust, just like Lassie."

I smiled and nodded.

"They would have been rather uninteresting films if Lassie had stayed at home and slept in their driveway all day!"

After 23 rescue missions, we had to admit defeat. Brenden and I agreed Jack had made his point.

"Well, if he wants to move back here again, he's welcome," Brenden said, scratching Jack's ear.

"And if he wants to stay at mine, he's welcome too," I added.

In future, it would be up to Jack to decide where he wanted to reside. For a while, he took to living at both houses, but gradually his visits back to Glenmadrie became shorter and less frequent, before fizzling out entirely.

Lesley wasn't delighted with the outcome, but at least by then she had become accustomed to the idea.

***

Compared to the quiet 'close friends and immediate family only' English affairs, Irish funerals can be rather a surprise, especially for us Blow-ins inexperienced in such things. My first inkling of a difference occurred not long after we arrived in Ireland, when one of my clients phoned to cancel a golf lesson at the last minute.

"I'm sorry, Nick," Chris said, "but I've got to go to a funeral."

"Oh dear," I replied, almost overwhelmed with empathetic concern. "Were you close?"

"Not at all. I never met the man," he admitted, somewhat shamelessly. "But it'll be a good spread and a chance to meet up with some friends."

The following week, in the absence of another untimely death, Chris explained some of the rituals surrounding funerals in Ireland. He happened to be a retired history teacher, so I presumed he was as well informed as anyone on the matter.

"Irish funerals are rooted in tradition," he began. "The wake has a certain formula, a history, centred around the Roman Catholic church. Death notices are very important. They're a bit like the reading of the wedding banns as a way of keeping the community informed. Although these days most people check the local papers or radio.

"Years ago, the body was washed by a local woman and then laid out in the largest room covered in a white sheet. The clocks were stopped and any mirrors turned around. They used to have tobacco and a pipe in the room and every male caller was expected to have a puff."

"And plenty of food and drink?" I added.

"That would come later," Chris replied. "From time of death until the burial, someone would be with the body at all times. Until the body was prepared, there wouldn't even be any crying, for fear it would attract evil spirits. Once everything was ready, the keening could begin."

"Keening? Is that like the wailing and brow-beating I witnessed in Africa?" I asked.

"I guess," he shrugged, perhaps indicating he'd never been to Africa. "In Ireland, the head keener was called the Caointhe and would lead the crying, with perhaps some poetry and a few songs thrown in for variety."

I laughed.

"Back then," he continued, "wakes went on for several days and nights. There's a theory the singing and merriment came about less as a celebration of life, more in an effort to keep everyone awake!"

"Are these sorts of wakes common now?"

Chris shook his head.

"These days there's usually a good turnout. Especially if it's for someone well known or respected. In that case, it's not unusual for the entire village to attend."

"I've seen that a couple of times." I nodded. "The first time, I got caught in traffic for 20 minutes. I thought it was for a local hurling match, but then I noticed most people were wearing suits or black ties."

"Aye," he smiled. "You could easily make that mistake. Anyway, nowadays people visit the deceased's house during the wake to pay their respects. Mourners might have a cup of tea and a sandwich, then share a few stories about him that's passed. It's very much a community affair with a chance to catch up with friends and have a good gossip." Chris gave me an irreverent grin. "If you're lucky, you get to do it all again at the funeral!"

It was Muriel's wish to be cremated and for her ashes to be sprinkled along with those of her late husband back in England. Cremations in Ireland are not unheard of, but they are certainly not commonplace. Consequently, the nearest crematorium was in Cork, some two and a half hours away. With the only attendees likely to be Pat, Dizzy, Judy, Lesley and me, we elected to have a small funeral service locally and, sometime later, a memorial in England for family and acquaintances from back home.

Eamon and his wife did a wonderful job preparing the hall for the service. The coffin was decked with beautiful flowers and a framed photograph of Mum from happier and healthier times. There was plenty of chairs and enough food and drink to feed a small army. Not being religious people, we hadn't planned on engaging the services of a priest, but Eamon was quick to offer some sage advice.

"Most people here are church goers," he said. "Having a priest present will help them to pray and mourn."

Although Mum's death hadn't been mentioned in the local death notices, on the evening of the service, we were surprised and gratified to discover several of our neighbours had come to pay their respects – even though they had never met Muriel. I spotted Old Tom and young Tiernan at the back of the hall. Dressed in their best suits, they looked slightly uncomfortable and unsure of themselves. Seeing two friendly and familiar faces at such an emotionally difficult time, we couldn't have been more grateful – and I told them so.

Lesley was too upset to trust her voice, so she had asked me to be the master of ceremonies. I kicked things off by thanking everyone for coming and then read some extracts from the letters and emails we'd received from friends and family back in England. After sharing a potted version of Muriel's life story. I finished off with a few comments of my own.

"Somebody once said 'It's nice to be important, but it's more important to be nice'. Muriel was never rich and she wasn't famous, she was really just a very small pebble in a very large pond. However, like a pebble falling into a pond, she created ripples that touched many lives, and that made her important to anyone who knew her.

"Mum was delighted when Lesley and I married. She was ecstatic when our daughter Joanne was born just a year later. The support she gave to us when we were a young married couple was crucial in helping us to become the people we are today and the same can be said for her granddaughter.

"Muriel was a genuinely nice person. Although shy, she was a good friend to have. She was honest, but she only spoke well of people. She was a generous person, giving freely of herself, always prepared to make time for people, even if they were sometimes too busy to reciprocate. Muriel was a loving wife, a caring mother, an excellent grandmother, a doting great-grandmother and a good friend to many people. That makes her important. She will be sadly missed by those who knew her, and rightly so.

"Lesley and I brought Muriel to live with us in Ireland when her health began to fail. It was our intention to make her final years as comfortable and pleasant as possible. That was not something we could do alone. Although she had trouble articulating how she felt, we know Muriel was very appreciative of the warm welcome she received from everybody here. On her behalf, Lesley and I would like to express our heartfelt gratitude to those people who selflessly supported us with such passion and professionalism. Without your help, it would not have been possible to do what we have done."

After Judy had played Muriel's favourite song on her guitar, we moved on to the religious service. The priest had cancelled at the last moment and when his hastily arranged replacement repeatedly called Muriel by the wrong name, I could almost hear her chortling from within her coffin. Muriel had little time for religion, but she certainly enjoyed a good laugh. We'll miss her.

25 – Back to Normal

Like a gyroscope knocked off-kilter before spinning back into stability, our lives quickly returned to something resembling normality.

Since Mum came to live with us, Lesley had given up baking for the market and closed her dance club. At the same time, I'd all but stopped teaching golf and declared myself a fulltime author. These decisions were driven by the twin cattle prods of the failing Irish economy and the time restrictions of being fulltime carers. Whereas our time was once more our own, if anything, the economy was worse – particularly in the rural west. On the upside, we were still debt free and had a decent enough income from investments and book sales to stay afloat, provided we managed our finances prudently. Without work commitments, Lesley was now free to garden whenever she wished and for as long as she wanted. Similarly, I could plan a few games of golf.

Beyond the simple shared pleasures of going to a show or taking a trip to town together, my first instinct had been to book a holiday. Perhaps we should have a couple of weeks on a sunny beach somewhere, or revisit Egypt to once again cruise the mighty Nile and gaze in awe at the pyramids, The Valley of the Kings and The Temple of Luxor? Goodness knows we deserved a break and it didn't seem an unduly extravagant proposal – or so I thought.

"Frankly, dear," Lesley said in her kindest voice, "I'm sick of the sight of you!"

"Huh?" I exclaimed.

We were in the garden, throwing some seed for the chickens. Unaware of this threat to my deep-seated abandonment issues, the three hens pecked hopefully at the ground around our feet.

"I said I want to go alone," she said.

My little face had fallen in mock disbelief, but she had a point. For months we'd practically been prisoners in our own home – albeit voluntary inmates. During that time Lesley and I had hardly been away from each other for more than an hour. What with absence making the heart grow fonder and all that, perhaps we would benefit from having some time apart.

Back indoors, Lesley continued her pitch.

"You could go off and play golf for a few days," she suggested. "You enjoyed that trip to Portugal."

"That's true," I conceded. Lost in thought, I stroked my chin. "I was invited to play over there in a pro-am recently, but I didn't really fancy going alone."

"Or you could play here in Ireland," she suggested.

"I like that idea," I nodded enthusiastically. "Andrew and I could go together. There's loads of great Irish courses we haven't seen."

"That sounds like a great plan." With her victory in sight, my wife smiled. "Besides, I want to go to some of the summer Round Dances over in England," Lesley continued. "Also, taking separate holidays will save us the trouble and expense of arranging a house sitter."

"And you'll know someone is looking after the garden and dogs while you are away," I added.

"And the chickens."

I nodded. "Them too."

"Well, that's that settled then," Lesley said, clapping her hands together.

"Agreed." I nodded stoically and pointed toward my desktop computer. "Let's begin by booking you a trip to England. You haven't seen Joanne for ages."

***

So it came to pass that, bracketed by dozens of days out together visiting garden centres, attending concerts, visiting garden centres, touring museums, shopping and visiting garden centres, during that year we took our holidays apart. Lesley rekindled her love of dancing and spent a week with her cousin who was visiting from Australia. Along with trips to visit my family in England, I played more golf than I had for years. Inspired by the idea, my professional colleague, Andrew, had bounded into action and organised an Irish minitour for us and two amateur golfing friends. During that (largely) glorious summer, we played at Woodstock golf club near Ennis, Portumna, Birr, Druids Glenn, Powerscourt, Ballykisteen, Mullingar and Glasson. The courses were in great condition, the staff welcoming, the hotels were excellent and the golf wasn't bad either. By the end of our minitour, I felt rejuvenated and relaxed.

Taking our holidays apart that year may not have caused our hearts to grow fonder, but my wife's urge to hit me with a spade definitely diminished.

***

Lesley's first trip to England that year coincided with her 60th birthday. Being a loving husband, I conspired with Joanne to arrange a surprise treat for the old girl. Along with her pensioner's discount at wonderful Colchester Zoo, Lesley got a VIP pass to be zoo keeper for the day.

"It was great!" she said, her excited voice crackling over the phone. "We got to pet and feed the ring-tailed lemurs."

"I know," I replied, squinting at my phone. "I'm looking at the pictures now. Joanne just sent them."

It was so nice to see my wife and daughter happy and smiling.

"We had a lovely day," she replied. "Thank you so much."

"I'm glad you enjoyed it."

"I'll have to go now," Lesley said. "We're going out tonight and I need a shower. I think one of the lemurs got overexcited and peed on me!"

It was my turn to smile.

***

Unshackled from the constraints of needing to keep a low profile whenever Felix was around, like a nondescript bud developing into a beautiful rose, Oliver's character blossomed. This handsome beige tabby kitten quickly transformed from a shy flower into the class clown. Although it was fun to watch him goofing around, not everyone at Glenmadrie appreciated his antics.

"Gerroff!" Lesley shouted.

Oliver was bouncing around on the polytunnel roof, chasing butterflies and bees.

"He isn't doing any harm," I laughed.

"He's digging his claws into the plastic," she replied. "It's going to get ripped!"

Lesley was right. The little cat was charging along the curved polythene, using his wickedly sharp claws to avoid slipping down the sides. Although the polytunnel had remained mercifully undamaged during Jack's 'playing with plastic' phase, it wasn't going to survive another storm if it acquired thousands of nicks and cuts. I did a quick calculation. Replacing the polythene would take several days of work and cost around €400.

"Oliver!" I yelled. "Gerroff!"

The truculent feline paused mid-pounce and turned in my direction, his warm green eyes sparkling with mischief. I imagined him saying, "*Moi?*"

"Come on," I insisted. "Get down."

After a moment of careful contemplation, Oliver discarded my suggestion like an empty sweet packet and bounded after another butterfly. My ever more strident calls were ignored until Lesley resolved the situation with the hosepipe.

With the polytunnel now off limits, Oliver expanded his search for interesting and exciting places to play.

"Gerroff!" Lesley shouted. Oliver was sitting on the pile of seed at the centre of the bird table and playfully swatting at any wildlife which dared to come near.

"Hoy! Gerroff!" I groaned, sleepily. It was 4am and a certain tabby cat was running along the conservatory roof, chasing the windblown leaves and making more noise than an elephant in wooden clogs.

"Gerroff!" Lesley screamed. Halfway through his nightly 'mad half-hour' Oliver was hanging from our living room curtains and looking for something to swat. Perhaps convinced he was a superhero, our nutty cat dived onto the couch and set about digging his claws into the leather.

"Gerroff!" we shouted in unison.

Walking through the garden, I ducked under a low branch. As fast as lightening, a tabby paw scythed through the air and with puckish glee, flicked the hat from my head. Peering into the foliage, I saw two green eyes twinkling impishly. Reaching into the branches, I gently stroked Oliver's head as he rolled his chin and purred loudly.

"Gerroff," I whispered affectionally.

***

I saw a piece on the news the other morning regarding the successful delivery of a parcel to a house in rural Ireland, despite the address on the label being totally unreadable. The world was agog, social media heaved with excited chatter and the press were overawed with the mystery of how the parcel reached its correct destination. Here such miracles are almost commonplace thanks to the intrepid staff at An Post and their knowledge of their area and customers.

When we first visited Ireland in search of our dream home, Lesley and I quickly discovered the best way to navigate was with the aid of an Ordnance Survey map, a magnifying glass, and some corrective guidance from the village shop. We never failed to find our destination, although sometimes it took a while.

Our first task upon taking ownership of Glenmadrie was to visit our local post office and announce our presence. Since then, we have always received our post even when it was only addressed to: Lesley, Clare, Ireland. That being said, international parcels can be rather more tricky.

Despite our close ties with America and the UK, many online retailers still consider Ireland to be an unsuitable destination for their products. A small proportion of parcels never reach Ireland, heading instead for far flung places like Australia, Israel, or France with all the enthusiasm of a drunk homing pigeon. Such confusion is understandable. After all, depending on how the mood takes you Ireland can be referred to as: Southern Ireland, Ireland, Eire, The Republic of Ireland, or just ROI. The tracking data for those parcels which do arrive usually has just three entries:

1. Your parcel has been dispatched.
2. We have no idea where your parcel is.
3. Your parcel has been delivered!

Rumour has it there is a Bermuda Triangle for courier drivers somewhere in the green and hilly wilds of County Clare. Amongst the tangle of leafy lanes, unsignposted junctions and mobile phone blind spots, there must be a pub called The Backend of Beyond. I imagine it is a welcoming place, with a warm fire, good beer, friendly staff, and a car park bursting with hundreds of abandoned delivery vans.

Because of the high turnover of courier drivers we seldom see the same person twice. I have spent many happy hours on the phone trying to direct a delivery driver to our house. At times I felt like an air traffic controller guiding a crippled aircraft to land safely. Although we now have a carefully developed series of instructions with easily identifiable waypoints, sometimes it's just quicker to drive to the local post office and wait for the courier to arrive.

One quirk of rural Ireland which first endeared us to this beautiful place was the lack of postal codes. For many years we struggled to explain this omission to any company with a computer or an online booking form. The technology simply couldn't cope with the blank postcode box and refused to complete the transaction. The residents of rural Ireland proudly wore this affront like a badge of honour, until the day we heard the shocking news – Ireland was going to get postal codes!

In most countries, to help those good people at the post office deliver letters and parcels, it is common practice to use a zip code, or some other style of postal code designed for the country in question. Zip codes and postal codes are very common. Germany introduced them in 1941 at the height of World War Two. Argentina introduced them in 1958, the UK in 1959, and the USA in 1963. By 2015, almost every country on the planet was using some sort of zip code – with the exception of Ireland. There were a few good reasons for this delay.

1.   Frankly, as a nation, we're quite resistant to new-fangled ideas. Although it can become quite tedious, explaining to outsiders how we manage to get around and make a living, despite being so cruelly disadvantaged.

2.   We've been finding each other's houses for centuries, without the need for digitized codes. When you move in, you simply visit the local postmaster and tell them where you live. They will say something like, "Oh, you mean Bill's old place," and that will become the moniker for your residence, even though Bill was chronologically only the third in a long line of owners, but evidently first in regard to notoriety.

3.   We quite like the rebelliousness of entering a string of zeros into the postcode box of online forms and being able to tell foreigners that we don't have, or need, post codes.

British post codes are really simple. They are just a code for an address in reverse. For example, take the English postcode CM7 3DT. The UK has 121 postal areas. CM is the code for the district of Chelmsford, and 7 is the sub-code for the town of

Braintree. The number 3 directs postmen and delivery drivers to the southeast of the town and DT takes them to Howard Close. So, a letter addressed to: 201, CM7 3DT, UK, would easily reach 201, Howard Close, Braintree, Essex, England, United Kingdom – if there were such an address. Each element of the postcode is a unique but logical identifier for part of the eventual destination. It's so simple an idea that you couldn't cock it up if you tried. Or could you?

In 2005, the Irish government announced they were going to design a unique postal code system named Eircode. Not for them the stuffy system used by those tricky Brits, or the tried-and-tested German structure, or the logical American ZIP codes, or even something based on the new-fangled GPS system. Ireland would go it alone. Ten years, and €27 million later, having roundly ignored advice from all sides, the new Eircode system was unveiled. The good people of Ireland gave a collective snort of disbelief and said, "Well that's never going to work!"

I recall a discussion I had with Brian, a client who happened to be a postman.

"Are these Eircodes really just random letters and numbers, or is there some system being applied?" I asked.

"No. The lettering is deliberately haphazard," he replied, smiling over his beer. "Having spent so much on designing the system, they couldn't risk delivery drivers using the Eircodes without paying for them. So, each city was allocated an arbitrary letter, which appears at the beginning of the Eircode. These letters bear no relationship to the city name. For example, Galway is H, Cork city is T, and P and E. Tipperary will be designated E, but an F is for North Roscommon and Sligo. County Clare, Limerick, and parts of Kerry will use a V. The second part of the Eircode is randomly generated, meaning it is impossible to identify two linked addresses, even if they share a dividing wall."

"It sounds fantastically complicated," I laughed. "Perhaps it's like a Mensa question. If Waterford is X, County Laois is R, and Ennis is V, how many apples has Sally got?"

Brian snorted.

"Did every house get an Eircode?" I asked.

"Well, every property in Ireland was allocated an Eircode. If someone didn't get one, it was because Eircode didn't know their house existed, or because they thought the house was in a different field, or because they made a mistake."

"And how are these mistakes to be rectified?"

His eyes narrowed. "Why do you ask?"

"There's a special website set up to help people check their Eircodes," I explained. "According to the map, my Eircode will send people to a muddy farm track up by the forest."

He pulled a face before answering, as if he were trying to suck something from between his front teeth.

"If your address was inadvertently changed during the issuing of Eircodes, there's absolutely nothing you can do about it." Brian smiled benevolently and patted me on the shoulder. "My advice is to order some new stationery, change the sign on your house, inform your friends, and get over it."

Not to worry. Devoid of an Eircode, our post still finds its way to Glenmadrie. The other day we received a letter addressed to our old house in England, but with the useful footnote of County Clare, ROI. If you want to send a letter to Ireland, you can try adding an Eircode – it might work. Alternatively, you can deliver it by hand. Everyone here would be pleased to see you.

***

My final holiday trip of the year coincided with my niece's wedding in England. I flew over early to visit my daughter and spent a few happy days chasing my energetic grandson around the garden, the zoo and every soft play area in Essex. After such a long period of comparative inactivity, it was good to get the old bones moving again and there is no more demanding fitness coach than a hyperactive toddler.

Towards the end of the week, I travelled with Joanne and Mark up to Norfolk for the wedding. The venue was a delightful old hotel near to Cromer, on the north Norfolk coast, a location once favoured as a quiet retreat by none other than Winston Churchill.

My mother arrived in the afternoon, so the family had a meal together, a walk down to the beach and then retired to the bar, where we chatted late into the night. It was all very pleasant. At one point during the evening, I got chatting to one of my sister's friends. He was a retired teacher and a keen runner. Older than me by around ten years, he looked fit and healthy, whereas I felt bloated and tired. When I was training and teaching karate back in Essex, I ran five kilometres at least three times a week. Sitting there quietly sipping my lime juice and soda water, I couldn't remember the last time I'd been out running, or why I'd stopped. Unlike Essex, County Clare is extremely hilly. Perhaps I'd subconsciously compensated for abandoning my exercise routine with my vigorous daily dog walks up through the forest. With a silent toast to myself, I vowed to buy some running shoes as soon as I got home.

With a few hours to waste the following morning, I took an early breakfast and headed over to the hotel golf course for a quick nine holes before the wedding service began. The course was so-so, and using borrowed clubs, so was the golf, but the view from the highest point of the course was worth the walk.

I spent many of my teenage years in Norfolk so the scenery was familiar. Looking north, I could see the towns of Sheringham to my left, Cromer to the right and inbetween, the misty grey-blue of the North Sea blending seamlessly into the cloudless sky. Unlike the lush green countryside of County Clare, with its rolling hills and cooling Atlantic air, Cromer felt hot, dry and dusty. After a long drought-striven summer, the sandy earth had dried out turning the crusty grass pale beige. It took me back to the summer heatwave of 1976, when Britain baked in wall-to-wall sunshine for 66 days. Standing at the top of the hill, I recalled that long school holiday, carefree days lounging in the garden, trying to catch grass hoppers and playing golf. Most mornings, with my golf bag slung over my shoulder, I made the seven mile trip to Royal Norwich golf club on my Raleigh racing bicycle, played 36 holes and cycled home again in time for tea. Even though I would be spending the whole day exposed to the scorching summer sun, I never carried a water bottle, wore sunscreen, or a hat. Kids were tough in those days. But then again, perhaps that carefree lifestyle is why I've had skin cancer!

The wedding went well and the afterparty was an enjoyably raucous and joyful affair. The music was great, with many rock and roll classics and, although I stuck to orange squash all night, I somehow found the bravado to enter the dancefloor. Drunk on adrenalin and keen to burn off some excess calories, I inelegantly spun, clumped and hopped my way through the evening, only to be comprehensively out danced by my 88-year-old mother!

Naturally, for most people, the highlight of the week was the wedding ceremony. It was certainly memorable.

I was sitting alongside a very pleasant dark-haired Polish girl who was discreetly bottle feeding her new born baby. We were on the second row from the front and off to one side. During that awkward moment of expectant silence which follows the words 'Speak now, or forever hold your peace' the baby filled its nappy with a noise not unlike someone stepping into a wellington boot filled with warm custard. As the sound reverberated around the room, all eyes instantly swung in my direction.

Unwilling to out the true offender and powerless to defend my innocence, all I could do was turn my blushing face towards my accusers and mouth, "I'm so sorry."

Once the laughter had subsided, the Polish girl patted my knee and whispered kindly, "You're my hero!"

26 – Fit to Drop

Back in Ireland, I hotfooted my way to the cheapest shoe shop and splashed out the thick end of ten euros on a nice pair of lightweight running shoes. To compliment this extravagant purchase, I stopped off at one of those oddly named European discount retailers in search of some running kit. After sorting through the bins of windscreen wipers, colouring books, computer accessories, cordless drills and garden tools, I found the section dedicated to sportswear. Sandwiched between the end-of-line swimwear and the new range of ski suits, was a small pile of clothing deemed suitable for exercise. Unfamiliar with the protocol with regard to running attire, I chose something I felt was functional, fashionable and adaptable. My wife thought otherwise.

"What on earth are you wearing?" she asked, her hand failing to completely cover her smirk.

"It's my new running kit," I replied, making the classic strongman pose. "It's very flexible."

"You look like an overweight wasp," she laughed. "Why ever did you choose black with gold stripes?"

"It was the only colour they had left," I explained.

"Well it clashes terribly with your white socks and pale blue trainers!"

"Pfft! You have no sense of style." I goofed a haughty expression and waved her insults away. "Anyway, tracksuits are very fashionable."

"They were – about 30 years ago!" she laughed. "Anyway, that's not a tracksuit. It's made of lycra and probably intended for cycling. You haven't ridden your bike for years. It's probably gone rusty by now."

"This suit is very stretchy." I did a couple of deep knee bends to demonstrate.

"Please don't do that." Lesley pointed at my crotch and looked away. "That lycra is rather too revealing, even on a cold day."

***

Aside from my slowly spreading waistline, the main inspiration behind this sudden desire to exercise was my good friend, Andrew Rich.

After falling from his horse a couple of years earlier, he had been almost unable to walk. He spent several of our golf games driving his father's buggy, or hobbling ponderously along the fairway, wincing at every step. His recuperation was slow and the physio painful, but his condition gradually improved – even if his golf didn't. Perhaps because he was feeling podgy after such a long period of inactivity, Andrew took up cycling and, as his body healed, he switched to running.

For many people, simply recovering some mobility and fitness would have been enough, but Andrew is made of sterner stuff. In October, I watched in awe (from the comfort of my couch) as he completed the Dublin Marathon in a time of 6:01:46. It was an incredible achievement and I'm proud to be his friend.

My return to running had been going well. At first I'd needed to pause after just a few hundred metres, bent over and sucking air while I waited for the sparkly bits to clear from my vision, but with perseverance and repetition I was able to complete the route without stopping. Over a month, I gradually built up to a point where I was covering five kilometres, three times a week. Although I was only running to lose a little weight and improve my fitness, I was pleased to see my times were dropping almost as quickly as the excess pounds. The first two thirds of my looped route was along the main road, which curved gently downhill, but the last kilometre, leading back to Glenmadrie, was up a steep and undulating single track lane. Running uphill is never easy and the uneven surface made the tough climb much harder. The road along the entire length of my course was cambered to assist drainage, but the sideways slope of the narrow tarmac on that final leg was so severe, it usually felt as if I was running across someone's roof.

One Friday morning, with the air cool and my adrenaline flowing, I covered the first four kilometres in record time. Feeling particularly energetic, I pushed hard up the final hill before easing into a gentler trotting motion along the final stretch. Perhaps my legs were tightening up, or maybe the uneven road camber put some extra strain on my aching muscles, but suddenly I felt as if a mouse was trapped under my left sock. I paused momentarily to check for vermin before moving on. Three strides later I felt as if a dog was now trying to bite the mouse – and my leg. After massaging my left calf for a minute, I tried walking, but whatever I did, the leg would not take my weight. In the end, swearing like a drunken sailor, I had to hop the last 400 metres back to the house.

It can take more than a month to heal a torn Achilles tendon. The treatment is centred around rest and avoiding activities which aggravate the injury. In the best Irish tradition, I waited a fortnight before setting off on another run. I covered less than a kilometre before admitting defeat and hobbling home.

Unable to run or walk for any great distance, it seemed my winter exercise would be limited to hitting golf balls in the garden and catching up on some DIY.

***

"There's plenty to do," Lesley said.

We were in our lounge eating a lunchtime sandwich. Lesley was sitting in an armchair and I was on the couch, with my left leg elevated on a stool.

"Like what?" I asked. Although I had already written a snagging list, in my experience, it was always a good idea to seek a second opinion. I found my wife to be far more supportive of my ideas if she thought she'd suggested them first.

Lesley gleefully counted off the jobs on her fingers. "Cutting and splitting wood for the fire. Clearing the pond of all that weed and grass. Then there's house repairs to do."

"I've got to replace some of that clearlite," I added. "Quite a few sheets are cracked. It's great for letting in the light, but once it gets brittle and sun damaged, it's no match for our windy weather."

"Do the guttering while you're up there," she replied. "It's full of moss from the roof and it overflows every time it rains."

Although these jobs were already on my list, I nodded anyway.

"You'll have to help me with the pond," I said. "Once I've pulled the weed and thrown it on the embankment, you can put it in the wheelbarrow. It's a good job I bought those waders."

"It's best to leave the weed on the side for a couple of days," she explained. "So the bugs can escape back into the water."

"Okay. Whatever you want." I pointed at the window.

275

"Hello. This is new."

Lady, our unruly foxhound had been out in the garden. While Lesley and I were talking, she had suddenly appeared at the sitting room window. Standing on her hind legs, with her paws on the windowsill, she was peering at me through the glass as if to say, "Why aren't you paying me any attention?"

Dissatisfied with my inaction, she looked away before tapping loudly on the glass with her paw.

"I think she wants to come in!" Lesley laughed.

"I'll wait until she barks at the door," I replied, patting my sore leg.

But Lady was unimpressed. Her tapping became louder and more strident. She had decided this was to be her new way of demanding entry and she wasn't going to move until I rose to my feet and headed towards the front door. With a sigh, I heaved myself upright. As soon as my bum left the couch, like an actor completing a soliloquy, Lady gave a nod of satisfaction at a job well done and disappeared stage left.

My wife and I shared a look and burst out laughing.

***

I spent the thick end of two weeks replacing and repairing the storm damaged clearlite roofing. The job took longer than I had anticipated because, rather than just replacing the damaged sheets, I decided to remove and refit the entire roof. Working 12 feet up, balancing on four-inch rafters slick with sleet and ice, whilst holding a ten-foot sheet of clearlite and trying to stop it flapping in the wind is a good way to test your nerve. I was understandably satisfied when the job was finished without incident. I put my tools away, a happy man. The December weather was again turning cold and wet, but now our wood store and walkways would remain dry. After a trip to the local recycling centre to dispose of the off-cuts and the old sections of clearlite, I was looking forward to a quiet weekend and a well-earned rest.

On Saturday afternoon, Lesley went out to see some friends and to do a little shopping. With the house to myself, I walked the dogs and then pottered about, tidying up and enjoying our rural solitude. My only other job on that day would be to take Lesley to the airport in the evening, as she was flying to England for a week to visit our daughter and grandson.

A little before sunset, I'd just let the dogs into the courtyard and was admiring how well my new roof had kept the sleet and rain away, when I noticed there was a steady drip of water from the guttering at the south end of the house. As this was directly above the roofing I had just replaced, I was a little miffed I had not spotted the leak during the two weeks I had been up there. Nevertheless, it was a simple matter to nip up the ladder and clean out the obstruction. All I had to do was walk along the corrugated iron roof, place a couple of stout boards across the new clearlite to spread the load, and carefully shimmy my way across until I could reach the gutter.

I have given much thought as to why I did what I did next. Maybe I was tired and rushing to complete the job before it got dark, perhaps I had become overconfident, it's possible I just made a mistake, because wet clearlite and corrugated iron can look almost identical in the half-light of dusk. Whatever the reason, with two roof boards still tucked under my arm and wearing heavy wellington boots, I stepped off the corrugated iron and onto the fragile plastic roof.

Over the years, I have had several falls. Some from ladders and a few from trees, along with the usual slips, trips and jumps most active people will experience during their lives. Typically, there is a brief moment as part of your brain says 'You're going to fall!' and this is followed by a slightly briefer moment while you look for somewhere soft to land. Sometimes there is an appreciable slowing in the passage of time, so you can conveniently enjoy the main feature entitled 'Your life, in a flash' – albeit without popcorn and adverts.

I experienced none of this. Hearing a sharp cracking sound from beneath my feet, I paused mid-stride in puzzlement, wondering if there was perhaps ice on the roof. Suddenly the clearlite fractured. There was no sensation of falling, or a replay of the key moments in my life – which would have been rather boring in any case. From my viewpoint, the observable world abruptly travelled upwards at an incredible speed. With the wind whistling past my ears, I plunged helplessly into the darkness below. Just as I was bracing my legs to tuck and roll like a parachutist, a lorry hit me squarely in the centre of my back and my world exploded in darkness and pain.

My ears were ringing and somewhere a distant voice was calling.

I attempted to open my eyes, but failed.

The voice was calling again. Gradually, the words filtered through to my befuddled brain.

"Oh no," she groaned. "Oh no!"

But why? Then I remembered the lorry. Obviously, I was lying on a cold and uncomfortable road with my wife leaning over my battered body.

"Oh no," Lesley cried. "Oh no…"

My eyes flickered open and things gradually came into focus. High above me, through the twilight darkness, I could see a hole in the clearlight roof. The voice wasn't my wife's, it was mine, subconsciously responding to the pain in my back. Cautiously turning my head, I stared in puzzlement at my surroundings. To my right I could see our woodpile and at my shoulder, some garden tools. To my left was a concrete wall with an arched window and, beyond that, our courtyard. I was in our outdoors wood store. It was almost dark and I could see snow falling. But where was the lorry? Surely I was hit by a lorry. Where was it?

Bent over backwards with my arms above my head, I was being stretched like a man on a rack. My right leg was out straight, but the left was twisted behind and underneath me at an almost impossible angle. To make some sense of my surroundings, I cautiously brought my arms down and felt about in the darkness. There was no lorry, but I was spread-eagled across some sort of a hard metal structure. It surrounded me like an uncomfortable seat, only this chair was tipped at an awkward angle and seemed to contain some garden peat. It was our steel wheelbarrow.

Closing my eyes, I visualised what had just happened. Falling through the roof into the woodstore below, I had narrowly missed being impaled on Lesley's garden fork and spade. It was a lucky escape, but not fortunate enough. By some measure of bad luck, my heels had hit the handle edge of the wheelbarrow, hard enough to bend the steel frame and twist the thick metal body. Under the force of the impact, the wheelbarrow tipped. Like a man slipping on a banana skin, my feet shot forwards and I flipped onto my back, just in time to collide with the rising reinforced metal edge of the wheelbarrow with all the force of a speeding lorry.

The baleful calling had stopped, only to be replaced by another more familiar sound. It was the distinctive grrup-grrup-grrup Amber made whenever she wanted me to throw a toy for her to chase. The little dog was standing to my left and nudging her ball expectantly with her nose.

"You've got to be kidding me!" I grunted, wincing as pain lanced through my back. "I'm sorry, Amber, but I don't think I should move."

Unimpressed with my excuse, Amber barked again.

"You'll have to wait until Mummy gets home, just like me."

Undeterred, the little dog circled her ball and woofed some more.

"Sorry, baby," I groaned.

Ten minutes later I was shivering uncontrollably.

"It's probably shock," I told myself, unconvincingly. Although shock was likely after such a fall, the true cause of my shivering was the plunging temperature. As I'd only planned to be outdoors for a few minutes, I hadn't worn a coat. Unsure of my injuries, it would be wise to wait until Lesley returned from visiting her friend. On the other hand, if I remained outdoors for much longer I risked freezing to death. With the decision made, I gradually untangled myself from the wheelbarrow. Then, with utmost caution, I rolled onto my front and began crawling towards the house – pausing only to throw the ball for Amber.

It took me ten minutes to make my way indoors and another five to pull myself upright. After a quick inventory, I delivered the damage report. Apart from several cuts to my face and hands from the broken clearlite and a six inch long graze along my spine starting just above my belt, most of the pain was centred on the ribs on the right side of my back. Half-crouching like a man who'd recently been kicked in the groin, I was still hanging onto the back of a kitchen chair when Lesley bustled in and headed directly for the stairs.

"I need a pee!" she shouted over her shoulder. "I lost track of time. We'll have to get a move on, otherwise I'll be late for my flight!"

Used to Lesley's dramatic bustling entrances, the dogs and I waited patiently for her to return. Once she had attended to her ablutions and fussed the pooches, Lesley finally noticed my unusual posture and sickly white face.

"What's the matter with you?" she asked, frowning.

"I fell off the roof," I explained.

"Well that was a silly thing to do," she tutted, with mock indifference.

"I know," I groaned. "Silly me. Although I can confirm Ireland's gravity is in working order, I'm afraid your new wheelbarrow is wrecked."

"Are you hurt?" she asked, her voice suddenly tinged with genuine concern.

"A bit," I nodded. "It hurts like hell when I take a deep breath. I think I've cracked a rib."

"Oh no!"

Perhaps in a subconscious effort to stop what she said next, my dear wife's hand covered her mouth.

"Will you still be able to drive me to the airport?"

"How are you feeling?" Joanne asked. "Mummy said you fell off the roof."

"I fell through the roof," I corrected, "and landed in the woodshed and flattened your mother's new wheelbarrow."

"That must have been painful. Are you okay? She said you hurt your back."

"I'm very sore," I admitted. "I may have cracked a rib somewhere. It certainly hurts when I breathe."

"You're lucky it's all you broke, you silly sod!" she chided, playfully.

"Actually, I think I've snapped a bone in my left wrist too," I added. "My left ankle is swollen and black and I'm pretty sure I've busted my big toe. I broke the same toe doing karate some years ago, so I know how it feels. The funny thing is, my back was so sore, I didn't notice the other injuries until I was driving home after dropping Mummy at the airport."

"Hang on…" Joanne covered the telephone with her hand as she shouted the news to Lesley. "Mummy says you should go to the hospital."

"I'll go and see my doctor tomorrow," I sighed. "There's nobody else here to care for the animals. If I go to A&E on a Sunday, I'll probably be there all night."

"Are you lying down and resting?" she asked.

"Don't worry. There's golf on the television, so I'm spending the day on the recliner couch, popping painkillers and taking it easy. It's where I slept last night. Sitting up is slightly more comfortable than trying to lay down. I'm only getting up to visit the loo, let the dogs out and to get more drugs."

The last bit was rather a white lie. Earlier, and with extreme caution, I'd gone back onto the roof to replace the damaged section of clearlight. Stupid as it may seem, it felt like a risk worth taking. I had surmised, with bad weather forecast, the repair was essential. Besides, I wanted to get back on the bike as soon as possible – so to speak. That being said, I must have looked like a frightened kitten crawling across that corrugated roof, and it wasn't just because of my injuries. I now knew it would take a while to rebuild my confidence for working at height.

First thing Monday morning, I limped into the local surgery. Doctor Mark didn't even examine me. Upon hearing my story, he gave me a letter and told me to drive directly to the local hospital for some X-rays.

An hour later, I parked my car at Ennis General hospital and, like a man trying to hold a coin between the cheeks of his bottom, hobbled through the front door. I recognised the receptionist as one of Lesley's former dance students. She was a lovely lady with a ready smile and flowing ginger hair.

"It's such a shame your wife had to close her club," she said. "I was really enjoying those evenings out."

"Lesley enjoyed them too," I smiled and nodded. "She was sorry when it came to an end."

"And how is her mother?"

"I'm afraid she passed away earlier this year," I replied.

"Oh, I'm so sorry. Please give your wife my best wishes."

"Thank you." I nodded again.

"So what brings you here today?"

"Rather stupidly, I fell off the roof," I explained, handing over the letter. "My doctor has sent me here for some X-rays."

She read the letter and shook her head.

"I'm sorry, but you can't have X-rays without seeing a doctor first." She shrugged apologetically and pointed to my right. "Take a seat and someone will see you shortly."

While I waited, I sent Joanne a text.

"I'm at Ennis, waiting for an X-ray. Tell Mummy I'm fine."

"Mummy asked if the dogs are okay?" Joanne messaged back.

I smiled. It was typical of my wife to prioritise the dogs over me.

"Yes. They had a big breakfast and I put down an extra bowl of water in case I'm delayed."

Any further conversation was put on hold when I heard a nurse calling my name.

Because of the austerity cuts within the health service, Ennis hospital's Accident and Emergency department had recently been downgraded to a small injury clinic, which only opened from 8am to 8pm. The decision had met with a lot of local opposition, and rightly so, but to no avail. Outwardly, the department looked little different to when Lesley visited with her twisted ankle, but the structural changes ran deep, as I was about to discover.

After the nurse had recorded my details, a doctor came over.

"And why are you here today?" he asked, smiling as if I were a gameshow contestant.

"I'm afraid I had a bit of a tumble." I pointed at the letter clipped to my chart. "My doctor's sent me here for some X-rays."

The doctor asked me what had happened. Once I'd recounted the events of the previous day, he read the letter, looked quickly at my swollen wrist and blackened ankle, before asking me to pull up my shirt so he could examine my aching back.

"I think I may have cracked a rib," I groaned, twisting to point behind me with my thumb. "It hurts when I breathe."

"Lie down please," the doctor said, gently placing his hand on my shoulder.

I complied, grunting in discomfort.

"Now, don't move." His kindly voice was suddenly stern. "You may have broken your back."

"What?" In surprise, I tried to sit up, but his hand kept me firmly in place.

"Please stay very still," he said. "Based on the swelling in your back and the mechanism of the injury, I suspect you may have an unstable spinal fracture."

Despite my determined protestations, he remained resolute in his diagnoses and added a dire warning of the risk of permanent paralysis should the bones move. Eventually, I complied.

"We'll know more once you've had an X-ray." He smiled and patted my hand. "The ambulance will be here soon."

"Ambulance!" I exclaimed. "Why an ambulance? The X-ray department is just down the corridor!"

"I'm sorry." He gave a helpless shrug. "The radiology department here is no longer equipped for spinal injuries. We're transporting you to Limerick University hospital."

Although I was confident my back was only bruised, with perhaps a broken rib or two, given the risk of incurring a lifechanging injury, I meekly complied. After what felt like hours laid perfectly still and counting all 77 ceiling tiles, the ambulance arrived.

"But I drove here!" I complained, when they explained the

transfer procedure. Can't I just lay on a stretcher?"

"Sorry mate," the paramedic said, "but we can't take the risk."

I rolled my eyes and groaned.

Like a Christmas gift wrapped by an overzealous six year old, I was fitted with a neck brace and immobilised within a bright orange inflatable body splint before being strapped onto a stretcher. While the ambulance made haste towards Limerick, the paramedic went about his business. Unable to see anything other than the ceiling of the ambulance, or hold a conversation over the wailing siren, I closed my eyes and concentrated on controlling my rising nausea. I was momentarily distracted by some pushing and tugging at the far end of the trolley and idly wondered if someone was trying to steal my shoes. Suddenly, there was a searing pain in my foot.

"Owwww!" I wailed, somewhat louder than the siren. "What the hell was that?"

The paramedic leaned over and shouted into my face. He'd been eating cheese and onion crisps.

"I was just squeezing your toes to check if you had any feeling."

"Please don't do that again," I replied. "That toe's probably broken and so is the ankle."

"It is a bit black," he agreed. "I'm afraid I had to cut your shoe to get it off. Still, it's a positive sign you have feeling."

"Not if someone's squeezing your broken toe it isn't," I growled, a bit selfishly.

As the ambulance crew bade me farewell at the hospital, I apologised for my outburst of anger – and breakfast.

"Happens all the time," the paramedic casually waved away my concerns. "Motion sickness is very common."

***

"What time did you get back?" Lesley asked, her voice crackly and distant over the phone.

"It was just after nine," I replied.

"The dogs must have been frantic."

"They'd been very good, no mess or anything," I reported. "Mind you, they were all desperate to go outside. They've had their supper and an extra treat too."

After caring for the dogs, I'd hobbled up the path to check on our chickens. Although I'd taken the precaution of leaving them locked in their cage, there was a slight risk some opportunistic and determined predator had made an attack. Fortunately all was well. Our three chooks were snuggled up in their coop and fast asleep, so all I had to do was close the door.

Back indoors, I saw Oliver had emerged from wherever he'd been hiding. I found him sitting atop the tumble dryer, with one leg pointing skywards while he diligently cleaned his bottom. To highlight his irritation at being abandoned for a day, he made a point of ignoring me for a few minutes, before grudgingly hopping down to eat his dinner. I tickled his ear and was rewarded with a rumbling purr.

With my zookeeper duties complete, I made myself a sandwich and sat down to call Lesley.

"So what's the prognosis?" she asked. "Are you a cripple?"

I shook my head.

"There was no spinal break visible on the X-ray, thank goodness."

"What about the other injuries?" she asked. "Your ribs, wrist and ankle, are they broken?"

"I think so, but I don't know for sure," I replied. "I'll go and see Doctor Mark when you get back home."

"Didn't they check you over at the hospital?"

I sighed. "They only X-rayed my spine."

"What?" Lesley exclaimed.

"The A&E was really busy. It looked like a war zone casualty department," I explained. "There was a three hour wait before I went for the X-ray and another hour or so before the radiologist's report came through. I asked the doctor about the other injuries, but he told me I'd have to go back to the small injuries clinic at Ennis. Of course by that time they were shut. To be honest, once I'd been given the all clear, I just wanted to go home – especially as I only had one shoe and I was missing both socks!"

"I'm not surprised you felt that way. You've had a horrible day," Lesley sighed. "Hang on, your car was still at Ennis hospital. How did you get home?."

"Andrew rescued me. He'd messaged me about something earlier," I explained. "When I mentioned I was at the hospital and likely to be stranded, he came straight over and gave me a lift back to Ennis."

"What a good friend he is," my wife said.

I could only agree.

In the aftermath of that fall, I got to thinking about luck and friendship.

I felt lucky to have such good friends. People like Andrew, who would drop everything they were doing to come to the aid of a friend in need, were beyond value. I will always be grateful for his assistance that day and for the effort he made organising our earlier mini golf tour of Ireland. At a time when I was feeling low after Muriel's passing, those fun weeks of carefree golf and long conversations late into the night were just the tonic I needed. Then there were Lesley's friends Pat and Bill.

So that Lesley didn't have to cut her holiday short, Pat, a retired nurse, kindly offered to come to Glenmadrie if I needed assistance with dressing and cooking. In the end, I didn't need her help, but at the time the offer was priceless. For his part, Bill was happy to take me car shopping in Limerick a few days later. I'd finally made the decision to part with our Skoda estate, particularly since it was dented so badly by the health service lorry. My plan to have its replacement ready and waiting for when Lesley came home was in tatters, until Bill came to the rescue. With his help, I found a lovely second-hand Volvo estate and transported it to our local garage where it was serviced and valeted just in time for Lesley's return. My wife was delighted with her new toy and we were both grateful to Pat and Bill for their friendship and support.

I didn't consider myself a lucky person, I wasn't even sure if there was such a thing, but I was fortunate. I was fortunate to be born in a time of peace, in an affluent country where I had endless opportunities and prospects – most of which I wastefully squandered. I was fortunate to meet and marry Lesley and to be a parent to a healthy and intelligent daughter. And we were incredibly fortunate to move to Ireland and begin a new life with barely a bump along the way. But lucky? I know I was lucky once in my life, because I was lucky that fall didn't cause my death or leave me in a wheelchair.

The other day I read the dreadfully sad story of a 22-year-old girl who slipped in some mud and fell whilst out walking. Like a clown skidding on a banana peel, she lost her footing and landed flat on her back. A casual onlooker might have laughed before offering a friendly hand. Most likely she'd be winded and embarrassed, with nothing more than a muddy bum to show for her misadventure. But in this case she was unlucky. Landing poorly, she shattered part of her spine and was paralysed.

Then there was Jason, the younger brother of a golfing client. He was in his early 40s, with a wife and three young children. Jason was attending a family party to celebrate the New Year. He'd had a few drinks, but not too many. Walking down the stairs after visiting the toilet at his brother's house, he lost his footing, fell backwards and struck his head. It was an insignificant fall, followed by a minor bump, but somehow the impact broke his neck. Even though there was a doctor at the party, Jason could not be saved.

These are but two of a dozen such stories I've heard since my fall. Perhaps in other circumstances, they'd have passed me by almost unnoticed, like a cloud briefly obscuring the sun from shining on my otherwise perfect life. But these days I find myself asking, "Why them and not me?"

My fall was substantial with a particularly violent ending. After seeing a photograph of the location, the doctor at Limerick hospital declared I was the luckiest person he'd seen all year.

"Given the distance you fell and the way you landed, you were almost certain to have broken your back," he said. "Frankly, it's a miracle you didn't."

Although my back wasn't broken, my wrist was. I'd also cracked a rib, broken a toe, badly injured my ankle, torn or twisted a bunch of other muscles and tendons, and lost a sock. However, those are wounds I wear with pride. It seems us old people don't bounce back like we once did, so my injuries will take a long time to heal. I know I won't return to running for a while, but I don't mind. I am a lucky man, with good friends who, if asked, would drop everything to come to my aid, or help me look for my socks.

28 – A Taste of Honey

Modern technology has a lot to answer for, some good and some bad. In our case, it resulted in the arrival of a new dog to our happy home.

It all started after I changed mobile phone providers.

As usual, I was welcomed as a new customer with the gift of a shiny new smartphone. Now, I'm quite tech savvy, particularly for someone who grew up long before the idea of the internet was even a glint in Mr. Tim BL's eye. That being said, I was still pretty impressed with the capabilities of my new HTC phone and enthralled with its numerous exciting but utterly pointless features. On the other hand, I'm nearly as paranoid about my privacy as a pot-smoking spy. So it might surprise you to learn I didn't follow my usual protocol of disabling every feature and only using my phone for making calls, sending texts, or as a glorified paperweight.

With the clever interactive features enabled, HTC soon became my virtual friend, watching my every action and making useful suggestions for what to buy while I recuperated on my couch. Consequently, just after I had casually searched for one of those drone helicopters, as a gift for my son-in-law, my smartphone enthusiastically took up the challenge and started bombarding me with suggestions as to how I could spend my money on unrelated electrical items.

"I see you were searching for a drone helicopter," HTC said. "Perhaps you might be interested in this robot lawnmower?"

"Not really," I laughed. "That's a 12-inch solar powered lawnmower, fine for a tiny back garden in sunny Surrey, but hardly suitable for four acres of wet meadow grass in rain-lashed Ireland. Besides, I already have a perfectly adequate lawn tractor."

A few minutes later, my phone pinged again.

"I see you were searching for a drone helicopter," HTC said, "perhaps you might be interested in this remote controlled car?"

"No thanks," I tutted, whilst surreptitiously trying to figure out what 'push notifications' were and if I should turn them off. Before I could, my phone pinged again.

"I see you were searching for HTC phone instructions," HTC said, without a hint of irony, "perhaps I can interest you in this advert for an HTC phone."

I involuntarily ground my teeth and politely declined by banging my new HTC phone on the table. Lesley glared at me. Nevertheless, a few moments later, my phone pinged again.

"I see you were searching for electrical items," HTC said, "so perhaps I can interest you in this electric dog."

"What?"

"An electric dog," HTC casually repeated.

"You're kidding me," I said.

"I kid you not – it's an electric dog."

"Show me."

It was a small electric robot dog, nearly new for just €30.

"My goodness!" I showed Lesley the advert. "Look, I've found the answer to all of our problems!"

"Ha! What a great idea! I bet it's clean, obedient and better behaved than this lot." She nodded towards our three lovable pooches. Like the unfortunate victims of a canine train wreck, they lay scattered around the fireplace quietly leaking noxious gas.

"I'm not so sure," I grinned. "Knowing our luck it would probably drip oil on the rug and need new batteries every week."

"I guess…still, it is kind of cute looking…" She left the clue hanging.

"And about as useful as a chocolate teapot," I countered, trying to defend my wallet. "For the life of me, I can't imagine why someone would buy a robot dog, let alone try to sell one."

"I guess they bought it and now they're trying to sell it," she replied, stating the obvious.

"Well, they can jolly well keep it," I laughed. "Afterall, a robot dog is for life, not just for Christmas."

"I suppose you're right," Lesley sighed, clearly meaning the exact opposite, even though she usually despised such extravagant electrical oddities.

"Perhaps we should get another dog?" My suggestion was casual and made without much enthusiasm, but I guessed what Lesley was thinking.

She gave me a look which suggested getting another dog was a wonderful idea, but at the same time completely mad and irresponsible. Confused, I looked to our alpha dog for advice.

"What do you think, Lady, should we get another dog?"

Lady lifted her head and gave me a sour look. She clarified her opinion by letting off a loud fart.

"Well, I guess that settles it!" I opened the window for some much-needed ventilation. "No more dogs!"

And we would have left it there had HTC not intervened.

It was approaching Christmas, the time of the year where Ireland's climate encourages most sensible people to stay indoors and enjoy the twin pleasures of a warm fire and old movies. We were indulging ourselves in the delights of Gregory Peck at the peak of his acting skills in Captain Horatio Hornblower, when my smartphone decided to interrupt.

"Hi Nick, I see you've been looking at dogs."

"No, I haven't!" I replied, for once I was firmly confident in my user history.

"Yes you have, I distinctly remember you looking at this Electric Dog…"

"You're mistaken," I said. "It wasn't an animal, it was electric."

"And a dog…" I imagined HTC giving me a sly smile.

"I can see what you're thinking, but Electric Dog would come under computers and the like," I explained.

"I understand… So dogs it is! Here's a picture of a puppy which is for sale and may be of interest to you."

"Oh for God's sake! I said computers, not dogs, and I'm not really interested in another computer – or a so-called smart phone, thank you very much!" I angrily poked at the screen with my finger. "Now, how do I delete this advert for a pupp– oh my God it's so cute!" I held out the phone for Lesley to see. "Look at this little doggy!"

And so it began. Every evening, as regular as clockwork, my phone would chime to announce the arrival of the latest batch of adverts, featuring variously delightful dogs and puppies for sale or rehoming. At first it became a soft form of entertainment, like window shopping for houses at the obviously extortionate end of the price scale, but soon the oohs and aahs became more considered. I'm not really sure at what point we transitioned from idle speculation and adorable canine daydreams, to serious dog hunting. I suppose it was around the time we hypothetically discussed what sort of dog we would prefer.

We were genuinely concerned introducing a mature dog into

our relatively well-balanced pack of old ladies might lead to problems, so we agreed a puppy would be the best option. Initially, Lesley was keen on the idea of getting another Lhasa Apso, but they are rare in the West of Ireland, primarily because short-legged dogs with long fur are about as inappropriate for muddy fields and wet grass as a supercar is for our narrow lanes and potholed farm tracks. We toyed with the idea of a Border Collie puppy. They were all insufferably cute and available in their hundreds, but they are working dogs and need to be worked hard to remain healthy in body and mind. Both Lady and Kia were rescued from the pound and we would have been delighted to go down that route again, had there been a puppy available, but it was not to be. And there was another consideration.

Almost everyone who has ever been a dog owner knows the dreadful pain we suffer when a beloved pet dies. Dogs fill our lives with such joy and passion. They are our constant companions, never needing time alone, or space to grow, and they are always there for us, with a head on the knee, or a lick of the hand as soon as we need some comfort. Overflowing with unconditional love and friendship, they are so prevalent in our days their passing can leave a void so vast it can never be filled. We may be able to get over the death of another human, perhaps by imagining they have gone on to a better place. Our heart may still grieve, but life will go on and our friends and family will somehow fill the vacuum death has created. But there is something different about our relationship with dogs.

Dogs may not be our whole life, but they make our lives whole. Only children and dogs give their love unconditionally, in a way which makes you want to be as good a person as they already think you are. Children grow up and become people with their own lives and perhaps their own dogs. Only dogs will provide such silently devoted companionship. Their presence is constant, their attention total (particularly if you're eating biscuits) and their love is unwavering. Each dog is so unique in its interaction with our lives they can never be replaced or replicated. Once gone, they are lost forever, but the open wounds they have left in our hearts will never heal. It is their only fault. So Lesley and I decided one more dog would be enough and our special dog would be a golden retriever puppy.

Once we had made a decision, it was time to put the

technology to work. Inevitably, my HTC thought otherwise.

"I noticed you were searching for golden retriever puppies," it said. "Here are some adverts for puppets which may interest you."

And then…

"I noticed you were searching for golden retriever puppies. Here is an advert for gold flint garden gravel which may interest you."

Or…

"Chinese golden urns."

Or…

"Golf ball retriever."

Eventually, with a combination of threats and IT skills, I managed to convince HTC we really were looking for a goldie puppy. Grudgingly it complied and showed me some adverts. There were several litters of puppies for sale, possibly because it was so close to Christmas. Lesley was keen to ensure we only bought from a good and reputable breeder, or preferably a family. So we discarded any suspicious looking adverts, principally those with a sales history showing repeated breeding, or any with pictures of puppies in a permanent breeding enclosure. That certainly thinned our choices. However, there was one advert we found to be particularly promising. The pictures showed several puppies playing with a child in a kitchen, which suggested a domestic seller, and although the puppies were priced slightly below the average, the seller was demanding evidence his dogs were going to a good home. Several phone calls later, along with a lot of map reading and a trip to the cashpoint, we were on our way.

Gareth was a friendly family man and farmer. He had bred his golden retrievers for the first time and was now selling the litter. He readily agreed to our request to see all of the puppies and the parents in the home before we committed to buying, so we arranged to meet at his farmhouse that evening. The farm was hidden deep in the winter darkness of west Clare about 20 miles the other side of Ennis and about an hour's drive from our house.

On the assumption we were going to buy a puppy eventually, we stopped at a pet supermarket on the way to buy some essential supplies. Like excited parents at the mother and baby superstore, we filled our trolley with glee. There would be no hand-me-downs for our golden puppy! We selected a new dog bed, a collar and lead, some bowls, various toys and chews and a sack of the finest puppy food. The bill was only slightly less than the cost of the puppy and left me wondering if we should have bought the electric dog after all.

Despite the inky darkness and the lack of any relevant road signs, we navigated our way through the cold drizzle and found the farm with surprising ease. In typical Irish fashion, we were greeted at the door by Gareth and his wife, Mary, and welcomed into their home as if we were old friends visiting from afar. They led us past the living room, all decked out with Christmas decorations, and into the warmth of their kitchen where we could get to know each other. Or at least that was the plan, but it was difficult to have even a short chat with the farmer and his wife, whilst eight gorgeous golden retriever puppies were demanding our attention.

Not much bigger than a domestic cat, all eight puppies were almost identically cute, with soft snow-white fur, stained with a little hint of vanilla on the ears and across the snout, and fat black noses which made a perfect triangle, along with the dark chocolate of their captivating eyes. Instantly we were in puppy heaven, tickling, stroking and petting any dog within reach. I was almost bowled over by a jumble of excited fur, as four of the puppies scrambled over each other in a desperate attempt to get the most attention. In retrospect, it wasn't a good idea to wear my best black trousers, but I didn't care. As I rocked back on my heels for balance, I glanced at my wife and saw from the look of delight on her face, we would soon be the proud owners of a golden retriever puppy.

After the initial chaos subsided, Gareth politely excused himself from the conversation and went out to the yard to fetch the parent dogs, leaving Lesley and me to chat with his wife. I tried to join in the conversation, but there were two women talking and the puppies would not be denied the attention, so I crouched down and put both hands to good use.

Mary watched me for a moment before asking, "Was it just the one you'd be wanting, or have you space for more?"

Lesley beamed a huge smile at me. "How many shall we take?" she teased.

"Eight would be fun, but I think we'll have to settle for one."
I scanned the furry gaggle of gorgeous pups. "But which one?"

After the initial excitement of meeting someone new dissipated, the puppies were beginning to turn their attention to other matters. Some were sniffing around the base of the cooker, perhaps attracted by the memory of roast beef, others were by the door, possibly looking for their mother. A couple had curled up under the table, unsure of the excitement, but too tired to care. However, one puppy sat confidently at my feet and politely demanded my attention. I gently picked her up and held her in the crook of my elbow, while I stroked her fat little tummy. She accepted my attention with a contented sigh, snuggling her face deeper into my sweater as she closed her eyes.

"I think I'm in love," I whispered to Lesley, with a smile.

That exquisite moment of affection was rudely interrupted when Gareth came back into the kitchen with the puppies' parents. They were attractive and excitable dogs, but obviously well cared-for. There was an undignified scramble as seven of the puppies fought to get to mummy and the prospect of some milk. She joined in the fun by doing a little dance in an attempt to keep her teats away from their hungry mouths and needle-sharp teeth. Even the pup in my arms was taking notice of the commotion, so regretfully I put her down, all the time hoping she wouldn't become lost to me forever within the group of eight near-identical puppies. I needn't have worried. Five minutes later, the little furball was once again back at my feet, full of milk and waiting patiently to be picked up. As before, content and trusting, the puppy snuggled into the crook of my arm and closed her eyes. Not to be left out, Lesley came over and joined in the petting and stroking. A little calm was restored as Gareth took the parents outside again. It was time to get down to business. Mary took the lead.

"It looks like she's chosen you," she said, stating the obvious with a gleeful smile.

"It certainly seems that way," Lesley cooed.

With the shaking of hands, the exchange of good wishes and a not insignificant amount of cash, the deed was done, and we were the proud owners of a new dog – or more likely her new slaves!

We had a long drive ahead and it was already late as we

finally set off for home. The journey along unfamiliar roads was not made any easier by the steady drizzle which turned the oncoming headlights into a succession of greasy flares on the windscreen. During a break in the traffic, I glanced at Lesley who was sitting in the front seat and cuddling the puppy. In our excitement, we had not thought to bring a blanket, so our new friend was safely wrapped in Lesley's best coat. By the faint light of the dashboard clock, I was able to see my wife was gently stroking the little dog and smiling like a new parent.

"So, what shall we call her?" I asked, hoping the conversation would help to keep me awake until we got home. Lesley looked down at the puppy. She gently stroked its soft white fur and the honey coloured tips of its ears.

"How about Goldie?" she asked.

"I think that's what every other golden retriever on the planet is called."

"Blondie?" Lesley suggested.

I pulled a face and sucked my teeth. "A bit obvious don't you think? Anyway, I wasn't a big fan of her music."

Lesley gave my arm a warning thump. "You suggest something."

"What about Kim?"

"Kim's a boy's name."

"Sally?"

"Won't work." Lesley shook her head. "We had a next door neighbour in England called Sally. She had jet black hair."

"Let's call her Joanne," I quipped.

"I don't think our daughter would approve of us calling our dog by her name."

"At least she'll come when we call her."

"I wouldn't bet on it," she said, with heavy irony.

There was a natural pause in the conversation while we got on with the quiet business of driving and dog petting. I thought about our daughter, her husband and our grandson, David. They were happily preparing for Christmas at their new home in England. David was almost two years old and excited at the prospect of his first proper Christmas. They were due to visit us in January. I reached over and gave the little head a stroke with my fingertips.

"I hope she stays this soft," I said. "David's going to have a fit."

"I can't wait to see his face. He's never been in a house full of dogs, it should be fun."

A name popped into my mind.

"Should we call it Honey?" I suggested.

"Honey…" Lesley repeated the word, in a gentle whisper, testing its suitability. "Honey… Yes, that could work."

"Do you think so?"

"What about it little one?" My wife gave the tiny pup a stroke between the ears. "Shall we call you Honey?"

Honey lifted her sleepy head and, after a moment's careful consideration, promptly regurgitated her supper over Lesley's best coat.

"Well, that's settled then," I said, as I pulled off the road and handed Lesley the roll of kitchen towels all experienced dog owners carry in their cars. "We shall call you Honey."

And so Honey was christened in a Volvo on a rainy night in December whilst Lesley was liberally splattered with milk. A fair exchange in anyone's book.

When we arrived back at Glenmadrie, Jack was waiting patiently on our doorstep. He would probably only stay for a couple of days, as had become his habit, but his appearance couldn't have been better timed.

After such a tumultuous year, it seems our lives were back in order and we were once again a family, living the dream in rural County Clare.

The end.

You can read more of Nick and Lesley Albert's Irish exploits, in Fresh Eggs and Dog Beds Book Five. It's scheduled for publication in 2022.

About the author

Nick Albert was born in England and raised in a Royal Air Force family. After leaving college in 1979, he worked in retail management for several years, before moving into financial services as a training manager. In the mid-1980s he qualified as a martial arts instructor, and began a parallel career coaching sport. In search of a simpler life, and the opportunity to write full-time, he and his wife, relocated to the rural west of Ireland in 2003.

Contact the author

www.nickalbert.co.uk
nickalbert@outlook.com

Chat with the author, other memoir authors, and readers at We Love Memoirs:
https://www.facebook.com/groups/welovememoirs/

Ant Press Books

If you enjoyed this book, you may also enjoy these Ant Press titles:

MEMOIRS
Chickens, Mules and Two Old Fools by Victoria Twead (Wall Street Journal Top 10 bestseller)
Two Old Fools ~ Olé! by Victoria Twead
Two Old Fools on a Camel by Victoria Twead (thrice New York Times bestseller)
Two Old Fools in Spain Again by Victoria Twead
Two Old Fools in Turmoil by Victoria Twead
Two Old Fools Down Under by Victoria Twead
One Young Fool in Dorset (The Prequel) by Victoria Twead
One Young Fool in South Africa (The Prequel) by Joe and Victoria Twead
Two Old Fools Boxset, Books 1-3 by Victoria Twead
Fat Dogs and French Estates ~ Part I by Beth Haslam
Fat Dogs and French Estates ~ Part II by Beth Haslam
Fat Dogs and French Estates ~ Part III by Beth Haslam
Fat Dogs and French Estates ~ Part IV by Beth Haslam
Fat Dogs and French Estates ~ Part V by Beth Haslam
Fat Dogs and French Estates ~ Boxset, Parts 1-3 by Beth Haslam
From Moulin Rouge to Gaudi's City by EJ Bauer
From Gaudi's City to Granada's Red Palace by EJ Bauer
South to Barcelona: A New Life in Spain by Vernon Lacey
Simon Ships Out: How One Brave, Stray Cat Became a Worldwide Hero by Jacky Donovan
Smoky: How a Tiny Yorkshire Terrier Became a World War II American Army Hero, Therapy Dog and Hollywood Star by Jacky Donovan
Smart as a Whip: A Madcap Journey of Laughter, Love, Disasters and Triumphs by Jacky Donovan
Heartprints of Africa: A Family's Story of Faith, Love, Adventure, and Turmoil by Cinda Adams Brooks
How not to be a Soldier: My Antics in the British Army by Lorna McCann
Moment of Surrender: My Journey Through Prescription Drug Addiction to Hope and Renewal by Pj Laube

One of its Legs are Both the Same by Mike Cavanagh
A Pocket Full of Days, Part 1 by Mike Cavanagh
A Pocket Full of Days, Part 2 by Mike Cavanagh
Horizon Fever by A E Filby
Horizon Fever 2 by A E Filby
Completely Cats - Stories with Cattitude by Beth Haslam and Zoe Marr
Fresh Eggs and Dog Beds: Living the Dream in Rural Ireland by Nick Albert
Fresh Eggs and Dog Beds 2: Still Living the Dream in Rural Ireland by Nick Albert
Fresh Eggs and Dog Beds 3: More Living the Dream in Rural Ireland by Nick Albert
Fresh Eggs and Dog Beds 4: More Living the Dream in Rural Ireland by Nick Albert Don't Do It Like This: How NOT to move to Spain by Joe Cawley, Victoria Twead and Alan Parks
Longing for Africa: Journeys Inspired by the Life of Jane Goodall. Part One: Ethiopia by Annie Schrank
Longing for Africa: Journeys Inspired by the Life of Jane Goodall. Part Two: Kenya by Annie Schrank
A Kiss Behind the Castanets: My Love Affair with Spain by Jean Roberts
Life Beyond the Castanets: My Love Affair with Spain by Jean Roberts
The Sunny Side of the Alps: From Scotland to Slovenia on a Shoestring by Roy Clark

FICTION
Parched by Andrew C Branham
A is for Abigail by Victoria Twead (Sixpenny Cross 1)
B is for Bella by Victoria Twead (Sixpenny Cross 2)
C is for the Captain by Victoria Twead (Sixpenny Cross 3)
D is for Dexter by Victoria Twead
The Sixpenny Cross Collection, Vols 1-3 by Victoria Twead

NON FICTION
How to Write a Bestselling Memoir by Victoria Twead
Two Old Fools in the Kitchen, Part 1 by Victoria Twead

CHILDREN'S BOOKS
Seacat Simon: The Little Cat Who Became a Big Hero by Jacky Donovan
Morgan and the Martians by Victoria Twead

LARGE PRINT
Chickens, Mules and Two Old Fools by Victoria Twead (Wall Street Journal Top 10 bestseller)
Two Old Fools ~ Olé! by Victoria Twead
Two Old Fools on a Camel by Victoria Twead (thrice New York Times bestseller)
Two Old Fools in Spain Again by Victoria Twead
Two Old Fools in Turmoil by Victoria Twead
Two Old Fools Down Under by Victoria Twead
One Young Fool in Dorset (The Prequel) by Victoria Twead
One Young Fool in South Africa (The Prequel) by Joe and Victoria Twead
Fat Dogs and French Estates ~ Part I by Beth Haslam
Fat Dogs and French Estates ~ Part II by Beth Haslam
Fat Dogs and French Estates ~ Part III by Beth Haslam
Fat Dogs and French Estates ~ Part IV by Beth Haslam
A Kiss Behind the Castanets: My Love Affair with Spain by Jean Roberts

Chat with the author, other memoir authors, and readers at
We Love Memoirs:
https://www.facebook.com/groups/welovememoirs/

Printed in Great Britain
by Amazon

77261122R00172